Linux Tidbits

So you want to check out the world of Linux? You won't be sorry! Linux is an up-and-coming operating system that's right for everyone from the most timid to the most adventurous of computer users. Take this card along with you on your journey—it'll help you remember some of the features that set Linux apart from the rest of the crowd.

Can I Place an Order from a KDE Menu?

Sorry, wrong kind of menu. KDE provides you with a graphical user interface (GUI)—and lots of menus that help to make your tasks easier. Here are some noteworthy things to know about working with lists and menus:

➤ Commands are typically located in menus.

➤ Application menus are traditionally located under the window's title bar.

➤ Working with menus is similar to working with buttons. Clicking on a menu button (also called menu item) opens the menu to reveal the commands.

➤ You can click and drag on menus. The option under your cursor when you release the mouse becomes the selected command.

➤ If the menu displays an arrow, the command offers submenus. You can treat submenus the same as menus.

➤ An ellipsis (…) marks a command that opens a window or dialog box.

➤ Commands can also be invoked by typing a keyboard accelerator (typically, this is Ctrl plus a character).

➤ Menus that display an underscore (_) under a letter can be opened via the keyboard by pressing Alt+letter.

➤ Dimmed commands are currently unavailable and cannot be selected.

➤ Choice lists open a drop-down list of options from which you can choose.

What if I Don't Want to Use Menus or GUIs?

Linux can take care of that for you too! GUIs are one way to use Linux—shells are another. Some of the more common shells:

Shell	Description
Bourne	Simplistic. It doesn't offer things that are especially useful in a shell, like command-line editing.
ksh	The Korn shell. It's more of a UNIX flavor (at one point, it was only available if you had a specific brand of UNIX installed).
csh	The C shell. This interactive like other shells, but it uses a different kind of grammar and syntax. It was the first to offer a command history.
tcsh	Enhanced C shell (csh). With this shell you get command and filename completion as well as command-line editing capability.
bash	The "Bourne Again Shell." This is the default shell of most Linux distributions. It offers command-line editing and filename completion.
zsh	Newest shell. Structured like most previous shells, this one is compatible with the Bourne shell.

Note: To check to see what shell you are running, type: `echo $SHELL`

QUE®

cut here

The Complete Idiot's Guide: Linux Command Reference

What Can I Do with Files and Directories?

Command	Result
ls	List files
ls -a	List all files, including hidden ones
ls -s	List files and their size
ls -F	List files with characters to show file type
ls -t	Sort files by time, new files first
pwd	Print the working directory
mv	Move a file
cp	Copy a file
rm	Delete a file
cd	Change to a directory
mkdir	Create a directory
rmdir	Delete a directory
mvdir	Move a directory

Could You Help Me Out?!

Command	Result
man	Retrieves a manual page
apropos	Lets you search for keywords
whatis	Prints a one-line description of the command
info	Produces the GNU Info pages
whereis	Finds the path to the tool you want to use

What Else Can I Get this Shell to Do?

Command	Result
passwd	Lets you change your password
chsh	Changes your current shell
who	Tells you who is logged into the system (in a network setting)
w	Tells you who is logged in and what they're doing
date	Prints the current date and time
cal	Produces a calendar
wc	Count lines and words in files
spell	Spell check a file
free	Displays how much memory is available
du	Shows how much disk space is being used
df	Reveals how much of your system's disk space is available

Should I Know Anything Else about Commands?

Character	Function
;	Separates commands
()	Groups a string of commands
\|	Pipe
&	Tells the command to run in background
' " \	Characters used in quoting
$	Substitutes variables
* ? ~ + - [] ! @	Metacharacter

Note: Shell commands are case sensitive. So BASH, bash, Bash, and BasH all are different commands to the shell.

Typically commands you enter will be lowercase.

THE COMPLETE IDIOT'S GUIDE® TO

Linux

by Manuel Alberto Ricart

A Division of Macmillan Computer Publishing
201 W. 103rd Street, Indianapolis, IN 46290

The Complete Idiot's Guide to Linux

Copyright © 1998 by *Que Corpation*

International Standard Book Number: 0-7897-1826-x

Library of Congress Catalog Card Number: 98-87629

Printed in the United States of America

First Printing: December 1998

00 99 4 3 2

Trademarks

Warning and Disclaimer

Executive Editor
Grace Buechlein

Development Editors
Laura Bulcher
Gregory Harris

Managing Editor
Brice Gosnell

Project Editor
Kevin Laseau

Copy Editor
Marilyn Stone

Indexer
Rebecca Hornyak

Proofreader
Betsy Deeter-Smith

Technical Editors
Aron Hsiao
Jeff Perkins

Illustrator
Judd Winick

Software Development Specialist
Jack Belbot

Interior Design
Nathan Clement

Cover Design
Michael Freeland

Layout Technicians
Ayanna Lacey
Heather Hiatt Miller
Amy Parker

Contents at a Glance

Part 4: Appendixes **287**

Contents

15 Help Please 163

16 Permissions: Protecting and Sharing Your Work 173

About the Author

Manuel Alberto Ricart is a trainer and engineer for Paradigm Research, Inc. (http://www.pri.com), a Silicon Valley–based training company. Alberto develops instructional materials for Java and Internet programming technologies. Paradigm Research, Inc. delivers its training materials to a number of *Fortune* 500 and notable high-tech companies, including Hewlett-Packard, MCI, Ford, and Netscape Communications, Inc.

Alberto has been involved with computers since the late 1970s, when he was introduced to programming on a then–state-of-the-art IBM system 32, which had a whopping 32KB of RAM and a tiny hard disk. Since then, he has developed a number of software products for the Macintosh operating system (OS), the NEXTSTEP OS, and, more recently, Java. Alberto has also provided UNIX and Internet networking support to a wide range of clients since the mid-1980s. He holds both bachelor's (1987) and master's (1989) degrees from the University of Wisconsin-Milwaukee.

In 1992, he founded a software company, SmartSoft, Inc., that developed a wide range of commercial object-oriented software tools for the NEXTSTEP/OPENSTEP (UNIX) OS. His products were sold worldwide.

In 1995, he cofounded a second firm dedicated to building Internet solutions that enabled companies to harness the Internet for business. His specialty is dynamic content-driven intranets and electronic commerce solutions. He has developed custom technologies used by notable companies such as Oshkosh B'Gosh and Warburg Pincus Funds.

Alberto specializes in the invention and design of software products and tools. His focus is Internet and Web core technologies such as the Apache and Netscape Web servers, Perl, JavaScript, Java, and all the other technologies required to support them, such as UNIX network connectivity and administration. Since 1996, Alberto has used Linux extensively in the development and deployment of many Internet Web sites and intranet projects.

His book *Apache Server Survival Guide* (published by sams.net, ISBN 1-57521-175-0) has been published in hard copy and included in two other electronic publications relating to the RedHat LINUX OS.

Alberto can be reached at alberto@pri.com, where he can usually be found tinkering with technologies all day long.

Dedication

To Diana, Julisa, Isabella, and Viviana: You make it all possible.

Tell Us What You Think!

As the reader of this book, *you* are our most important critic and commentator. We value your opinion and want to know what we're doing right, what we could do better, what areas you'd like to see us publish in, and any other words of wisdom you're willing to pass our way.

As the Executive Editor for the Operating Systems team at Macmillan Computer Publishing, I welcome your comments. You can fax, email, or write me directly to let me know what you did or didn't like about this book—as well as what we can do to make our books stronger.

Please note that I cannot help you with technical problems related to the topic of this book, and that due to the high volume of mail I receive, I might not be able to reply to every message.

When you write, please be sure to include this book's title and author as well as your name and phone or fax number. I will carefully review your comments and share them with the author and editors who worked on the book.

Fax: 317-581-4663

E-mail: opsys@mcp.com

Mail: Executive Editor
 Operating Systems
 Macmillan Computer Publishing
 201 West 103rd Street
 Indianapolis, IN 46290 USA

1, 2, 3 Go!

Welcome to Linux! It's the software that is grabbing the world's attention as a reliable and powerful operating system (OS). At the time of this writing, Linux and Windows NT are the only OSs gaining market share. Most other OSs are either stagnant or are losing their share to Linux or Windows NT.

How to Use This Book

This book is a gentle introduction to Linux, and as such, it is not intended as a comprehensive guide. On the contrary, great effort has gone into this book to keep it from becoming yet another comprehensive reference guide. I've been selective about covering the topics you are most likely to use early in your Linux hacking career.

One of the interesting things about Linux, and UNIX in general, is that learning new ways and tools is almost an endless task. There are many tools—too many to cover even in several "comprehensive" volumes. Much of the comprehensive and exhaustive reference for Linux is readily available in various forms, some of which will be installed into your computer as part of the installation process.

In contrast, this book focuses on how to make you self-sufficient. It teaches you two ways of working with Linux: using the X graphical environment (with KDE) and using the shell, the command line interpreter so closely associated with UNIX. And, if you are managing your own Linux computer, there are some administrative tasks that you need to learn how to do.

So how is this book organized? Installation and first-time configuration instructions are located in Appendix A, "Linux Installation." Appendix B, "OpenLinux Compatibility Guide," provides you with an up-to-date list of the ever-growing and ever-changing list of hardware that is known to be compatible with Linux. While mapping your installation plan, you should verify that your hardware is listed and known to be compatible with OpenLinux.

After your initial Linux installation and configuration, start with Part 1, "Working with Linux in a Graphical Environment—The KDE Desktop," and read the chapters in order. (We've structured the chapters counting on you doing so.) Part 2, "Working on the Command Line," introduces similar concepts as Part I, this time using a shell instead of a graphical user interface. Last, Part 3, "Essential System Tasks Under Linux," focuses on various administration tasks that you'll need to do occasionally. Keep in mind that while you are learning Linux, you are also learning UNIX. What you learn here will transfer with little modification into other UNIX environments.

Have fun getting to know your new operating system!

Why Linux?

So why all the attention? UNIX has been around for a number of years, and although believed by some to be the only choice among *real* OSs, it has remained in the vertical market arena until very recently. But what does this mean? UNIX (or Linux, which is based on UNIX) provides a very robust environment in which to run and deploy applications. By design, it offers the following features:

➤ Multiuser support

➤ Security

➤ Full multitasking

➤ Networking support for client and server applications

➤ Source code

These are features that some of the PC OSs available today don't offer, or they have been added as an afterthought. These are all very important features, especially in the context of today's networked environments where computers share information.

Unlike Windows-based systems, UNIX is able to support multiple users concurrently. A single UNIX/Linux computer can have multiple users working on it (running programs, accessing files, and other services) at the same time, either seamlessly across a network or through a directly attached console (a screen and keyboard).

As a result, UNIX and Linux offer an environment where many (hundreds) of users can simultaneously access a system, if the system has enough resources. With so many potential users, how do you protect important files from unauthorized access? Linux's UNIX roots handle security transparently, not as an afterthought, but as part of the Linux way of life. In order for you to work on the computer, you have to sign in.

Security isn't Linux's only kudo. It's also an expert juggler! How else could you simultaneously support multiple users? Linux is a multitasking OS. It juggles multiple programs and users at the same time, creating the illusion that each user is working on his or her own computer. Obviously, only a little tiny bit of work can be done in a slice of time, but the illusion is well maintained. Other OSs that claim to be multitasking usually don't scale well. When a few users are accessing the services, performance rapidly decreases. The juggling illusion becomes reality for platforms that support multiple processors. The computer can, in fact, juggle multiple things at the same time. The Linux OS takes advantage of these hardware configurations and makes use of the additional processing power to increase performance to new levels—usually with better results than the original OS the hardware was designed for.

Many of today's computers rely on a networked environment. "The network is the computer" ᔆᴹ is the famous slogan for Sun Microsystems, a large UNIX vendor. The network is indeed the computer. Information exchange via email, the Web, and other mechanisms is an everyday fact. Linux can not only participate as a client for such

services, but it can also offer them to other PCs and workstations. Linux, in fact, powers many Internet service providers (ISPs) and the users who access the ISP's services. It is well tested and reliable.

Not many commercial environments provide the source code to how they work, and then do so freely. That's where Linux steps out from the crowd! Having the source code allows information service (IS) departments, or hackers as well, to customize the particular behavior of the OS or a program distributed with it to fit a particular need. Companies concerned about security issues can examine how the software really works and make their own evaluations and adjustments. In the event of a problem, someone with the right background can generate a fix, usually within hours of a problem or security issue being discovered. Compare that to waiting for days, weeks, or months for bug fixes—the norm that most of us have come to expect with other OSs. For the student, having access to the source code provides insight into how systems are made and built.

On the downside, UNIX and UNIX-like OSs have lacked ergonomics on the surface, providing confusing interfaces that vary from program to program and vendor to vendor, and generally aren't intuitive for nonexpert-type users. Mainstream application developers not seeing profitability with these environments have chosen to keep their wares on other, more profitable OS platforms. But that attitude is rapidly changing in the Linux market.

With its newfound popularity, Linux has encouraged big software developers such as Oracle, Sybase, Corel, and many others to develop versions of their applications for Linux systems. The world is beginning to take Linux seriously—and a little sponsoring goes a long way! This in itself has generated additional media interest, and Linux coverage has changed from a curiosity in obscure publications to a viable business option and alternative to heavyweight products from other companies. This is great news, because the more developers entering the Linux arena, the more popular and accessible this OS environment becomes!

With the advent of Linux, the infrastructure (the guts of what makes UNIX so robust) suddenly is available free of charge. In a world where a desktop license for the average commercial UNIX is several thousands of dollars, this is indeed a very good breakthrough. It has eased Linux into environments where UNIX would never have been considered due to price constraints.

No doubt much of its popularity starts with it being available for its nice price: free for the download or for under $50 if you want it packaged into a CD—or if you bought this book, you got an even better deal! It most definitely is priced to sell. Commercial distributions of Linux include additional commercial software that further enhances its value for resolving additional business-type problems.

Also helping with the Linux craze is the advent of the Internet. Many people requiring a robust environment to handle their Internet services, such as the World Wide Web, email, and others, have traditionally considered UNIX to be the natural for this.

From the beginning, most of the things you hear about today were available and developed there first. Macintosh and Windows-based machines only recently (in UNIX terms) have become networked. But even today, they still don't have the same robustness when playing server roles. UNIX machines have been participating in networks since almost the inception of networks.

Linux is a new concept for UNIX. It is freely available and supports cutting edge hardware, not to mention it's much easier to use than the UNIX systems that preceded it. That's not saying that rough edges are not to be found, however. Although Linux is not particularly difficult to learn, any difficulty comes with the increase in functionality. All powerful and flexible things are usually complicated; to say that Linux isn't powerful would deny its flexibility and complexity. New desktop environments, such as the K Desktop Environment (or KDE for short), are promising high-quality user interfaces that provide cutting-edge features previously unavailable to UNIX-like systems. Revitalized ergonomics provide a price-feature comparison not previously possible.

Included with this book is Caldera's OpenLinux 1.3. Caldera has positioned its Linux distribution as the commercial strength, reliable version of Linux. Some of its features are very nice when compared with the other popular distribution (RedHat). The additional add-ins provided by Caldera (Sybase, NetWare support, and so on) make it easy for OpenLinux to migrate to your workplace.

Recently, the city of Medina, Washington (population 3,082) selected OpenLinux to implement its document management system. The reason for this move was related to the 40,000+ construction permits, blueprints, change orders, and other documents related to the construction of the $53 million home that Microsoft's Bill Gates built there. The city's choice came at the realization that there was no more room for any future paperwork, and it would be required either to build a new town hall or to install a document management system. Naturally, Microsoft Windows NT was looked into as a potential solution, but after realizing that the OpenLinux solution would cost less than 10% of the NT solution, OpenLinux won the city's business. Talk about irony!

After such a persuasive argument about Linux being an up-and-coming OS, aren't you ready to get started? That's just what this book is designed to help you do—get started with Linux. If you are experienced with other OSs, this book will develop your Linux basic skills. One goal has been to make you productive right from the start. This book will take you from installing Linux to doing basic things and even to doing some system administration things.

Conventions

The Complete Idiot's Guide to Linux is designed to help you get up and running with your new Linux OS. In doing so, this book uses the following conventions:

> ➤ **Bold** indicates text that you type, items you select, click and press, and text that you see on your screen.

➤ You'll see monospace text for URLs, onscreen messages and command output.

➤ Any words that are being defined or emphasized will appear in *italics*.

Also, be sure to watch for these features:

Check This Out

You'll find "Check This Out" sections throughout the book. I'll use them to point out things that are noteworthy, stuff to be leery of, great tips—basically, they'll be full of information that will add to your understanding of Linux and maybe even make you say, "Wow!"

Techno Talk

Everyone knows that technical subjects sometimes leave you scratching your head wondering what that long-winded explanation just meant. Well, have no fear. I'll turn to "Techno Talk" boxes to let you know when to read carefully. This is where I'll highlight terms, methods or brainy stuff that you don't necessarily need to know, but that certainly helps you make more sense out of Linux.

Note

The "Note" boxes will be used to pass along cross-references pointing you to other parts of the book or for anything that I feel is something you should take a look at.

Acknowledgments

Writing a book is a monumental task that touches on the lives of many people. As usual, my personal monumental tasks get in queue during those times I tend to have more than enough to do. I am still trying to figure out a way of making the process easy on me and my family. Ideals are nice things.

To my beautiful and wonderful wife, Diana, and my three beautiful girls, Julisa, Isabella, and Viviana, this book is for you. I know I blew a summer for the second time. I think I know how you feel.

Knowing that single individuals cannot accomplish monumental tasks, many thanks are also needed for people whom I have never met in person, yet their periodical emails and phone calls made them seem closer than they are:

Laura Bulcher for making sure that I wrote what I meant to say.

Grace Buechlein for facilitating the many opportunities and making it all possible.

Aron Hsiao and Jeff Perkins for playing the reader's role and verifying that my writings are not fiction and that what I said works exactly how I say it does. (Any discrepancies are their fault and not mine ☺.)

All others, anonymous editors and formatters whose names I have no idea of, for making the production of this book a reality.

And, finally, Mr. Zero, Stephen Asbury—a friend since the NeXT days, with whom I share the unique pragmatic understanding of the good and evil in technology—for patiently listening to my colorful complaints while developing the "uphill" portion of this book.

Note

Linux is an evolving operating system. That's why it's all the more important for you to check the Caldera Systems Web site regularly for company announcements and software patches. Here's where you can find information specific to the release of Linux included with this book: http://www.calderasystems.com Be sure to take a look at the "News & Features" section for news, reviews and product updates.

Part 1

Working with Linux in a Graphical Environment—The KDE Desktop

Okay, so you've installed Linux (Part 4 walks you through that), and you're ready to face the beast. Guess what: You're in for a surprise! Part 1 gives you a look at the kindler, gentler side of Linux—the K Desktop Environment, or KDE. The chapters in this section walk you through working with applications, teaching your files who's boss, and communicating on the Web. We even take a look at how to customize KDE so that it looks and works the way you want it to. Are you ready to get this adventure started? Slide into your walking shoes, grab some snacks for the trip, and let's get moving!

The First Login on the KDE Desktop

This section assumes that you have already installed Caldera OpenLinux. If you didn't read the introduction, I recommend that you do so now, as the introduction explains the logical order for this book and some of the conventions used throughout.

In This Chapter

➤ Getting into Linux

➤ A first look at Linux under KDE

➤ Useful mouse and keyboard techniques

➤ Shutting down Linux

In this chapter you will learn how to get in and out of Linux using the K Desktop Environment, or KDE for short. KDE is a graphical user environment where you use icons, menus, and windows to do your work. You'll embark on a short tour of the screen and some of the user-interface (UI) elements provided by the KDE environment.

Logging In

Before you can use Linux, you have to log in. Logging in allows you to use the computer and protects your work from other users by allowing only you to access your files. Linux is a multiuser operating system in which many users can work at the same time. Login ensures that only authorized users are able to work with the computer.

If you installed Caldera OpenLinux and KDE (which is installed by default with the standard system install) as I suggest in Appendix A, your login prompt will look similar to this:

```
Caldera OpenLinux(TM)
Version 1.3
Copyright 1996-1998 Caldera Systems, Inc.

login:
```

The login process is simple: You provide your *username* and *password*. Your username and password are established when you install the system. If you are using an already configured system, you will need to contact your system administrator to find out what these are.

If you make a mistake while typing your username or password, you can press the Backspace key to erase the characters you want to retype. Note that you will not see your password on the screen as you type it. Not echoing your password to the screen helps to protect you and your account from nearby prying eyes.

After you have entered the correct information, the login panel will disappear, and you'll enter your desktop. If you made a mistake typing your password, you will see a message telling you that your login was incorrect and that you need to reenter your login and password again.

On a successful login, you will be let into the system. However you will be facing a text interface. To start up the graphical interface type **kde** at the prompt. (Note: Having to manually start the kde appears to be a bug with Caldera OpenLinux 1.3 and may be fixed by future patches available at the Caldera Web site.)

The KDE Desktop

A *desktop* is where you do your work on the computer. It is the workspace where you can start and run programs, create files, organize files, and do whatever it is you want to do with your computer. When you first enter your desktop, it will look similar to the one shown in the following figure.

Linux looks like this with the KDE desktop active.

If you have used other operating systems with a graphical user interface (GUI—you might hear some people pronounce this term "gooey," but the correct usage is "G-U-I"), you can probably go right to it and get some work done. The KDE desktop is similar to other windowed environments such as any flavor of Windows or the Macintosh; there are, however, some small and not-so-small differences in the way some things work.

Let's take a look at the KDE desktop components:

➤ The *panel* at the bottom of the screen

➤ The *taskbar* at the top of the screen

➤ The *desktop*

The Panel

The *panel* is the bar with icons at the bottom of your screen. It is used to launch applications; each of the icons represents an application, a command, or a menu (menus have a black triangle on them). Menus provide access to other features and applications.

The panel offers facilities for switching among various *virtual desktops*. With virtual desktops, you can reduce the clutter in your screen by running applications under separate desktops. You can switch between desktops easily by clicking a button (on the panel these buttons are labeled One, Two, Three, and Four). You will learn more about virtual desktops in Chapter 4, "Working with Applications."

The panel gives you access to applications and virtual desktops.

The Application Starter gives you access to your applications and the ability to log out of the system.

The Taskbar

The bar at the top of the screen is called the *taskbar*. Whenever you start a new application, a new button is displayed that's named after the application. Each of these buttons represents a task or application executing in the KDE environment. Clicking the mouse on a task button takes you to the application. The button that looks pressed belongs to the currently active application. If the application is hidden, its name is displayed in parenthesis. To show the application, just click its button. Right-clicking a button displays a menu that allows you to control some options of the application's window.

Each button on the taskbar represents a running application.

Both the panel and taskbar are services provided by an application called KPanel that runs whenever you log into your system and work under the KDE.

The Desktop

The *desktop* is the colored area between the taskbar and the panel. Individual program windows float above it. Under KDE you have several desktops. You control which desktop you are in by clicking on the buttons in the panel labeled "One," "Two," "Three," and "Four."

Another way to switch among desktops is to middle-click an empty area on the desktop. Doing so will display a menu that allows you to switch among desktops and applications.

The desktop can be used as a temporary location to place files and other things you are currently working on.

Applications

Applications are programs that present information in a window that you can open or close from your desktop. KEdit, the application pictured in the following figure, is a simple text editor you can use for editing files. To launch KEdit, you just click its icon on the panel.

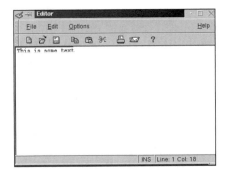

KEdit: a simple text editor that is easy to use.

KEdit, like most applications, has menus. Menus are located directly below the application's title bar. (KEdit's menus include File, Edit, Options, and Help.) *Menus* list commands that you can choose to make the application do something.

Using the Mouse

The *cursor* is usually a small black arrow that moves when you move the mouse. You use the cursor to point at objects. The appearance of the cursor will change depending on what you are pointing at.

Other variations of the cursor include:

➤ I-beam for editing text

➤ X when your cursor is over the desktop

Other inhabitants of your desktop are icons. *Icons* are a graphic representation of files, applications, or other things that live in your computer.

You can do almost everything on your computer using your mouse, with the exception of typing text. The mouse controls the location of the cursor. You slide the mouse to point at an object on the screen. If you run out of room while sliding the mouse, you can just pick it up and put it back down somewhere else on the mouse pad; the cursor won't move while the mouse is in the air. No matter how far you move the mouse, the cursor will stay on the screen.

Basic Mouse Actions

When you get the mouse to point at something, an icon or a word, you use the mouse button to perform one of these actions:

➤ *Click:* Without moving the mouse, press and release the left mouse button.

➤ *Right-click:* Without moving the mouse, press and release the right mouse button.

➤ *Middle-click:* Without moving the mouse, press and release the middle mouse button. If your mouse has only two buttons, press them both at the same time to simulate the middle button click. (This feels better with a three button mouse, though.)

➤ *Press:* Without moving the mouse, press the left mouse button and hold it down.

➤ *Drag:* Hold down the mouse button, move the cursor (you're still holding the button, right?), and then release the mouse button. The secret to a successful drag is to resist the temptation to let go until the object you're dragging is exactly where you want it.

➤ *Double-click:* Click twice in quick succession. If you click over text, the I-beam cursor is placed between characters. If you double-click, you select the word you are working on. Some applications might use triple-clicking to select a paragraph or perform some other application defined function.

Buttons, Menus, and Text Fields

The basic controls of a modern UI can be grouped into three categories:

➤ Buttons

➤ Lists and menus

➤ Text fields

Buttons

Buttons often are in application windows to give you easy access to certain commands. Buttons come in a variety of shapes and sizes. They are usually labeled with text and graphics indicating what they do. To activate a button, you click on it. If the button is just an image, when you move the cursor over it, the button might draw a border around itself to let you know that it is indeed a button and that you can click it. If you hover over a button for a while, the button might display a "tool tip" telling you what the button does.

Dimmed buttons are not active and cannot be clicked. (Well, you could click them, but nothing will happen.) Buttons appear dimmed either because their functionality is unavailable or their function is not applicable at the moment.

Buttons often look like this; note the change in color on an activated button.

These icons are buttons too!

Most applications have a toolbar with buttons. Move the cursor over an icon, and a border will appear around the button along with a tool tip, or text that tells you what the button does.

If after you start clicking a button, you decide you don't want to click it after all, just move the cursor off the button before releasing the mouse.

Some buttons, called *check boxes*, allow you to enable multiple options available to your application. Check boxes under X Windows are rendered as squares.

You can select multiple check boxes in a group.

Other buttons, known as *radio buttons,* allow you to enable only a single option in the group. Clicking on a different option disables the previously selected option as it enables the new one. Radio buttons under X Windows are rendered as diamonds.

Radio buttons are called so because they're like the radio buttons in your car stereo: They can only be set to one thing at a time.

15

You can only pick one
radio button in a group.

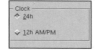

Tabs are another kind of button. They allow an application to group and display information and controls in a limited amount of space. By clicking on a tab, you reveal a different set of controls and information.

The Options tab stores
some controls...

...while the Desktops tab
in the same panel stores
an entirely different set of
controls.

Sliders are used to set a value that is in a range. To use the slider, drag its knob to the desired value or position.

Sliders allow you to set a
value in a constrained
range, like choosing a vol-
ume level on your stereo.

Lists and Menus

You tell an application what to do using commands. Commands typically are in menus. Applications have menus right under their window's title bar.

Working with menus is similar to working with buttons. If you click a menu button (also called *menu item*), the menu opens, and you can then click one of its commands.

You can also click and drag on a menu. The option under your cursor when you release the mouse becomes the selected command.

If the menu displays an arrow, the command offers submenus. You can treat submenus in much the same way as menus.

In a hierarchical menu, clicking a menu item displaying an arrow opens a submenu with additional commands or submenus.

An ellipsis (...) marks a command that opens a window or dialog box. Never be afraid to explore menu commands with an ellipsis, because you can always cancel the dialog box with no adverse effect.

Commands can also be invoked by typing a keyboard accelerator. For example, you can invoke the Open Terminal command by typing Ctrl+T while the K File Manager (or KFM) window displayed in the previous figure active. A different application might use Ctrl+T for a different purpose.

Menus that display an underscore (_) under a letter can be opened with the keyboard by pressing Alt+*letter*.

Dimmed commands are currently unavailable and cannot be selected.

Choice lists are similar to menus. They open a drop-down list of options from which you can choose. While still holding the mouse button, drag your mouse until the cursor points to the option you want. Release the mouse to select the option. Choice lists that sport a text field (described next) are called "Combo Boxes," because they allow you to select from a menu or type a new choice and they are a combination of controls.

The choice list looks like this before it is activated...

...like this while you're making a selection...

...and like this after you release the mouse.

17

Text Fields

When an application requires additional information in the form of text, you enter that information into a text field or its larger cousin, the text area. A label typically indicates the purpose of the text field.

This dialog box requires text input.

When working with a text field, an I-beam cursor is displayed, indicating that you can type text there. To move to another field or to give a field focus, click on it.

To select a portion of the text, click the mouse button where you want to begin the selection and drag to where you want to end it. (In some applications, you can also click and then Shift+click the selection's end.)

To select text, click the mouse where you want to begin a selection...

...and then drag to where you want the selection to end. The selected text is highlighted, and typing replaces the current selection.

Manipulating Controls with the Keyboard

You can move around controls and forms (a collection of controls) by pressing the Tab key. The currently active control will display a black outline to indicate that it is selected. You can then use your keyboard to change its current setting, type data if the control is a text field, or select it if it's some sort of button.

You can use your keyboard's arrow keys to change the setting of a slider.

If the control can be clicked, you can probably also activate it by pressing the Spacebar while the control is selected.

To move backward, you can press Shift+Tab.

Ending the Work Session

At the end of your work session, you can log out. If you don't expect to use your computer for a day or two, you should turn it off. Remember to save your work before you do any of these things. The procedure of shutting down your system is critical to the health of your disk, so don't just switch off the power button!

To log out, choose Logout from the application starter (the X icon) or click the logout icon in the KDE panel. If you have applications open, you will get a "Session prepared for logout" dialog showing what data you are likely to lose. You can then change your mind at this point if you need to go back and save information.

Check This Out

Don't turn off the power to your computer until the computer says that the system has been halted. Otherwise, you can damage your computer.

To turn off your computer, first log out and then choose Shutdown on the login panel. On the panel that appears choose Shutdown again. After your computer has been halted, you can power it off.

To restart your computerinstead of simply halting it, logout and then, on the login panel, choose Shutdown. In the resulting dialog box, chose Restart.

If for some strange reason your desktop ever stops responding, you can force an exit by pressing Ctrl+Alt+Backspace. Doing so will terminate the X server (KDE) and take you back to the console. Here again is one of the benefits of Linux: You can exit a locked-up GUI without having to reboot your machine.

Working with Windows

In This Chapter

➤ Working with windows

➤ Opening and closing windows

➤ Iconifying and maximizing windows

➤ Sticking windows to the desktop

Under Linux, you can work in your choice of interface: One is the console (a text-based interface generated by one of several shell programs); the other is with a graphical user interface (GUI) such as the X Window System, more commonly known as X Windows. In the GUI, windows represent applications and documents. Even if the window is just a fancy interface to the console, a windowed environment makes you more productive because you are able to interact with multiple applications and programs at the same time.

Techno Talk

Unlike other operating systems, X Windows, the windowing environment on UNIX and UNIX-like environments like Linux, allows you to choose your interface. In X Windows terms, the look and feel of your windows are provided by a window manager.

The window manager defines what the user interface looks and feels like. KDE is a window manager with many additional and desirable features, but you can substitute it with others. Some are already built into your system.

Windows and Panels

KDE windows behave similar to their counterparts in other operating systems. Windows typically fall into two categories:

➤ Standard application windows

➤ Dialogs and panels

A standard application window is where you do your work in an application. If you are writing a letter, for example, you typically do so on a standard window like the one pictured in the next figure. Each application presents different functionality on a window. A Web browser displays a Web page in a window. A file manager, where you manage your files and folders, also works in a window.

KEdit, a text editor, offers a good illustration of an application window and its elements.

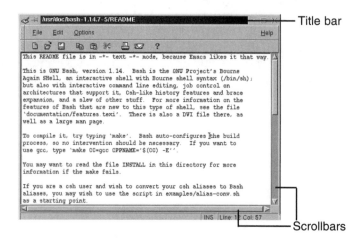

Windows have a *title bar* at the top that shows the window's name. Typically, this name will be the name of the application or the document you are working on. Other times, a dialog might display some other informative message in this area. KDE title bars that are too small for their title display an interesting animation: The title bounces back and forth in a frenetic ping-pong dance.

Windows also typically have *scrollbars*, slider-type controls along the right side and bottom of a window, to move around the view of your document. Scrollbars appear when your document is larger than the window can display.

Dialog boxes and panels are windows that let you enter information to tell the application what to do. You typically see them in response to issuing a menu command or by activating some application functionality that requires your confirmation, such as quitting the application, saving a file, and so on.

Other panels allow you to enter additional information needed by the command. For example, the Find panel in the KEdit application requires information about the text you want to find.

Some panels, called *dialogs*, ask you a question and provide buttons for you to supply an answer. Other dialogs just inform you of some event taking place and require your acknowledgment to dismiss the box.

A panel can have text fields, in which you supply additional text information to a command, and controls, in which you specify additional options to the command.

The relief of around the Yes button means that you can operate the button by pressing the Enter or Return key on your keyboard.

Some panels just provide buttons for you to select from among a multiple options.

Some dialog boxes simply require you to acknowledge them to dismiss them.

Window Controls

Windows provide several manipulation controls. Many of these controls are displayed on the window's title bar area.

The title bar area of a KDE window has several buttons.

The window button displays a menu with window manipulation commands. Most of the commands you see there are also accessible through other buttons in the title bar. Sometimes this button is displayed as a small icon representing the application. In this case, the little icon is the window button.

The Stick or Pin button will "stick" a window so that the window is available from any virtual desktop.

The Iconify button collapses a window into the taskbar. Clicking its task button on the taskbar will make the window reappear on the desktop.

The Maximize/Restore button expands the window to its maximum size possible in your screen. Clicking it a second time restores it to its previous size.

The Close button closes the window and terminates the application.

The Active Window

To work with a window, the window needs to be focused or active. The *active window* is one that has the dark title bar. It is the one that will receive keystrokes if you started typing. There can only be one active window at any one time.

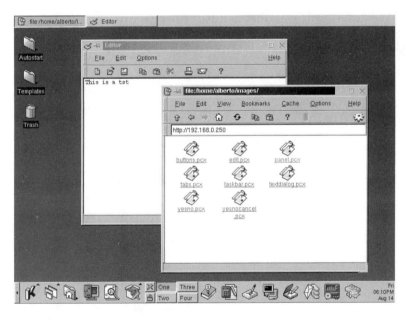

Active windows have dark title bars and are able to receive keyboard input. Inactive windows have a grayed title bar.

How you activate a window will depend on the focus policy. Essentially, there are two main ways you can activate a window: The first is by clicking on the window (the default setting in KDE); the other is by moving the cursor over the window you want active (default on other window managers).

25

I like the click to change active windows, because I can activate a window and bring it to the front by clicking anywhere on it. The other policy, although potentially saving you some clicks in the course of a day, require that you are careful where you park your mouse.

Accessing Windows that Overlap

It is possible for windows to completely overlap so that one completely covers another. In this situation, you might have to iconify a window to get it out of the way or access the window you want through a menu or the taskbar.

The Windowlist menu in the panel gives you access to all your open windows. It provides a convenient way to access a window that is covered by another.

Scrollbars

If the window is too small to display the contents of the document you are viewing, the window will display scrollbars. Scrollbars are placed along the bottom if the document is wider than the window or to the right if the document is taller than the window.

Scrollbars allow you to view a document that is larger than can fit in a window.

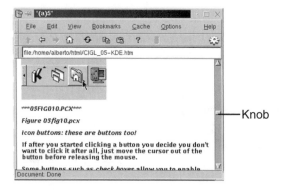

A scrollbar works like a slider: You move its knob (also called the "thumb") up and down (or left and right), and the document scrolls in that direction. You can also press the arrow buttons at the ends of the scrollbar to scroll continuously. If you click on the scrollbar area, the document will scroll one unit, line, or page, depending on how the application behaves.

Resizing Windows

Windows can be resized by grabbing them on one of their edges or corners. When you are in the resize zone, the cursor will change to the window resize cursor (see Chapter 1, "The First Login on the KDE Desktop."

To resize a window in one dimension, grab one of its edges. To resize on both dimensions at the same time, drag from a corner.

Moving a Window

You can move a window around by dragging it by its title bar. As you drag, the window will follow your cursor. When you have placed the window where you want it, release the mouse button.

Another way of moving a window is by using the move command available under the window menu. (You can also obtain a window menu by right-clicking the window's title bar.)

Finally, if you press the Alt key and press the mouse button anywhere on a window (not just the title bar), the window will move anywhere you drag your mouse.

Moving a window by dragging its title bar.

Closing a Window

When you are finished working with a document or application, you can close it by clicking its close button on the title bar. If the document needs saving, the application should prompt you to save changes. You usually don't have to worry about shutting down an application and accidentally losing your work! But because some applications might not be consistent, it's always a good idea to save a document before you close its window; otherwise, changes could be lost. Windows can also be closed by issuing the Close command from the window menu.

Navigating through the File System

The computer keeps and organizes information in files and folders. A file can be a chapter for your best-selling novel or an image scan of your favorite place on earth. A file can also be a program or application used to create other files. A folder can contain other folders and files, which in turn can contain more folders and files, nested as many levels as you want.

The files and folders in your computer make up the file system. At the very top of your computer's file system is a root folder that contains all files and directories stored in your computer.

Each file and folder in your computer has a name that identifies its contents. For example, a folder containing your email files might aptly be named "Mail." A file containing your to-do list might be called "todo."

Filenames in Linux can be up to 256 characters in length. They can contain numbers and uppercase and lowercase letters. You can use most characters; however, there are some that you should avoid. Characters such as the asterisk (*), question mark (?), ampersand (&), vertical bar (¦), circumflex (^), quote ("), and apostrophe (') should

never be used, as these characters are special to the shell. Characters such as dash (-) and spaces should not be used because they will be hard to work with and delete through a shell. (The dash is used to specify program arguments. Some tools will get confused when the name of a file begins with a dash, because they will think that you are specifying arguments instead of a filename.) The space will make the shell think that you are specifying two different files. (Surround it with quotes to access it from a shell.) You should avoid these characters even if you only intend to work through KDE or another graphical environment.

In addition to their descriptive name, files and folders have a pathname that identifies their location in the file system. The pathname lists all the folders, starting at the root, that you must traverse to reach the file. All names in the file path are separated by a slash (/). A slash at the beginning of the pathname represents the root folder.

This is Linux's hierarchical file system.

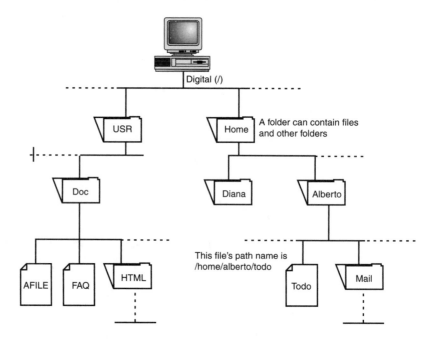

Everything you do under Linux will require that you interact with the file system. Under Linux there are two ways you can access your files:

➤ Through a graphical environment like KDE

➤ Through a shell or command prompt

This section focuses on using the graphic tool K File Manager (KFM), which is part of the KDE environment. Other X environments provide their own tools or, as a last resort, xfm (The X File Manager).

The File System Through KFM

KFM is the file manager for KDE. KFM provides *network-transparent* file access. This term means that if your computer is connected to a network, you can use the graphical interface to access resources stored in other computers using standard internet protocols such as FTP (File Transfer Protocol) or HTTP (Hypertext Transfer Protocol, the protocol used by the Web). This functionality is very powerful, as it allows you to browse information located on your disk or on a computer in China with equal ease.

In KFM, icons represent files and folders. Uniform Resource Locators (URLs) represent file paths. An URL is like a file path on steroids: It specifies the location of a file (a resource) that you can access using various protocols. URLs typically provide

Check This Out

Accessing files through a shell is covered in detail in Chapter 11, "Shells and Consoles."

➤ The protocol (how to access the resource)

➤ A machine name (the machine storing the resource)

➤ The path to the resource

Unless you've been away from civilization during the past few years, you have heard about the Internet—and probably are familiar with Internet addresses such as `http://www.aol.com` or `http://www.yahoo.com`. These addresses are URLs.

File URLs look similar to HTTP URLs: `file:/home/alberto`. One obvious difference is that the protocol used is called `file` instead of `http`. The file protocol specifies a file in a local computer, your computer. The other difference is that there's only one slash after the colon instead of the two you might have seen or used while accessing the Web.

A KFM window provides you with menus, a tool bar with navigation tools, a location field where you enter file paths and URLs, and a status area for messages and additional information about a file.

Typically you open a KFM window by clicking the home button on the panel. Other features of the KFM window include:

➤ Toolbar — Provides you with shortcuts to move around in the file system and for manipulating files.

➤ Location field — Specifies the URL you are browsing.

➤ Status area — Displays information about files and file selections. (at the bottom on the window)

➤ Home button (KFM) — Click this button to create a file viewer window.

The root directory as displayed by KFM looks like this. Note the additional information displayed in the status area for the vmlinuz *file.*

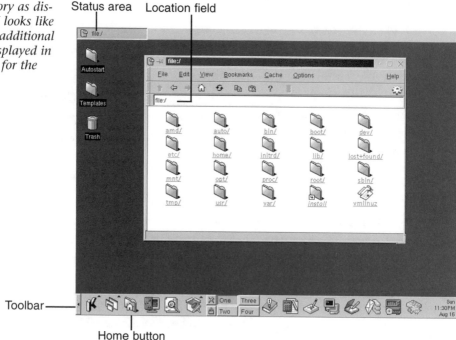

The KFM Navigation Toolbar

The KFM toolbar provides you with convenient buttons for moving between directories and manipulating files:

➤ The Up button will move you one folder up from your current location.

➤ The Back button will move you to your previous location. If you have entered directories in the location bar, the back button will move you in reverse order of your navigation history.

➤ The Forward button will move forward in your navigation history. (You must have used the back button for this one to be enabled.)

➤ The Home button will take you to your home directory.

➤ The Refresh button will reload the directory and make any changes you have made visible.

➤ The Copy and Paste buttons are explained in Chapter 6, "Organizing Your Files."

➤ The Help button opens up the help program with information about KDE.

➤ The Task button is animated when a lengthy task is taking place. If you click it, you can create a new KFM window.

KFM's toolbar provides various buttons to assist you in navigating the file system.

Opening a Folder

You open a folder to see what other files and folders it contains. When you open a folder, the KFM window displays the contents of the new directory. Initially, KFM displays files as large icons. Other view formats are available from the View menu.

To open a directory, just click on it. You can also use your keyboard's arrow keys to move among icons. To open the selected file, press Enter. The keyboard technique allows you to "select" a file. Because KFM uses a single click to open a file, it's difficult to select files with the mouse: A single click can take you into a directory you didn't mean to open. Future versions of KFM will allow you to use a double-click to open a directory.

To view a folder's contents in a new window, right-click the folder.

To select a folder without opening it, click on it while pressing the Ctrl key.

Dot files—files with a name beginning with a period (.)—are typically omitted from file listings. To view dot files with KFM, select the Show Dot Files command from the View menu.

When you open a directory, the view displaying the contents of the previous folder is replaced with the contents of the new folder.

Opening a File

You open a file to see its contents, just like a folder. When you open a file, KFM opens the file by running the application associated with the file. If the application is not currently running, KFM starts it up for you. When the application opens, it displays your file.

If the file is an application, KFM simply starts the application.

To select a file without opening it, click on it while pressing the Ctrl key.

KFM uses various methods to try to figure the type of a file. One of the methods it uses is to look at the file extension (typically a three-character name following a period at the end of a filename). Another method peeks at the contents of the file.

If KFM cannot figure out what application opens your file, the file will display an icon with a question mark.

The unknown file icon looks like this.

If you try to open such a file, KFM will prompt you for the application to use.

When KFM doesn't know how to open a file, it prompts you for the name of the program to use, which you can type in the text field provided.

If you click the Browser button on this panel, KFM displays a list of applications it knows about.

A Tree View

KFM provides a tree view that you can use to easily jump among folders. You can enable tree views through the Show Tree option in the View menu.

The Show Tree command displays three folders: the root folder (/), a shortcut to your own home directory called "My Home," and a directory called "Desktop."

Check This Out

To associate a file with a KDE application, see Chapter 10, "Customizing KDE."

The tree view allows you to easily move among folders. Opened folders display a down arrow.

A File List

You can list the contents of the current folder in such a way that it includes additional information about each of the files, such as its size, owner, and permissions and the time it was last modified. To view additional file details, choose the Long View option in the View menu.

The Long View option provides more information about a file.

What the Listing Means

When you display the contents of a folder using Long View, the following additional information is displayed in a table format:

➤ Name of the file

➤ Permissions

➤ File owner

➤ File group

➤ File size

➤ Last modification time

Let's examine these components in more detail.

File Size

This refers to the size of the file in bytes. A *byte* represents one character of information. 1024 characters represent 1K (Kilobyte) of data. One Megabyte is 1024K.

Last Changed

The time and date that the file was last modified is shown. The time is displayed using 24-hour military time, where 6:00PM is represented as 18:00 and midnight is 0:00.

File Owner

The username represents the owner of the file or folder. This is typically the user who created it. The owner of a file can grant permissions to the file so that others may be able to access and read the file.

File Group

On a multiuser system like Linux, multiple users can be assigned to a group. A group allows its members to more easily share files. Groups and owners are closely related with permissions.

Permissions

All files in the file system have three sets of permissions. One set exists for the owner of the file, one for the group of the file, and one for other users. These permission sets allow the owner of a file to control who can access the files he or she creates.

Permissions work because all users are required to log into Linux before having access to the computer. Whenever you access a file, the system checks to see if you have the proper permissions on the file. If you don't, the system rejects your request. There are several levels of permission:

➤ Read permissions (r) indicate who can read the file

➤ Write permissions (w) indicate who can modify the file

➤ Execute permissions (x) indicate who can run a program or read a directory

➤ Absence of permission is shown by a dash (-)

Permissions are specified as three groups; here's how the permissions read:

> **-rw-r--r--** owner permissions to read and write
>
> -rw-**r**--**r**-- group permissions to read
>
> -rw-r--**r**-- others permissions to read
>
> **d**rwxr-xr-x a "d" marks a folder or "directory"
>
> **l**rwxrwxrwx an "l" marks a link to a file or folder

Bookmarks

KFM is able to remember locations in your file system through "bookmarks." A *bookmark* allows you to save a location so you can quickly return to it no matter how deep it is. In this regard, they function like Web bookmarks.

To create a bookmark:

1. Navigate to the desired location using KFM
2. Choose the Add Bookmark command under the Bookmarks menu

Bookmarks can be accessed through the Bookmarks menu available from the KFM window or by right-clicking on an empty area of your desktop.

Selecting Files and Folders

In KFM you can select multiple files with the mouse if you hold down the Ctrl key while making your selection. From the keyboard, you can use the arrow keys to move among icons. To select an icon, press the Spacebar. To open the icon, press Enter.

Using the keyboard to select multiple files. The box around the icon indicates the current icon. To move to another icon, use the arrow keys.

Working with Applications

In This Chapter

➤ Various ways you can launch and stop applications

➤ How to work with multiple applications

➤ How to use virtual desktops

➤ A list of some of the KDE applications that you might find in your application starter

Both KDE and Linux come with a number of applications ready to use. This chapter teaches you how to work with applications in a graphical environment. You'll see that working with multiple applications at the same time is very easy under a graphical environment such as KDE.

Applications, Programs, and Tools

So what is the difference between an application, a program, and a tool? All of them are programs. A *program* is something that runs in your computer.

In general, an *application* is a program that is interactive, uses a graphical user interface (GUI), and is flexible for a number of tasks.

A *tool* can sometimes be interactive and guide you through various steps, but it is more limited in scope. Typically, tools run in the command line, but depending on the tool, it could also have a GUI.

In this book I use the terms interchangeably; however, most of the time, an application is a program that runs under X Windows (or KDE), and a tool runs under a shell. We talk about tools and shells in Part II.

Manually Starting an Application

There are several ways you can start an application:

➤ If the application appears on the panel, you can click its icon.

➤ If you are browsing using KFM and you see the applications icon in a window, you can also click it to start it up.

➤ If you know the name of the application's program file, or "binary," you can type it into a shell to launch it. (You will get information on how to work with a shell in Part 2 of this book, "Working on the Command Line.")

➤ Finally, if the application is available on the Application Starter (K Menu), you can launch it by picking the appropriate entry in the menu. The Application starter is shown in the following figure.

When an application is launched, Linux will load it into memory and start it. After a few seconds of disk activity, you will see its window appear. A task button is also added to the taskbar to represent it.

Pick an application to start it.

Executable shell program

Image file

Command line

The KDE Desktop gives you several ways of starting an application.

Application starter.

Shortcuts to frequently used applications

Documents or applications stored in Autostart are launched when you start the session. Applications can also be started by typing their name on the command line.

An application can also be started by clicking on the icon for a document associated with it. If you click on a document, its application will start up and display the contents of the document.

Working with Multiple Applications

Linux is a multitasking operating system. Working and running with multiple applications at the same time is easy under a graphical environment such as KDE. Even though many applications can run at the same time, there's only one active window.

Check This Out

Applications and documents are associated via kdelnk files. Kdelnk files have a .kdelnk extension. These files provide information that allows KFM to associate icons, documents, and applications. Having these associations allows KFM to open your document with an application when you click on a document's icon. For more information on .kdelnk files, see Chapter 10.

41

The active window displays a differently colored title bar, and its button on the taskbar appears to be pressed. The active application is the one that is able to receive keyboard input. Even though some of your applications are running in the background, that does not mean they are idle. If you have a lengthy operation running in one application, you can work on a different application while the other task completes in the background.

Switching Between Applications

There are two ways that you can switch between applications: If the application window you wish to make active is visible, you can click in it; or if the application is hiding or if its windows are displayed in a different desktop, click the task button representing the application in the taskbar (see the following figure).

Switching between applications.

Icon of the next application

Name of the next application

WordPerfect <2>

Currently running applications

You can also switch between applications by pressing Alt+Tab. If you keep the Alt key pressed and then hit Tab, you will see a series of icons representing all running applications. Hitting Tab again (while still holding the Alt key) will display the next application on the list. When you have found the application you want to make active, let go of the Alt key.

Hiding an Application

You can hide an application by clicking its iconify (also called minimize) button. The application is still running and available, but its windows are removed from the screen. A hidden application continues to display a button in the taskbar.

Say you're working with multiple applications and you're finished with one, but you think you will need the application again soon. It is faster and easier to hide it and keep it running than to quit and restart it later.

When you click the application's button in the taskbar, the application and its windows are restored to their previous location.

Virtual Desktops

In KDE you have the ability to work in more than one desktop at a time. This ability is useful if you perform different tasks that require various groups of applications running at the same time.

Using a virtual desktop is similar to hiding applications, except that when you move between desktops, all applications belonging to that desktop are restored to their previous state. For example, you can use one virtual desktop to compose your email and read Internet news, another for a task such as programming or writing, and yet another to play a game or do anything that strikes your fancy.

In KDE you can have up to eight different virtual desktops. By default, however, only four are available. (Later, in the section "Changing the Number of Virtual Desktops," you'll learn how to customize the number of desktops you have accessible.) Different desktops have different color backgrounds to help you tell them apart. By default, the virtual desktops are called One, Two, Three, and Four, but you can rename them as you see fit.

The Virtual desktops feature and KDE's Workspace Auto-restore feature make a powerful combination. You will find more information on the KDE Workspace Auto-restore feature later in the section "The KDE Workspace Auto-restore Feature."

Switching Between Desktops

To switch between virtual desktops, click the desktop button in the panel (see the following figure). If you like keyboard commands, you can also press Ctrl+F*n*, where *n* is the number of the virtual desktop you want to view. You can also press Ctrl+Tab to cycle between the various desktops.

Virtual Desktop buttons

To switch between desktops, click the button for the desktop you want to visit.

If you click on a task button for an application that is active in a different desktop, you will also switch to that desktop.

To switch between applications and desktops and get a list of the current tasks organized by desktop, press Ctrl+Esc. (Alt+Esc also works for this purpose. And, you can use the Windowlist menu in the panel for this purpose. See "Accessing Windows that Overlap" in Chapter 2, "Working with Windows.")

Sending an Application to a Different Desktop

To send an application to a different desktop, you can use the window menu and pick the appropriate desktop from the To desktop submenu. The window menu is accessible from all KDE windows (see the following figure).

Use the To Desktop sub-menu to move an application to a different desktop.

Click to display window menu.

Alternatively, you can right-click the window's title bar to display a number of menu commands, including the To desktop submenu. Note that the icon displayed for this menu will be different depending on the application you are running.

When you send an application to a different desktop, the application disappears from the current desktop and reappears in its new desktop. To see the application again, view the desktop to which you sent it.

Sharing an Application Across Virtual Desktops

There are some applications that you must use in all desktops. A good example of this is the file manager. Instead of having multiple KFM windows in different desktops, it might be better to share the application with all desktops. You use the pin icon (also called the stick button) in a window for this purpose (see the following figure). Windows that have this button pressed will be accessible from all desktops.

To "pin" a window and make it visible from all desktops, click the pin icon on a window's title bar.

44

Pinning a window displays it in all desktops. In this figure, the KFM window is shared by all virtual desktops.

—KFM Window

Desktop Pager: Switching Between Applications and Desktops

KDE also includes a desktop pager application called, appropriately enough, Desktop Pager. A *desktop pager* is an application that provides a miniaturized view of all your virtual desktops and the windows they contain.

Switching between desktops and applications is just a matter of picking the right button and the application you want. Applications windows are labeled according to the application to which they belong.

Desktop Pager is available from the Application Starter menu under the System application group. You can also start the pager by issuing the command **kwmpager** on a shell.

Enabling the Active Desktop Borders Options

You can configure virtual desktops so that if you move a window and touch the edge of the screen, you automatically switch between desktops. This feature might feel more natural for moving applications across desktops. The desktops are arranged in the same geographic positions as shown on the panel and on the Desktop Pager tool (see the previous figure).

To enable the Active Desktop Borders feature, you'll need to access the KDE Control Center Application from the Application Starter Menu. Once the Control Center window appears, expand the Desktop category by clicking the plus sign next to it, and then choose the Desktop option. Check the Enable active desktop borders option (see the next figure). (This item is also available from the Application Starter by choosing the Settings menu, clicking Desktop, and then choosing Desktop from the submenu.)

The Desktop Pager (kwm-pager) displays buttons with a thumbnail view of all your virtual desktops. To change to a desktop, just click on the desktop button you want.

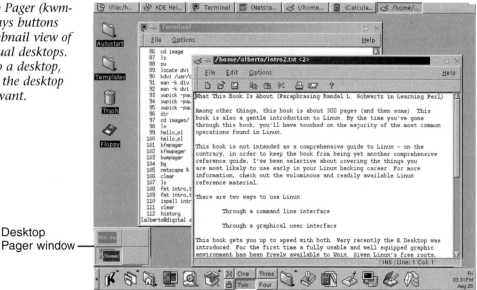

Desktop
Pager window

Check this option to
enable active borders.

You can enable Active Desktop Borders in this dialog box.

Controls how long
you must hit border
of screen prior to
changing desktops.

When option is
enabled, windows
snap near their
borders.

Controls where your pointer
will be when you are taken
to a different desktop

Changing the Number of Virtual Desktops

Depending on your work habits, you might need more or less than the initial four virtual desktops provided by KDE. If that is the case, you can have a maximum of eight desktops. To add more desktops to your KDE environment, go to the Application Starter (K menu on the panel), choose Panel, and select the Configure command. This displays the KPanel Configuration window. Pick the Desktops tab (see the following figure). Additional desktops can be added or removed by sliding the Visible slider.

Reveals desktop
configuration window

You can add up to eight virtual desktops using the KPanel Configuration window.

Name
your new
virtual
desktop

Controls
number of
vitural desk-
tops shown

Controls
width of
panel
buttons

Customizing the Look of a Virtual Desktop

You can control the look of a virtual desktop by activating the Application Starter, choosing Settings, selecting Desktop, and picking the Background tool. You'll see the Display Settings dialog box, which looks like this:

You can customize the look of your virtual desktops in the Display Settings dialog box.

Select the virtual desktop you want to customize

Sets background to flat color

Sets background to two colors

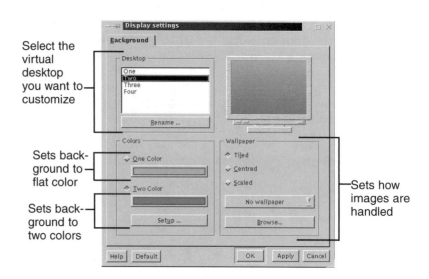

Sets how images are handled

Starting Applications Automatically

The KDE desktop has a special directory called Autostart. Any program or file in the Autostart directory automatically launches when you start a KDE session.

To put a file in the Autostart directory, navigate the KFM application to the directory containing the file you want. Click the file, drag it to the Autostart directory, and release the mouse button. KFM will display a menu giving you the choice to copy, move, or link the file to the Autostart directory. Choose link. The next time you log in to KDE, the document will open when you log in.

You can put links to directories and to applications in the Autostart directory. Links to directories result in a folder window to that directory that displays on the desktop when you log in. Links to applications result in having the application launched when you log in.

The KDE Workspace Auto-restore Feature

If you log out of the system without first quitting all opened applications, KDE will remember applications and documents you left open and restore them when you log in the next time. This feature can be useful if you work with multiple applications and you take a lot of care in organizing your various desktops.

For this feature to work, the application must be able to communicate with the KDE desktop. Typically, only KDE-aware (or X11-aware) applications are capable of performing this feature; command-line programs don't have this feature, so they don't work. If the application is sophisticated, it might also be able to remember the document you were editing and open it up for you. When you exit the workspace, KDE will warn you of applications that don't support this feature.

KDE Application Help: kdehelp

Most KDE applications provide a built-in help. This help system is accessible through the Help menu. Choosing the Contents command from the Help menu will open up the kdehelp viewer. This tool is a specialized browser for help information. If you are familiar with using a Web browser, you'll have no problems navigating this system. In short, text that is underlined is a hyperlink. Clicking on a hyperlink will take you to the location in the documentation where the topic is discussed.

The kdehelp tool is also accessible from the panel (see the following figure).

The kdehelp tool is a specialized Web browser for surfing KDE documentation.

Features of this window include:

➤ All KDE applications have a Help menu. Select the Contents command to open the kdehelp tool and choose Contents.

➤ Clicking underlined text will show you more detailed information about the underlined topic.

➤ The kdehelp tool can also be started by clicking the icon on your panel pointed out in the previous figure.

Exiting Applications

To exit an application, you can click the main window's close button or use the Exit command under the File menu. Because some applications you use won't behave consistently, it is always a good idea to save your document before you click a window's close button. Well-behaved applications should give you the opportunity to save your work before quitting.

Creating, Editing, and Saving Files

In This Chapter

➤ Creating a New File

➤ Opening Existing Files

➤ Working with the Open Panel

➤ Saving Changes to Your Documents

➤ Editing Text

Files store information on the computer's disk. When you type a letter to a friend in an editor window, the text you enter is stored in the computer's memory. Your letter is typically referred to as a *document*. If you quit the program without first saving your document to a file on your computer's disk, the information is lost. When you save your document to a file, you can later open it and continue editing it where you left off the last time you saved it.

In this chapter, you will learn to work with files from within an application: how to open and save files and how to save different copies of a file. This chapter also serves as an introduction on how to use a prototypical application such as the editor provided by KDE, KEdit. (KEdit is a simple text editor bundled with KDE.)

Creating and Saving Files

All KDE applications use similar menus and commands to save and open files. If the application you are using is not part of KDE or is not designed for the KDE environment, the interface will be a little different. Overall, however, it should be analogous to a KDE application, and you should be able to find your way around it.

Creating a New File

Typically, when you want to create a new file, you open an application and begin working. Usually, applications will start with an empty file (sometimes this is a document, but not always). If the application is already running, you might need to create a new document window, by either running a new instance of the application or using the application's New command. Typically, this command under KDE will be found under the File menu. Some applications allow you to work on multiple documents at the same time; some will allow you to edit only one document at a time. If your application only supports a single document at a time, you can bypass this limitation by launching another copy of the application. In the following figure you'll see KEdit (a text editor).

Creating a new file is as easy as choosing a menu command.

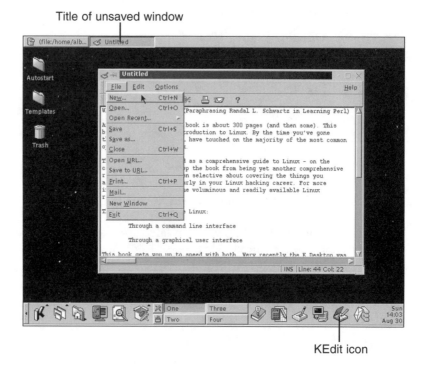

Title of unsaved window

KEdit icon

Features of this window include:

➤ The File menu, which provides commands for dealing with a document and the application such as New for creating new files, Open to open an existing file, Save to save a file, Close to close the document, and Exit to exit the application.

Choose New to create a new document. If you would like to work on several documents at the same time, you can use the New Window command or start another instance of the application.

➤ The KEdit icon is the 2nd icon from the right (pencil with the green cover): To start KEdit, click its icon on the panel.

➤ The title of an unsaved window is Untitled.

When you save your work in an application, it is stored in a file so that you can later read it or modify it. When you save a file for the first time, you give the file a name.

If you close the document window without saving your work, your work is lost because you did not save it to disk. Well-behaved programs will ask you to save your documents into a file before you exit them or before you close an unsaved window. Some not-so-well-behaved programs will readily discard your work without any warning. Stay away from programs that exhibit such behaviors.

Opening an Existing File

To open an existing file, you can use the Open command from the File menu (see the following figure). The Open command will present a panel that allows you to select a document to work with. You can use this panel to navigate through your folders (directories) until you find the document you want to edit.

Add/Go to a bookmark —— Create a new folder
Reload/refresh current folder —— Find a file
Go to your home folder —— Customizes the look and feel and behavior of open panel
Move one folder up

Folders available within the current folder

Filter designation

List of current files List an entry for directory tree

The Open panel lets you open an existing file for viewing, editing, and, in some cases, just selecting the file.

—— Location
—— Display files whose names begin with a period (.)

Instead of using the user interface controls to move between directories, sometimes it might be easier and faster to type the name of the path and name of the file in the Location field.

When you click on a file, the Open panel will disappear, and the document will load into the application.

Customizing the Open Panel

There are many options available to the Open panel that you can use to configure the way that files are displayed. To change your configuration, select the Configure button (see the previous figure).

You can customize many elements of the Open panel in this dialog box.

Open Panel Setting Customizations

Most of the customization settings are self-explanatory. My favorite customizations are to mix directories and files (see the following figure) and to uncheck the single click to open a file or directory. (Double-clicking to open reduces to possibility of opening the wrong file with a single click.)

The Open panel's display showing mixed directories and files.

Saving a New File

When you save a document for the first time, you create a file. As part of the process, you'll need to give the file a name. Documents are saved into files using the Save or Save As commands available under an application's File menu. Choosing the Save As command will prompt you for a name and a place to save your document. After your document is saved, using the Save command will update the contents of the file with any new changes you have made. If your file has not yet been saved, the Save command will behave the same as the Save As command: It will prompt you for a filename.

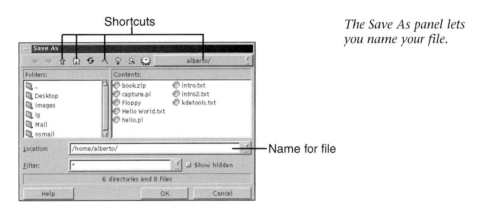

The Save As panel lets you name your file.

Features of this panel include:

➤ Shortcuts to move around files and directories similar to the Open panel buttons
➤ In the Folders window, select the folder where you want to put the file
➤ In Location space, type a name for the file

Click OK to save the file.

When you save your file, your work is saved to disk in the directory you specify. The document's title bar will change from `Untitled` to display the name and path where the file is stored (see the next figure).

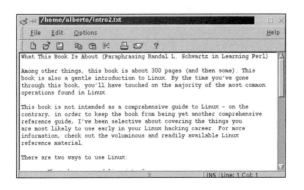

The title bar of a saved document displays its filename.

File Naming

You can name a file nearly anything you like. However, there are a few restrictions you'll need to observe.

The new filename cannot be in use by another file in the same directory. If this is the case, the existing file will be replaced with the new file.

Filenames are case sensitive; in other words, Linux considers introduction.txt and Introduction.txt to be different files.

Certain characters—such as the asterisk (*), question mark (?), ampersand (&), vertical bar (¦), circumflex (^), double quote ("), and apostrophe (')—should never be used, as these characters are special to the shell.

Characters such as the dash (-) and spaces should not be used because they will be hard to work with and delete when using a shell. The dash is used to specify program arguments. Some tools will not run properly when the name of a file begins with a dash, as the tools will behave as though you are specifying arguments instead of a filename. The space will make the shell think that you are specifying two different files (surround such names with quotes to access them from a shell). You should avoid these characters even if you only intend to work through KDE or another graphical environment.

Filenames will typically have an extension that indicates what type the file is. This extension is important because it tells KFM what application to use when opening the file by clicking on it.

Some common file types follow:

➤ .txt for text files

➤ .gif for GIF images

➤ .jpeg or .jpg for JPEG images

➤ .zip for zip files

➤ .gz for gzip compressed files

➤ .tar for tar archives

➤ .pl for Perl scripts

Saving Changes to Your Documents

If you modify a file after you create it, you'll need to save it again to store the new modifications. For this purpose, you use the Save command under the application's File menu.

You should save your files often during your work session to protect your work from being lost due to a program bug or power failure.

Saving a New Version

Many times while creating documents, it's easier to create a new document based on an existing one. You can reuse and modify an existing document while still maintaining the old document by using the Save As command to save the document to a different file. You can also use the Save As command to create different versions of your document. This way, you can revert to a previous version of your edits.

Text Editing Basics

Besides typing, there are a few editing basics that you should learn in order to work more effectively with the computer. Keep in mind that some of the actions described here won't work on all applications.

Most text editing works on the premise of a selection. A *selection* is text that has been highlighted by clicking and dragging. Normally when you highlight text, it is because it will be the target for other commands. Read on for more details on selecting text.

Selecting Text

To select text, click the cursor where you'd like to begin the selection and drag the mouse where you want to end the selection (see the next figure). The highlighted area is the selection. You can apply formatting and editing commands to the current selection.

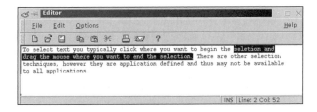

To select text, click where you want to begin the selection and drag to where you want to end it.

Some applications let you define a selection by clicking where you'd like to begin the selection and then Shift+clicking where you'd like to end it.

To select a word, you can double-click the mouse while the cursor is over a word. Some applications allow you to select a sentence if you triple-click over it, and some even allow you to select an entire paragraph if you click your mouse four times over the paragraph.

Copying and Moving Text

The commands to copy and move text in your document are in the Edit menu. To copy text from your document, select the text and choose the Copy command (see the following figure).

To copy information, select the text you want to copy and choose the Copy command from the Edit menu.

To move text, first select the text and then choose Cut from the Edit menu. Then click your mouse where you want to place the information and choose Paste from the Edit menu. Paste will insert text that you copied or cut. You can even use this technique to move text between applications.

Check This Out

Under X (and KDE!), a shortcut to the copy and paste routine is to select text as you normally do, move your cursor where you want to place a copy, and then middle-click the mouse. (Or as you learned in Chapter 1, "The First Login on the KDE Desktop," if you are using a two-button mouse, you can click both buttons simultaneously to simulate a middle click. However, for this to work, you must have specified the correct settings when you configured X Windows. See Appendix A, "Linux Installation.")

Text and information that you move in this way is placed in the clipboard. The *clipboard* is shared between running applications. This means that a selection you copy or move from one application can be inserted into another open application. Although this is true for most applications, some not-so-friendly applications don't make their clipboard available to the rest of the system.

Organizing Your Files

In This Chapter

➤ Creating Folders

➤ Working with Files and Folders

➤ Emptying the Trash

➤ Setting File and Folder Permissions

➤ KDE Templates

Getting Organized: Creating a Folder

Folders, or directories, allow you to group your files along some criteria. (For example, files for a book project all go in one folder, and files for your correspondence go in another.) This grouping capability will help you locate your files more easily. This will be more important as the number of files you create and store grows.

To create a folder using KFM, in an open KFM window, navigate with your mouse to the location where you want to create the new folder. Choose New from the File menu and choose Folder from the submenu.

After you have selected Folder from the submenu, a panel asking you for the name of the folder will be displayed (see the following figure). Type the name for the folder. (Pick a name as suggested in the section "File Naming" in Chapter 5, "Creating, Editing, and Saving Files.") Then press Enter.

New folders are empty by default and ready for you to add files and other folders to it. In the "KDE Templates" section later in the chapter, you'll learn how to customize the New command so that you can create files and folders that already contain other documents.

The New command under the File menu is customizable, which is why you have to navigate two menus to find the Folder option.

In this panel, type the name of the new folder you want to create.

Copying Files and Folders

You can copy files and folders into other folders. When you copy a folder, all the files and folders it contains are copied, too. In KFM, there are two ways that you can copy files and directories: using drag-and-drop and using the Clipboard with Copy and Paste.

Copying Files Using Drag and Drop

When you copy files using drag and drop, you click and drag the file you want to copy into another directory, onto the desktop, or into another KFM window. A menu appears asking you if you want to copy, move, or link the item (see the next figure).

Copying Files Using the Clipboard

You can also copy files and folders using the clipboard. To copy a file, select it (Ctrl+Click) and then choose Copy from the Edit menu. Navigate in the KFM window to the directory where you would like to place the copy and choose Paste from the Edit menu.

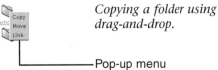

Copying a folder using drag-and-drop.

Pop-up menu

Moving Files and Folders

Moving files and folders is almost the same as copying the files using drag-and-drop. Instead of picking Copy from the pop-up menu, you pick Move (see the previous figure). Similar to copying a folder, if you move a folder, all files and folders inside the directory are also moved.

Linking Files and Folders

If you often find yourself copying files in order to have easy access to them, Linux has a better solution: links.

A *link* is a pointer to a file or folder that is somewhere else in the file system. A link looks and acts like the file or folder it points to. If you are viewing it through KFM, it will have the same icon (with the exception that it will have a little arrow next to it). When you open a link, you see the same file contents as the file the link points to.

Links are created in the same way you copy or move files using drag and drop. You click and drag the file you want to link into another folder or the desktop, and when you let go of the mouse button, you choose Link from the menu that is displayed.

This is what a linked folder looks like.

Replacing a File or a Folder

If you drag and drop a file whose name already exists in the directory, KFM will ask you if you would like to replace the original file or abort the operation (see the next figure).

Replacing a folder or a file permanently removes the file you are replacing. When you go to replace a file, KFM presents you with a dialog box that allows you to do one of three things: Rename the file (if you don't want to replace the original), skip the operation, or overwrite the file. If you drag multiple files, you can answer the dialog box a file at a time, or you can overwrite all files without any additional warnings.

Be careful when you replace files. It's important to remember that files that you overwrite are not recoverable.

If a file or directory with the same name already exists, you will be presented with this panel.

Deleting a File or Folder

To delete a file or a folder, select it and then choose Delete from the Edit menu. The file or folder will be destroyed after you confirm your action (see the following figure). Deleted files are not recoverable.

When you use the Delete command, you will be presented with this dialog box.

Moving a File or Folder to the Trash

A safer way to remove files than using Delete is to move them to the Trash. The Trash is a special folder on your Desktop where you can put files you want to get rid of. Instead of immediately being deleted, the file remains in the trash until you empty it. This allows you some extra time to ensure that you won't be needing the file.

To move a file to the trash, select it and then choose the Move to Trash command from the Edit menu.

You can also move files to the Trash using drag and drop. Just click on the file you want to move to the trash and, without letting go of the mouse button, drag the mouse over the Trash icon on your desktop; then release the mouse.

Retrieving a File or Folder from the Trash

Files moved into the Trash remain there until you empty the Trash. If you haven't emptied the Trash since you moved a file there, you can get it back. The Trash is just a special folder for holding documents you are about to delete. You can open it as you do other folders by clicking on it. To rescue a file, just click it and move it out of the Trash.

Emptying the Trash

As the amount of trash grows, you might wish to empty it to regain the disk space consumed by trashed files. To empty the Trash, right-click its icon and choose Empty Trash Bin from the menu that is displayed (see the following figure).

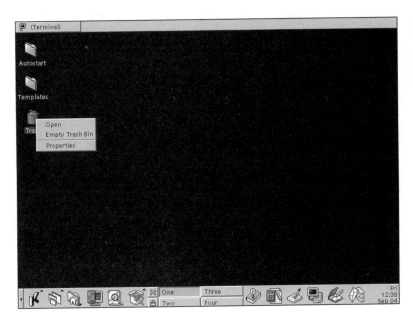

To empty the Trash, right-click the Trash Bin icon and choose Empty Trash Bin from the resulting menu.

File Properties

After you create a file or folder, most of the manipulations you'll perform will be in the form of renaming or changing permissions. KFM provides shortcuts to some of the operations described in previous sections by right-clicking on its icon. A context-sensitive menu will pop up to show you several options (see the next figure).

The KFM context-sensitive menu displays various options when you right-click on a file or folder.

The commands in a *context-sensitive menu* depend on what you click on—hence the name.

➤ Open with—Displays a panel where you can type the name of the application you want to use to open the selected file.

➤ Up—Navigates one directory up.

➤ Back—Navigates to the previous directory.

➤ Forward—If you used Back to get to this directory, you can return to your previous location with Forward.

➤ Cd—Focuses the current window to the selected directory.

➤ New View—Opens the directory in a new KFM window.

➤ Copy—Copies the file or directory to the Clipboard. You can then use the Paste command to place a copy of the file or directory you copied in the current directory.

➤ Move To Trash—Moves the selected file or directory to a special directory called Trash. This removes the files from their current location but doesn't delete them.

➤ Delete—Deletes the selected item.

➤ Add To Bookmarks—Adds the selected folder to your list of Bookmarks.

➤ Properties—Raises a panel that allows you to inspect and change information about the file, such as its permissions settings and its name.

Renaming a File or Folder

To rename a file or folder, right-click on the file or folder and choose Properties from the menu that is displayed. This will display a panel that allows you to rename the file (see the following figure).

When renaming a file, be careful not to change the file's extension, if it has one. The file extension consists of the three or more characters that follow a period at the end of the filename. The extension associates the file with an application.

There are many things that you should not rename. Everything inside your home directory is yours and can be renamed at will. Files in the Linux root directory or other system-oriented areas, however, should be left alone. Most users don't need to worry; as a general rule, Linux won't allow you to change anything which shouldn't be changed unless you are working in the superuser (root) account.

The General tab displays generic information about the file such as its name and path. To rename a file or folder, type a new name in the name text field and press Enter.

Setting File and Folder Permissions

The Properties panel also allows you to modify and set the permission settings for files and folders you create. Permissions are covered in great detail in Chapter 16, "Permissions: Protecting and Sharing Your Work." If you feel you need to control permissions, I recommend that you read this chapter first to understand the implications of the settings you change, as permissions is an advanced topic. This section explains how to change permissions using KFM and assumes that you understand these implications.

Permissions allow you to protect your files and folders from other users. By default, files you create will have a set of permissions assigned to them. When using KDE you can change file permissions using graphical controls. To get to the permissions panel, right-click a file or a folder and choose Properties from the menu that appears. Then choose the Permissions tab (see the next figure).

The Permissions tab displays a number of controls for setting the permissions of a file or folder. Each of the settings is duplicated for the User (Owner) of the file, a member of a Group assigned to the file, and Others. By setting values, you can control different levels of access for different users.

What Each of the Permissions Controls

Each file relates to a user in one or more roles (see the following figure):

➤ The user can be the owner of the file

➤ The user can be a member of a group granted permission on the file

➤ The user is neither the owner nor a member of the group

Each of these roles may have Read, Write, or Execute permissions, or a combination thereof.

Read permissions on a file or folder, allow you to see (read) its contents.

Write permissions on a file or folder, allow you to change its contents. In the case of folders, it might mean that you have permissions to add files to the directory.

Execute permissions are special. When set on a file, it indicates that the file is a program. If your role has Execute permissions, you are able to run the program. On directories, the Execute permissions also controls who can navigate into the directory. If you intend to copy files into a directory, your role must have Execute permissions on the directory.

Permissions can be altered a number of ways in the Permissions tab:

➤ The User row sets permission for the owner of the directory.

➤ The Group row sets permissions for members of the group.

➤ The Others row sets permissions for users that are neither the owner nor members of the group.

➤ The Owner field displays the name of the user that owns the file.

➤ The Group choice menu displays the name of the group assigned to this file. The choice menu is displayed if you are the owner of the file and you belong to more than one group.

➤ The Show Entries column enables users to see directory contents.

➤ The Write Entries column enables users to add or delete files from the directory.

➤ The Change Info column enables users to traverse the directory.

➤ The Special column enables special settings

The panel will look slightly different depending on whether you are working on a file or a folder. If you are working on file, the permissions columns will be called Read, Write, and Execute permissions. Otherwise, they will be called Show Entries (Read), Write Entries (Write), or Change Into (Execute). Although they have a different label, their functionality is exactly the same.

Understanding the Permissions Panel.

In the preceding figure of the Permissions Panel, the user (owner of the file) has Read and Write permissions; members of the group assigned to the file have Read and Write permissions; and other users are able to read the file but are not able to modify it because they lack write permissions.

A permission setting is enabled if it is checked. Permissions can only be assigned by the owner of the file or the superuser (root).

Don't change permissions on a file or folder unless you know what you are doing. For example, if you remove the Change Into settings (Execute permissions) for a folder, you will make it impossible for any user to navigate or open files in that folder.

Changing the Group of a File or Folder

If you are collaborating on a project with a group of other users, you might want to grant them access to a set of files and folders. When you create files or folders, they will be automatically assigned to your default group. If you are a member of other groups, you are able to reassign access for a different group to your files and folders.

To change the group memberships on a file or folder, right-click it and choose Properties from the menu; then choose the Permissions tab from the panel that is displayed.

To change the group of the file, click on the group choice menu to reveal the groups you belong to and select the one you want (see the next figure).

If you belong to more than one group you can assign a different group to your files.

Group you assign to your file has the group permissions specified in the panel.

KDE Templates

KDE provides a useful feature: Templates. Templates allow you to create prototypical documents and folder structures that you can easily reuse and customize.

When you place files and folders in the Templates directory on the Desktop, you are customizing what you will see under the New command in the File menu. The name of the files or folders you put there will be displayed in the submenu. When you want to create a customized copy of the template, just pick its name from the menu. A copy of the document or folder structure is created for you to customize. This is useful when you want to re-create some sort of directory or file organization. If you put plain files in this directory, you can use those files as a starting point for new documents without having to search for the directory.

Working with Disks

In This Chapter

➤ Starting a Superuser Session

➤ Configuring Floppy and CD-ROM Drives

➤ Granting Access to Disk Devices

➤ Working with Floppies and CD-ROMs

Working with disks in Linux is a little different than in other operating systems. In Linux and UNIX, disks are *mounted* into the file system. Mounting a file system incorporates the contents of a disk into the directory tree. When you are done working with the disk, you typically *unmount* it. Unmounting a file system removes it from the file tree. Mounting goes beyond disks. Volumes (network drives) available over the network can also be mounted and unmounted.

Volumes can be mounted anywhere on the file system. Under Linux, the default place where they are mounted is in /mnt. The /mnt directory will have a directory for at least your floppy disk and your CD-ROM drive; these directories will typically be named floppy and cdrom respectively. The floppy and cdrom directories are empty and only contain files and folders when a disk or volume is mounted to that directory. If you mount a volume on a directory that contains files, the contents of the directory are hidden from view and made inaccessible until the volume is unmounted.

Mounting a disk into the file system is, by default, a restricted action. To enable regular user access to these devices, you'll need to tell your system that it is OK for a user to mount the device. You'll learn how to do this next.

Configuring the System to Allow Users to Access the CD-ROM and the Floppy

The system keeps a configuration file for disks and where they are mounted in /etc/fstab. This configuration file is just a regular text file that you can edit using any text editor, including KEdit. However, permissions to modify this file are restricted to root, the superuser; to change and modify this file, you need to have this privilege.

You can obtain this privilege in two ways:

➤ You can exit the system, log in as root, and reenter the system

➤ You can start up a File Manager with superuser (root) privileges

For the sake of learning a new trick, let's walk through the second option.

Starting a Superuser KFM Session

To launch a KFM window as the superuser, you can go to the Application Starter|System and pick the File manager (Superuser Mode) command (see the following figure).

Launch a KFM window with superuser powers from the System submenu.

This will display a window asking you for the root password. After you enter it, a KFM window similar to the ones you've used before will be displayed.

Superuser KFM windows are distinguished from normal KFM windows by a red tab that tells you to exercise care when manipulating files and directories (see the next figure). One wrong manipulation can trash your system.

Red tab ———

A superuser KFM window has a red tab on the menu bar pane.

Type /etc/fstab and hit Enter in the location field on the root KFM window. A new KEdit will launch. This instance of KEdit inherits the superuser permissions, allowing you to modify the file.

After you finish editing the file, as explained in the section "Creating kdelnk Files for the Floppy and CD," close the KEdit window and the KFM root window to ensure that you don't use these empowered applications by mistake.

Enabling Regular Users to Access Disk Devices

Your /etc/fstab will contain text similar to this:

```
/dev/hda1 / ext2 defaults 0 1
/proc /proc proc defaults 0 0
/dev/hda5 none swap defaults 0 0
/dev/hdd /mnt/cdrom iso9660 ro,noauto,user 0 0
/dev/fd0 /mnt/floppy ext2 defaults,noauto 0 0
```

To enable any user to have access to the floppy, you'll need to modify the line that starts with /dev/fd. Typically, it will be called /dev/fd0 and is the device that represents the floppy disk. If you have multiple floppy disk drives, /dev/fd0 represents DOS drive A: (the first floppy drive), /dev/fd1 represents DOS drive B: (the second floppy drive), and so on. Floppy drive entries in /etc/fstab need to be modified to look like this:

```
/dev/fd0 /mnt/floppy auto user,defaults,noauto 0 0
```

In this entry I changed the ext2 to auto; this will allow the system to detect and read DOS and Windows floppies in addition to native Linux floppies. I also modified the options list by adding the *user* option before the defaults option. This will enable regular users to mount floppy disks. Note that there are no spaces between the commas and the options.

Techno Talk

Each line in the /etc/fstab file has the following format:

`device mountpath fstype options dump_order check_order`

➤ *device* specifies the name of the device file that represents the disk. UNIX devices such as your floppy disk are represented by device files. These are special files, and when accessed, they actually interact with your hardware. Device files reside in the /dev directory. When a program needs to use the device, it reads or writes to it as if it was a regular file. This simplifies the way programs talk to different hardware. For floppy disks, device filenames begin with /dev/fd. A number at the end of the filename allows for multiple devices of the same kind. Your CD-ROM will typically be /dev/cdrom, which is really a link to a more specific file, depending on whether your CD-ROM drive is an IDE drive, a SCSI drive, or some other type of drive.

➤ *mountpath* specifies where the device is mounted. Typically, this will be /mnt/floppy or /mnt/cdrom for your floppy and CD-ROM drives respectively.

➤ *fstype* specifies the format of the file system. If you specify auto, the system will attempt to detect the type of disk for you.

➤ *options* specifies a list of comma-separated options that tell the system how to handle the device. For example, there are options that tell the system the following: whether certain bits on the files should be interpreted, whether users should be able to mount the device, whether the device should be auto mounted at startup, or whether the device should be mounted read–write or read only. To read about all the options, you can use kdehelp (discussed in Chapter 4, "Working with Applications") or the man command (Chapter 15, "Help Please") and search the UNIX manual pages for fstab and mount.

➤ *dump_order* specifies the order in which file systems should be dumped by the dump program, a program used for backing up your file system to tape (see Chapter 19, "Backups: Safeguarding Your Work").

➤ *check_order* provides information for fsck (file system check) that specifies the order in which disks are checked. If your system is shut down inappropriately, the next time you boot your system, your disks will be checked for any errors. The number specified by this option tells the system in what order to perform the check. For more information on fsck, use the man command (Chapter 15).

To enable regular users to mount a floppy in /mnt/floppy, you need to add a comma (,) and then the **user** option to the list of options for the floppy device.

To enable use of the CD-ROM by regular users, you'll need to modify the entry that contains both the text **/mnt/cdrom** and the file system type iso9660. In my case, the entry for my IDE CD-ROM begins with **/dev/hdd**. To allow regular users to mount the CD-ROM drive, add a comma (,) and then the **user** option to the list of options for the CD-ROM device, like this:

```
/dev/hdd /mnt/cdrom auto ro,noauto,user 0 0
```

After you have completed your modifications, save the file and exit KEdit and the root KFM window.

Creating kdelnk *Files for the Floppy and CD*

After you make your CD and floppy drives accessible to all users, you will want to easily access the device through an icon. This will allow you to mount the volume using your mouse instead of having to use command line tools.

KDE has special files whose names have a .kdelnk extension. These files are used for several purposes, including to relate devices to icons. Although creating one of these files is a bit awkward, it is not difficult to do, especially if we use the device template that is built into the KDE.

To create an icon for your floppy drive, begin by right-clicking on the desktop. On the popup menu that appears, select New, and then Device. A window will appear, asking for a file name for your icon. Replace the default name "Device.kdelnk" with a name to represent your floppy drive, such as "Floppy.kdelnk." A new icon will appear on your desktop; the icon will be a question mark to indicate that the new device is not yet configured.

To configure the device, right-click on the icon and select Properties from the popup menu. This will cause KFM to display its window for configuring .kdelnk files. Select the Device tab at the top of the window to display options pertaining to mounting. In the box labeled Device, type **/dev/fd0**, but don't press Enter yet. Don't enter anything into the Mount Point or Filesystems boxes.

The new device icon must be configured before it will work. Since it hasn't been configured yet, it appears as a question mark.

KFM uses a special window to configure .kdelnk files.

Device filename

To configure a device icon:

➤ Select the Device tab at the top of the window.

➤ Enter the device filename in the Device box.

➤ Select an icon for the device while mounted.

➤ Select an icon for the device while not mounted.

You need to select two new icons for the device: one which will show when your floppy drive is mounted and another which will show when it is not. To select the icons, click on the button labeled Mounted Icon. Choose the icon that looks like a floppy disk with a little green light next to it, and click Ok. Now, click on the button labeled Unmounted Icon. This time, choose the icon which looks like a floppy disk without a little green light next to it, and click OK. Now, click the OK button at the bottom of the KFM window to accept your changes. On your desktop, you should see an icon that looks like a floppy disk.

Select Icon window. When you click on a button to select icons, KDE presents you with a panel where you can select an icon to represent your device. Typically there will be two icons per type. Icons with a green square next to them represent active devices. If you assign the pair, KDE will change the icon to provide visual feedback on mounted devices.

To configure your CD-ROM drive, follow the same steps, but name your icon file **CD-ROM.kdelnk**, enter **/dev/cdrom** into the Device box, and select the icons which closely resemble a CD in a personal CD player.

To test the device icons, insert a CD-ROM or floppy disk and click on the matching icon. A window will appear to inform you that the disk is being mounted. After a few moments, a KFM window will appear which displays the contents of the disk, now located at **/mnt/floppy** or **/mnt/cdrom**, depending on which device you're testing. Notice that a little green light has appeared next to the icon on your desktop; this indicates that the disk is currently mounted.

Before ejecting your floppy disk or CD, you must always ensure that it has been unmounted, otherwise you may lose data. To unmount the disk, right-click on the device icon and select the Unmount command. The little green light now disappears, indicating that your device has been unmounted. It is now safe to eject the device.

A KFM window listing files contained on a CD-ROM disk. The icon has changed to indicate that the device is mounted.

Copying Files to or from a Floppy

To copy files to and from your floppy drive, first you need to click on the floppy icon to display a KFM window focused to the device. You can then drag and drop files between the two KFM windows. Keep in mind that floppies have a limited capacity. If you try to copy a file that is larger than what fits on the floppy, the copy process will fail.

Currently there's no way to determine how much free space is available on a disk using graphical tools. The "Monitoring Your Disk" section of Chapter 22, "System Monitoring: Keeping an Eye on Your System," explains how to determine free space information using the command line. You will learn how to format a floppy disk at the end of this chapter.

Opening and Saving Files to a Floppy Disk

Opening and saving files to a floppy disk is the same as saving between directories. Just mount a floppy disk and save your file in the /mnt/floppy directory. Make sure that the file you are saving fits within the free space available on your disk.

Accessing the CD-ROM

Accessing a CD-ROM is essentially the same as accessing a floppy disk. To access the disk, you must have the CD mounted. The default mount point for the CD-ROM is /mnt/cdrom. If you click on the kdelnk file associated with the CD-ROM, KFM will open a window focused to the /mnt/cdrom where you can access your files.

Preparing a New Floppy Disk

KDE provides you with an application to format floppies, kfloppy. Kfloppy is accessible from the application starter utilities group (see the next figure).

The application allows you to select the drive and file system format to use for the floppy. Note that kfloppy can only format disks when the disk is not mounted.

Check This Out

When you format a disk, you erase all the files the disk contains. Ensure that the floppy disk does not contain files you'll need in the future before formatting.

Kfloppy allows you to format floppy disks.

The KDE Floppy Formater presents you with the following options when you want to prepare a floppy disk:

➤ Select the size and drive of your floppy disk.

➤ Select the density format. High density disks (HD) can store 1440K worth of information. Double density disks (DD) can store 720K.

➤ The file system choices are ext2fs (the native Linux filesystem, unreadable by DOS and Windows) or DOS format. DOS format will create disks which work equally well with Windows 95/98 long filenames or with MS-DOS filenames on older systems.

➤ After selecting your options, click format to initialize the disk.

➤ A quick erase doesn't do a low level format, it only creates a new filesystem on the disk.

➤ Full format does low level formatting of the floppy and creates a new file system on it.

➤ Click to exit the application.

Accessing the Network

In This Chapter

➤ Connecting to the Network

➤ Configuring a New Dialup Account

➤ Setting Up a Modem

These days, a computer that cannot access a network or the Internet is not interesting. Linux provides more networking services and network reliability than many other operating systems. Many of the networking technologies PCs have today owe their existence in grand part to UNIX. With Linux you have the ability not only to access the networking services as a client, but also to provide these services as a server. Many Web servers on the Internet are running under Linux because of its reliability and flexibility.

This chapter covers the basics of how to connect to the Internet using Linux.

How you connect your computer to the network will depend on the hardware you have. If your computer is participating on a network and you have direct access to the Internet from your network, all you need is an Ethernet card. If you installed your card before you installed Linux, the installation program configured the card so you can use it. The only thing you might need to do is configure your name services so that your computer knows how to access Domain Name System (DNS; covered in greater detail in the section "Configuring DNS Servers" later in this chapter). If you installed Linux prior to adding your network card, you'll have to use lisa to change your hardware configuration (see Chapter 21, "LISA—Linux Installation and System Administration Utility," for tips on how to use lisa).

If your computer doesn't have direct access to the Internet, you'll need to use your modem and set up a Point-to-Point Protocol (PPP) connection with an Internet service provider (ISP). An ISP provides connection services to the Internet for a modest monthly fee. When you connect to your ISP, your computer will be "on the Net," and you can use network services such as http (www), ftp, news, and so on.

Connecting to the Network Using a Dialup (PPP) Connection

Linux includes PPP and other protocols that you can use to connect to the Internet and private networks. PPP is by far the most popular dialup networking protocol supported by ISPs today. Typically, setting up PPP under UNIX has been a daunting task for the novice. Luckily, KDE provides a graphical tool, kppp, that you can use to configure a dialup connection easily.

Before you can connect, you will need to know the connection details to your ISP, such as dialup number, login, password, gateway, and DNS server IP addresses.

Adding an Internet Connection with Kppp

Before you can configure a PPP connection using kppp, you'll need to edit the /etc/ppp/options file. By default, this file can contain a line with the option lock. This option is for the PPP software to manage a lock on a connection and the hardware. Kppp does this itself, so you'll need to remove this option. To edit the /etc/ppp/options file, you need to have superuser (root) privileges. For this you can either log out of the system and log in as root or follow the procedure "Starting a Superuser KFM Session" as outlined in Chapter 7, "Working with Disks."

The only change that you might need to make to the file is to comment out the lock option (the only option by default on the /etc/ppp/options file). To comment something out, you put a pound or hash symbol (#) as the first letter in the line. Your edited file should look like this:

```
#lock
```

The pound symbol tells PPP to ignore the rest of the line. Save your file and exit any superuser KFM windows and KEdit sessions. If you opted for logging in as root, you should log in again using your own account. You are now ready to begin configuring a PPP connection to your ISP.

To start kppp, you can go to your application starter menu and choose kppp under the Internet program group. After selecting kppp, you will see a dialog box like the one pictured in the next figure.

If a connection were defined, you could select it, supply a login and password to your PPP account, and click Connect to dial it up. By default, there won't be any connections set up for you to use, so you'll have to define one. You do this by clicking the Setup button. This will present you with a window like the one depicted in the following figure.

Kppp can be started from the application starter menu under the Internet program group.

The Mini Command Line

The KDE Desktop provides you with an easy way to type commands without having to use a shell. The Mini Command Line is a small panel where you can type a command, program name, or even the path to a file to start a new KFM window. After you type in the command and hit Enter, the *minicli*, as this program is called, will go away and execute your command.

To access a minicli window, hit Alt+F2 on your keyboard. On the little panel that is displayed, type the name of a command or program you want to access. For example, type kppp to have that program launch.

Minicli can also open KFM windows. To open a KFM window focused to a directory, type the path to the directory in the minicli panel and hit Enter. If you specify the name of a file instead of a directory, the application registered for that file type will open (in many cases, this will be KEdit, the KDE editor).

To read man documentation pages, enter man:*programname*, where *programname* is the name of the tool or command you want to read about. See Chapter 15, "Help Please," for more information on using man.

The kppp window. The Connect to menu allows you to select the ISP you want to connect to. The Login ID and Password correspond to those assigned to you by your ISP. The Show Log Window box is useful for debugging your connection as you can see the details of the connection as it happens.

The kppp Configuration window is where you configure ISP settings.

List of entries

This is where you manage your current accounts and add new ones. Other features of this window include:

➤ Accounts tab—Shows all currently defined entries.

➤ Device tab—Click to set up the device where your modem is connected.

➤ Modem tab—Click to set special modem options.

➤ PPP tab—Click to set some options for kppp.

➤ About tab—Click to learn more about kppp.

➤ List of entries—Select an entry and click Edit to edit it.

➤ Edit button—Click to edit the currently selected entry.

➤ New button—Click to define a new account.

➤ Copy button—Click to duplicate an existing entry.

➤ Delete button—Click to delete the selected entry.

➤ Phone Costs, Reset Costs button, and View Logs button—Allow you to keep track of the time you are spending online. Useful for keeping track of your costs if your connection is billed by the minute.

When you click the New button, the New Account window appears, as shown in the following figure.

The Dialup Configuration offers several panels to set the dialup information, IP address for your machine, and DNS server settings, among other things.

IPS name
IPS's phone number
Select authentication mechanism

Adding a New Dialup Configuration

When you create an account, there are several things that you need to define. First you'll need to configure your dialup settings, by using the Dial tab in the New Account window. This window requires you to provide a name for your ISP. This name is displayed by the Connect to menu. The other information you need to provide is the phone number to your ISP's modem banks. The Authentication menu selects how to connect to your ISP. If your ISP supports connections from Windows 95/98/NT, chances are that the PAP authentication is all you need. Other authentication methods are available if that one doesn't work, but they require that you create a small "chat" script. I'll show you how to create one later in the section titled "Using a Login Script."

Configuring the IP Settings

Next you'll have to define your IP address settings for the connection. Special network devices, called routers, are responsible for delivering packets between networks. Most ISPs assign IPs dynamically. When your computer connects to the ISP, it will be assigned an IP address that it will use throughout the duration of your session. Next time you connect, you'll get a different number.

The PPP protocol can handle dynamically assigned IP addresses. The IP tab in the panel allows you specify the settings kppp should use, as you can see in the next figure.

So What Is All This IP Stuff, Anyway?

The Internet is a network of networks held together by a few protocols that define how information is routed and sent between computers. Information sent between computers is broken up into many small pieces (called packets or datagrams).

Packets are similar to mail you send through a post office. Each packet holds several pieces of information, including the address for the computer where it should be delivered, the address of the computer sending the message and the actual information, text, bits for an image, and so on.

When you hook up to the Internet, you become part of this large network. Your computer is identified uniquely (well, that is, if you are not behind a firewall), allowing you and other computers on the Net to talk to one another.

When you hear people talking about an IP, they are really talking about an IP address. In reality, IP stands for Internet Protocol, and its function is to wrap other protocols so that they can be delivered to the right computer using a network. The IP provides an envelope with the necessary information to get the packets from one computer to another. Therefore, for you to network on the Internet, you need to have some way to uniquely identify your computer. That's why you need an IP address.

Although IP provides information to send the data, it does not tell how the computers exchange this information. Other protocols that ride on top of IP do this. Data between computers on the Internet is typically transmitted using one of two major protocols: TCP or UDP.

The IP tab of the New Account window.

OK, Smarty-pants, So What's TCP, UDP, and PPP?

TCP stands for Transmission Control Protocol. TCP uses IP to pass information packets between computers. It is a connection protocol; computers connect to each other before sending information. The main advantage is that this connection protocol guarantees that packets you send are delivered and that the packets are put back together in the right order by the receiving computer. This is needed because information is broken into many small packets. Each packet has a serial number indicating its position on the data stream.

UDP stands for User Datagram Protocol. UDP is a connection-less protocol. It is a minimal protocol, and it is very fast. The only problem is that UDP doesn't make any guarantees that the data will get to its destination. Typically, UDP is used for sending very short messages between computers in which the time costs of establishing a TCP connection far exceed the needs. Most information sent via UDP is sent using just a single packet.

PPP is a mechanism for doing IP networking over serial lines (your modem). There other serial lines protocols, such as SLIP (Serial Line Internet Protocol), but PPP has established dominance partly because of its flexibility in not requiring a fixed IP address. PPP connections typically negotiate the IP address when you connect to your ISP.

Check the Dynamic IP Address button if your ISP assigns IPs dynamically. If you have a dedicated IP address (static address), enter that address and the subnet mask in the Static IP Address section. If you want kppp to temporarily set the domain and host name of your computer to the one matching the address assigned by your ISP, click Auto-configure hostname from this IP.

Configuring DNS Servers

Although your computer is very good about dealing with numbers and numeric IP addresses, humans are not. This is why phone numbers tend to be between seven and ten digits long and are broken into $3 \times 3 \times 4$ sequences. To solve this problem, addresses on a network are mapped to a machine name. It is easier for you to remember www.netscape.com than 207.200.73.73 (one of the addresses for that machine name).

To accomplish this task, special servers called DNS servers on the Internet keep track of the names and IPs assigned to different machines. When you ask to go to www.netscape.com, these servers are contacted, and the IP for the machine is returned to your computer. With this information, your computer can then make a request to www.netscape.com. Seems to make sense, right? But this is not exactly how it works from a technical standpoint. In reality, your computer will need to learn the address of a DNS server for the netscape.com domain, and then it will make a request to that server for the www.netscape.com machine.

As you might have inferred, this information is crucial to your ability to connect to other computers on the Internet. You provide information about your ISP's domain, including domain name and how to contact your ISP's DNS servers, in the DNS panel (see the next figure). This information is provided by your ISP and is a necessity if you want an Internet connection.

The kppp DNS panel collects information about your ISP.

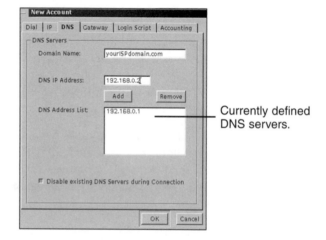

Currently defined DNS servers.

You should have at least two entries in the DNS Address List in case one of the servers is not available. Servers are queried in the order they are displayed.

If your computer is wired to a local network and you have DNS servers defined, you might want to disable those servers while your PPP connection is active. Click the Disable existing DNS Servers during Connection checkbox to do so.

Configuring the Gateway

The *gateway* is a special computer (a router) that connects other networks to your ISP's network. For your computer to access computers outside your ISP's network, you'll need to specify a gateway. This option also allows you to specify whether this connection should be used to access computers outside your local area network (see the following figure).

Configuring your gateway.

➤ Check Default Gateway to use an automatically assigned gateway.

➤ Check Static Gateway to specify a specific gateway (not recommended unless your ISP asks you to do this).

➤ Check Assign the Default Route to this Gateway to have your programs use this route to access the Internet. If you don't have another connection to the Internet, you should check this option.

Using a Login Script

It is possible that when accessing your ISP, your login sequence is nonstandard, or you must go through additional authentication steps. In these cases, you'll need to generate a login script in order to automate your dialup. Generating login scripts can be a challenging task, and your ISP should be able to provide you with an example of what to expect as well as instructions. To give you an idea on how to configure one, take a look at the following figure.

You add script terms by selecting an action such as Expect from the popup and then providing the text to expect in the text field. Next, click the Add button to insert the action into the list. The various terms, along with the information expected and the information sent when a match occurs, appears below.

Scripts are defined in a chat script. A *chat script* works by expecting certain text and then sending some other text in response. The previous figure has a very simple script that waits until the word login: is sent by the server. It then replies by sending the word Paricart, which is the login for this PPP account. After that it awaits the word word: (password) to which, in turn, the script replies with the text letmein. Typically expected text is abbreviated a little just in case the modem gets some garbage. In a world with error-correcting modems, this isn't that much of an issue anymore.

Defining a login script.

Pop-up menu

Various terms

Chat scripts can send/expect new lines if you type \n, and carriage returns with a \r. In addition, a chat script can instruct your modem to pause for a number of seconds, hang up, and so on. In practice, chat scripts are seldom simple and will require more steps than the one listed in the preceding paragraph (which does happen to work for my setup). If you need help writing a chat script, you should click on the Help button in the kppp window, as shown in the figure on page 82, and read the information about login script in the "Configuring an Account" section. Several more complex examples are listed there that you can use and adapt for your own needs.

Configuring the Modem Device

After you have an account configured, you'll have to identify your modem device to kppp. You'll need to go over your original notes identifying the COM port your modem uses under Windows. As an alternative, you can always try the four COM settings until you get it to work. To enable use of your modem as /dev/modem, you'll need to use lisa (see Chapter 21) or simply create a link from the /dev/ttySx to /dev/modem (see Chapter 12, "Working with Files on the Shell").

The modem devices are found under /dev/ttySx, where x is a number from 0 to 3. The various /dev/ttySx devices are mapped to the various COM ports. Table 8.1 shows a list of them.

Table 8.1 Device to COM Port Mappings

Modem Devices	COM Ports
/dev/ttyS0	COM1
/dev/ttyS1	COM2
/dev/ttyS2	COM3
/dev/ttyS3	COM4

Setting up the Modem Device with the kppp panel.

To configure your modem device, the following options must be set.

➤ Modem Device—Select the device representing your; see Table 8.1.

➤ Flow Control—Choose CRTSCTS to enable hardware flow control.

➤ Line Termination—Select CR/LF line termination.

➤ Connection Speed—Select a speed appropriate for your modem. Those using 14.4 kbps modems should select 57600 bps. Users with faster modems should select 115200 bps. If your modem experiences problems at the speed you select, you can lower it later.

➤ Modem Lock File—Specifies where the lock file will be placed; leave it as it is. If you try to fire up another connection and this file is found, kppp will check to see if the process owning the file exists. If it does, it will tell you that the modem is busy.

➤ Modem Timeout—Specifies how long to wait until giving up. Leave the 60 second defaults.

Debugging the Connection

If you have followed this far, your configuration should be ready for testing. Click OK at the bottom of the kppp Configuration window to accept your configuration changes. In the kppp window, select your provider, and check the Show Log Window option. This will display a window that shows you the information received from your ISP and the information sent by your computer or script. This tool is invaluable to see problem spots in your login scripts (see the next two figures).

PAP is used by most ISPs, as this is the default authentication scheme for Windows-powered machines.

Testing the connection.

Select your ISP entry.

Enter PAP authentication info here.

The debug window displays the information sent and received by your modem.

Connecting via Your Local Network

If access to the Internet is just across a network wire and your hardware was properly configured at install time, your network card should already be operational. The one thing you need to add is information about your DNS servers. DNS servers map machine names such as www.netscape.com to an IP address such as 207.200.73.73. Without DNS server entries, the only way for you to access a computer on the network is to know its IP!

Connecting to the Internet through your local network does not use the PPP, as discussed in earlier in the section.

To search DNS servers, you'll need to edit the file called /etc/resolv.conf. As you would expect, this file should be edited while having superuser privileges (root). Alternatively you can use lisa. (See Chapter 24 to define these network settings. Sometimes, editing the file directly is simpler and faster.)

In this file, you'll specify the IP addresses of your name servers as provided by your network administrator. My /etc/resolv.conf looks like this:

```
domain execpc.com
nameserver 165.207.1.3
nameserver 204.29.202.6
```

The keyword domain specifies the domain name for your network. The nameserver keyword specifies the IP addresses for DNS servers to search when resolving a name to its IP.

After you edit the file, you should be able to use any of your programs to access the network, provided your network hardware was properly configured at install time. If it wasn't, you'll have to use lisa—(see Chapter 21) to configure your network card and router (gateway) information.

Chapter 9

Communication: Web, FTP, Email, and News

<div style="border:1px solid">

In This Chapter

➤ Accessing the World Wide Web

➤ Transferring Files with FTP

➤ Sending and Receiving Email

➤ Participating in Newsgroups

</div>

Accessing the Web

Now that your connection is set, you can access the Web. Caldera's OpenLinux arrives preinstalled with Netscape Communicator. Netscape Communicator has all the tools you need to read news and email (Messenger), access the Web (Navigator), participate in discussion (news) groups (Collabra), and even develop your own HTML Web pages.

In KDE, KFM (the file viewer) is also network aware. KFM provides a basic browser capable of accessing simple Web sites. For quick and dirty Web surfing, KDE might provide all you need. For more extensive surfing, Navigator provides many more features and capabilities used by the more popular Web sites. Some of these features make viewing a Web site a more interactive experience. Netscape also takes full advantage of the strong networking capabilities and multitasking that Linux offers. Web sites seem to download and display much more quickly than they do on other platforms such as Windows or the Macintosh (see the next figure).

KFM's depiction of www.yahoo.com *Web site.*

To access the Web using KDE, connect to your ISP and type any Web address in the location field of a KFM browser. KFM will render that page as appropriate. To move to a different page or section of the Web site, click on a link. Links are typically seen as underlined text or even as an image. A *link* is an entry point (a hypertext reference) to another page with additional information. Links can be local to the Web site you are browsing, or they can be part of a different Web site. Links are what make the Web a web.

Not all browsers render the information the same way. Notice the difference between how KFM (in the previous figure) and Netscape render a page (in the following figure). Better Web sites exploit features found on Netscape and Internet Explorer. To get these enhanced pages, you must use Netscape Navigator. (Internet Explorer is not yet available for Linux, although some UNIX ports are starting to appear.)

Features of the standard browser window include:

➤ Location bar—Type a URL and hit Enter to go to that site.

➤ Back and Forward buttons—Back button enables you to move back to pages previously visited. If you go back, the forward button allows you to return to where you were last.

➤ Home button—Takes you by default to www.netscape.com, but you can use the Preferences command in the Edit menu to change your Navigator preferences for this action.

➤ The bookmark icon—Enables you to drag the address of the current page to your bookmark area (the area right below the location bar) so you can return easily to this page.

➤ Bookmark area—Bookmarked sites are available from these icons.

➤ Status area—Displays messages and the address of links your mouse hovers over.

➤ Links—Images or underlined text can represent a link to another page. Click the link to go to that page.

➤ Search button—Takes you to various search engines you can use to find information interesting to you.

➤ Navigator icon—Click to open a new Navigator (browser) window.

➤ Messenger icon—Click to access Messenger, the email component of Netscape Communicator.

➤ Collabra icon—Click to open a list of discussion groups (news groups) with the Collabra component.

➤ Composer icon—Click to open a text editor[nd]like application you can use for designing your own Web pages.

To access the Web using Netscape, invoke a minicli window (see "Mini Command Line" in Chapter 8, "Accessing the Network") and type `netscape`. You can also access Netscape Communicator from the Application Start menu under Applications. After a few seconds, you'll see some panels from Netscape telling you that it is creating a profile for you and a place to put cache files.

Bookmark area Bookmark icon

Netscape's depiction of the www.yahoo.com *Web site. Note that the presentation of the information is different than that shown in the previous figure.*

Location bar

Links

Collabra icon

Composer icon

Status area Navigator icon Messenger icon

FTP

FTP (File Transfer Protocol) is a protocol used to move files between computers. FTP under KDE is very simple: To go to a site, just enter an FTP URL in the location bar of a KFM window, like this:

```
ftp://somehost.somedomain.com
```

Somehost.somedomain.com is the fully qualified name of the machine you want to connect to. If that machine supports anonymous FTP, connections for which you don't need a login and password, KFM will display the contents available at that location. To navigate, use KFM as if it was your local hard disk. You can copy files between your local machine and the server or from the server to your local machine by dragging and dropping files between KFM windows (see the next figure).

To FTP a file using KFM, type the URL for the FTP site and browse for the file you want. Then click and drag the file to your desktop or to another KFM window focused to your local computer.

Because some files you transfer will be large, the speed of the copy will be much slower than you normally experience. But don't despair— the file will be transmitted across the wire.

If the server doesn't allow anonymous connections, you'll need to specify your login name, like this:

```
ftp://user@somehost.somedomain.com
```

user is your user name, followed by an at symbol (@), then followed by the fully qualified name of the machine. When you enter FTP URLs like this, more advanced programs raise a panel that asks you for your password.

You can also enter your password right in the URL; however, I don't recommend that you do this, as the password might be displayed for other people to see in the URL. KFM removes the password from the URL when you have connected. To supply your password on the URL, enter it like this:

```
ftp://user:password@somehost.somedomain.com
```

The username and password are separated by a colon (:), like this:

```
ftp://me:mypassword@ftp.netscape.com
```

The same technique for accessing files using FTP can be used with a browser such as Netscape Navigator. To access the site, enter the URL, and you are delivered. Instead of clicking and dragging to move files across the network, just right-click on the link and choose the Save Link As[el] command from the context-sensitive menu that is displayed. Use the Save panel that is displayed to navigate your way to the location where you want to save the file.

Email

KDE provides an email program called kmail that you can use to read and write email messages. Although this program gets the job done, I am a little partial toward Netscape Messenger, as it provides more features than kmail. One nice feature of kmail over Netscape Messenger, however, is that kmail can manage multiple email accounts for you. Netscape allows you to set up multiple remote IMAP mailboxes but only a single POP mail account. Most users have several POP mailboxes. IMAP, though more powerful and useful to power users, is not as popular between ISPs. I also like having a spell-checker accessible right from the application, as Netscape Messenger offers. At the time of this writing, kmail doesn't allow me to spell-check my messages. In this section, you will learn how to set up Netscape Messenger to handle your email.

The process of setting up your email reader is very similar for most email applications. You will need to know the following:

POP and IMAP? What's that?

IMAP and POP are two different protocols used to access your email.

IMAP stands for Interactive Message Access Protocol. It allows you to manipulate and organize a remote mailbox as if it were local to your computer—and it does it without the need to transfer your entire mailbox to your computer. This is cool because your mailbox is then centralized on the network. No matter what computer you use and where you are, your entire mailbox is accessible. Many ISPs don't like giving IMAP mailboxes, because users tend to collect copious amounts of email. For example, yours truly has an 80MB mailbox—yeah, there are things I should delete. But then again, disk space is cheap.

POP, which stands for Post Office Protocol, is a much simpler interface to your mailbox. It doesn't allow you to organize your inbox in any way, but it allows you to download your messages to a local mailbox for reading.

➤ Your email address

➤ The type of email account that you have (IMAP or POP)

➤ The username and password needed to access your account

➤ The name of the machine where your incoming mail is stored

➤ The name for the SMTP (outgoing) mail server

Configuring Your Identity for Netscape Messenger

In the identity panel, you provide information that will be included in your email, such as your "real" name and your email address (see following figure).

Identity panel in Netscape Preferences.

Click to reveal Identity panel

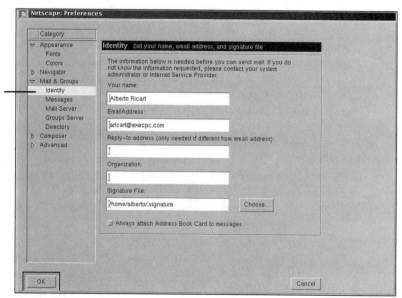

Configuring Your Mail Server

The next step in configuring your email program is to configure your mail servers so that Messenger can receive and send your email (see the following figure). Information to be entered here includes:

➤ Name of your email account (don't put a domain name on it).

➤ Name of mail server that sends your mail (SMTP).

➤ Name of mail server that stores email sent to you.

➤ Type of mail server. If it's a POP account, check whether if you want to leave incoming messages on the server (Otherwise messages are deleted from your ISP's server after they are downloaded. If it's an IMAP server, your mailboxes are kept on the server.

Click to access the
Mail Server panel

Name of email account

*Messenger's Mail Server
Configuration panel stores
information about sending
and receiving your email.*

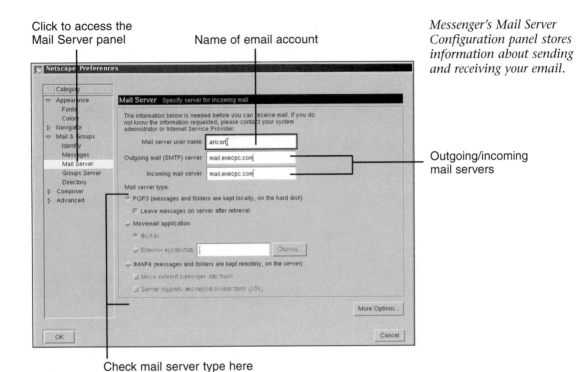

Outgoing/incoming
mail servers

Check mail server type here

Reading Email

After configuring your identity and mail server settings, Messenger is ready to send
and receive email. To start a Messenger session, choose the Messenger Mailbox com-
mand under the Communicator menu in a Navigator window. Messenger displays
four main areas (from top to bottom):

➤ Menus and buttons—Access to commands and functions

➤ Mailboxes—Access to separate mailboxes

➤ Mailbox contents

➤ Message body

See the following figure for a description of the most important buttons and areas.

Different buttons in the Messenger window include:

➤ Get Msg—Click to download new messages.

➤ New Msg—Click to compose a new message.

➤ Reply—Click to reply to sender of the current message.

➤ Forward—Click to send a copy of the current message to another person.

➤ Delete—Click to delete the message from your mailbox.

You can also organize your messages into different boxes. To select a different message
box, click the Inbox menu.

The Netscape Messenger window.

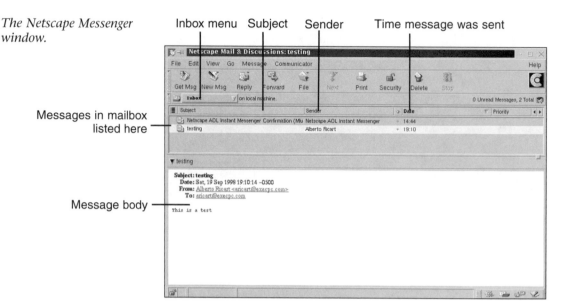

Inbox menu Subject Sender Time message was sent

Messages in mailbox listed here

Message body

Composing an Email Message

Sending email is just as easy as reading email. To send a message, click the New Msg button (see the previous figure). This will present you with a window where you can compose and address an email message like the one shown in the following figure. When done composing a message, click Send Now to forward your email message to your mail server for delivery.

Messenger's Compose Window—this is where you type a new email message.

Click to send message Click to attach files to your message

Recipient's email address

Message subject

Type message here

Formatting tools

Kmail is very similar in interface to Netscape's Messenger component. However, at the moment, Messenger is a more polished product with better tools and features.

News

If you have time to wander through Usenet, no doubt you will find a lot of useful and useless stuff. If you want to surf, you'll need a decent news reader. Again, the choices for you are several: under KDE you have knews, and under any X-Windows, including KDE, you have Netscape's Collabra.

Collabra doesn't make too much of a distinction between email and news. Although the configuration to access them is different, the result is similar. You use Collabra to subscribe to newsgroups that interest you, and then you use Messenger to read and post messages. Before you can read news, however, you need to download a list of what messages are available. When you click on one of them, the message is then downloaded and you can view it. If you want to post a message, you compose one basically like you compose an email message, but instead it is posted to a news server. From there the message is disseminated around the globe.

Configuring your system to use news is simple: You connect to a news server (nntp server; the name of this machine is provided by your ISP),

What Is Usenet?

Usenet is a worldwide distributed discussion system. It is made up of a classified hierarchy of topics grouped by subject (newsgroups). Messages are broadcast and propagated between news servers. Some groups are moderated, meaning that information posted by users needs to be approved prior to posting. Others are not moderated.

For a detailed description of what Usenet is and is not, see
`http://www.cis.ohio-state.edu/hypertext/faq/usenet/usenet/what-is/part1/faq.html`

and you download a very long and large list of newsgroups available from that server. (There are thousands and thousands of different groups.) You then select all the groups that interest you and start reading (see the next three figures). As a sanity check, you might want to assign an amount of time per day that you want to do this. It's very easy to get caught up in news reading and not realize that hours have flown by. As a choice, I tend not to look at newsgroups unless I am searching for specific information. Several years ago, I used to spend more than anyone's share reading news. Today I try to stay away; it's easy to get caught up in the noise.

If your ISP serves news under a special port, enter in the Port space; otherwise leave the default 119. Organizations also use news to distribute information. Some of these newsgroups are only available through a secure server that requires authentication; if your news server requires this, check the Secure checkbox next to the Port space.

The news configuration panel. To configure your news, use the Preferences command under the Edit menu in any Communicator window.

Name or IP address of news server

Click to access Groups Server panel

After you define your news server, you'll be presented with this window. Here, you can select the groups to join from those carried by your news server.

List of available news groups

Click to expand hierarchy

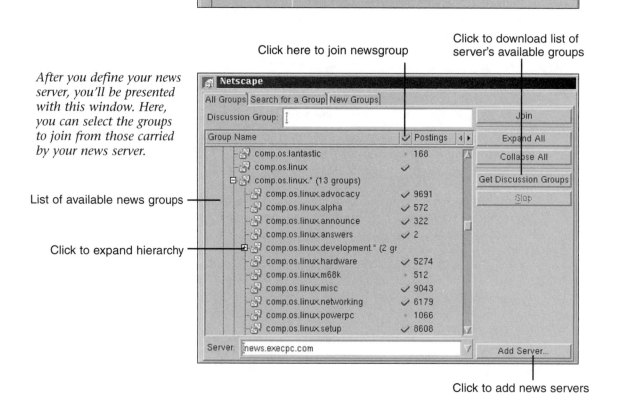

Click here to join newsgroup

Click to download list of server's available groups

Click to add news servers

If you know the name of a newsgroup that interests you, type it next to Discussion Group and click Join.

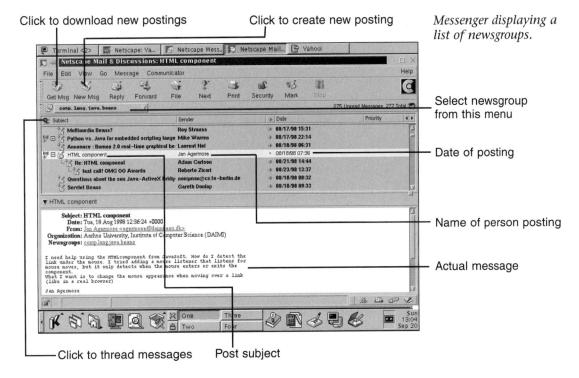

Messenger displaying a list of newsgroups.

Click to download new postings Click to create new posting

Select newsgroup from this menu

Date of posting

Name of person posting

Actual message

Click to thread messages Post subject

Use the Reply button to reply to a posting. If you hold it down, a menu will allow you to choose the reply method: to the group, to the poster, or to a combination of the two. A posting listed in bold indicates it hasn't been read yet.

Telnet

Telnet is an additional way to interact with another computer on the Internet. It is a command line[nd]only program that allows you to access a remote UNIX-like computer through a command line interface. Telnet is discussed in Chapter 17, "Command Toolbox: Usefull Shell Commands and Shortcuts."

Customizing KDE

In This Chapter

➤ Adding an Application to the Panel or Application Launcher

➤ Other KDE Options

➤ The KDE Control Center

KDE is fairly customizable; here's a quick guide on what you can do to customize your desktop. Most of KDE is customized through the use of kdelnk files (files that have a kdelnk extension). These files provide configuration information that KDE uses to associate files with applications, icons with applications and documents, devices such as disk drives with icons (see Chapter 7, "Working with Disks"), and others.

The KDE Panel can be customized in several ways. The following sections present some of the most useful.

Adding an Application to the Panel or Application Launcher

Adding an application to the panel is a simple two-step process. First, you'll need to create a kdelnk file that provides information about the application you want. This file will associate an executable program with an icon and its files. Then you install the kdelnk file by dragging it into the panel or putting it in a special directory where the application launcher will find it.

Creating a Kdelnk File that Represents an Application

Creating a .kdelnk file for an application is easy. The process is very similar to the process we used to create a .kdelnk file for your floppy and CD-ROM drives in Chapter 7, "Working with Disks." Right-click on an empty area of the Desktop. When the popup menu appears, select New and then Program. A window will appear, asking you to supply a name for this kdelnk file. Change the name from the default "Program.kdelnk" to a name which represents your program, for example, "Netscape.kdelnk." An icon which looks like a gear appears on your desktop.

After you have created the icon, right-click on it and choose the Properties command. This will present you with a panel like the one in the following figure.

This window controls the properties for the kdelnk file.

Click on the Execute tab to change the settings that associate the icon with the actual program. The Execute panel looks like the one in the next figure.

The execute tab allows you to associate a program with the kdelnk file.

106

If you know the location of the program file, just enter it into the Execute field. For example, the path to the Netscape program is `/opt/netscape/communicator/netscape`. If you don't know the exact path, you can also use the Browse button to find the file by hand.

Some programs use a special directory as their working directory where they keep files. When programs do this, they will routinely look in that working directory for the files associated with the program. Such programs would require having the Working directory field filled.

The Swallowing on panel option is for applications like the CD player that become a small icon on the panel when running. The Run in terminal button is for command line programs for which you want to provide an icon.

To associate an icon with the file, click the button containing the gear icon. This will bring up a panel you can use to select an icon for your program (see the next figure).

Use the Select icon panel to associate an icon with your program.

The Select icon panel has a popup menu that you can use to find icons in KDE's icon area in the `/opt/kde/share/icons` or in your home directory in the `kde/share/icons` directory. Note that this directory is typically invisible because it starts with a period; to display it in a KFM window, activate the Show Dot Files option in the View menu. Click on an icon you like, and click OK. (Netscape's icon is the one that looks like a ship's wheel.)

The final step in configuring the kdelnk file is to associate file types and the name of the program with the kdelnk file. This will allow KFM to associate the icon with the program when you are browsing the file system (see the following figure).

Check This Out

You can add your own icons using the Paint application. Icons are saved using the XPM format and are 32 pixels wide by 32 pixels high. If you store them in the kde/share/icons directory in your home directory, you'lll be able to associate them.

To associate your icon with the actual program, type the name of the program followed by a semicolon (;) in the Binary Pattern field. KDE will use this name to show the icon when you are browsing through the file system.

The Application tab associates file types and icons with the program. The comment area is displayed as a ToolTip when you hover your cursor over the icon.

The comment field is displayed as a ToolTip when you hover your mouse over an item displaying this icon.

The application name is the name for the program in your language. If you were editing this .kdelnk file by hand, you would be able to provide multiple translations to the application name.

The two lists at the bottom are special. The list on the left side represents the MIME (Multimedia Internet Mail Extensions) types that the application is able to open. MIME types are sometimes tricky to figure out, but in the case of Netscape, you'll want to associate the text/html type. To eliminate associations that don't match, select them from the left list and click the arrow pointing right (->). To add an association from the list, select the type you want and click the arrow pointing left (<-).

When you are done with your selections, click OK to save and dismiss the panel. The icon will change from a gear to the icon you selected for this program. The next step will make it visible to KFM.

Associating an Application with KFM and the Application Starter

To enable KFM to use the kdelnk file, you need to place it in a special directory. This directory will vary depending on whether you want to make the associations systemwide or just for your own personal workspace.

To install the file on your personal workspace, move it to the .kde/share/applnk directory or one of its subdirectories in your home directory. When you log out and back in, you'll be able to see the correct icon when you browse /opt/netscape/communicator/netscape. This action also has the effect of adding the item to your personal application menu.

To make the association take effect for all users in the system, place the link file in the /opt/kde/share/applnk directory or one of its subdirectories. Note that you will have to do this as the superuser (root). This also has the effect of adding the application to the application starter menu. Make sure that the files you add have the

permission mode set to 644 (readable and writable by root and readable by the group and others). See "Changing File Permissions" in Chapter 16, "Permissions: Protecting and Sharing Your Work."

Panel Management: Adding and Removing Applications

To add an application to the panel (the icon bar at the bottom of the screen), drag a kdelnk file, as created in the preceding section, to the panel. A button will be displayed that you can click to start the application.

To remove the application, simply right-click on its panel button and choose Remove.

Other KDE Options

KDE allows you to configure other settings related to the panel and the taskbar. To configure these settings, right-click on the panel in an empty area and choose Configure. You can also use the Configure command available from the Panel menu in the application starter. The various options are contained in three tabs (see the next two figures):

➤ Panel provides configuration settings to the location and appearance of the panel

➤ Options provides settings for configuring the menu ToolTips, Clock, and Auto-hide settings for the panel and taskbar

➤ Desktop provides options for controlling the number of virtual desktops (see Chapter 4, "Working with Applications")

The KPanel Configuration panel allows you to customize the location, behavior, and appearance of the panel and taskbars.

The Options tab allows you to configure settings, such as a display of ToolTips (information labels that tell you what a button or an icon does). You can also customize whether the panel and taskbar auto-hide and whether the clock displays. The Personal First button controls the order of menus in the application starter. Personal menus have a sphere icon.

The KDE Control Center

The KDE Control Center provides a unified place to change many settings related to KDE. This is where you can customize color settings, language preferences, screen savers, fonts, and so on. In addition, you can also fine-tune some hardware settings, such as mouse acceleration and keyboard repeat settings.

The KDE Control Center is available from the application starter and offers you the opportunity to customize your system to fit your preferences. Here's what the KDE Control Center looks like:

The KDE Control Center gives centralized access to many settings you can personalize.

What else can you do with KDE?

Well, let's say you aren't comfy-cozy with English. Guess what—KDE can be customized to the language of your choice! At last count, KDE supported about 25 different languages.

You can expect the KDE Control Center to offer more settings as the KDE environment matures.

This chapter concludes the tour through the KDE environment. In the Part 2, "Working on the Command Line," you'll be introduced to using Linux via the UNIX shell. Although the UNIX shell isn't as intuitive or sexy as KDE, it is definitely powerful. The other great advantage of the shell is that it is available in all UNIX implementations. So what you learn in the next section will apply to work that you might end up doing in other versions of UNIX.

Part 2
Working on the Command Line

Now that wasn't so bad was it? As you saw in Part 1, KDE helps make using Linux a breeze. But maybe you're thinking to yourself, "What did users do before KDE?" or "What if I'm just a rebel and I want to see the nuts and bolts of Linux?" We've got you covered! Part 2 shows you Linux features without the glitz of KDE—you get to try your hand at working on the command line. The chapters in this section talk about consoles, getting help, and shells (sorry, not the kind you find on the beach—it's not that kind of adventure). We even take a peek in the command toolbox at some useful shell commands and shortcuts. Well, if you're ready, the command line awaits!

Shells and Consoles

In This Chapter

➤ Introduction to the UNIX shell

➤ Basic shell navigation commands

Throughout the previous chapters I have focused on using Linux by using a graphical user interface (GUI or UI for short). If you use your computer as a workstation, that is how you'll use it most of the time. However, that is only half the story. Although KDE´s ergonomics are nice, they are not yet as polished as the graphical environment available to Windows or Macintosh users; but it is an excellent start.

At this point, you know how to work under Linux using KDE. And while the tour was not really technologically driven, I hope you feel confident enough to do quite a few things without the command line.

In this section of the book, I will tell you how to work on Linux (and UNIX!) using a command line. No matter how much you want to stay away from the command line, the truth is that this evil interface is actually quite powerful, and in certain ways it is indispensable. (Of course, the shell's interface isn't really evil; it just isn't as intuitive as a graphical environment such as KDE.) When you learn how to use a shell, you will have a powerful tool in your bag of tricks. Let's get our hands dirty for the first time using a shell.

The UNIX Command Prompt

The UNIX command prompt, or *shell,* as it's also called, provides you with direct access to the operating system. It is a command interpreter: It interprets and executes all of your commands. The shell is really just another program that sits between your keyboard, the operating system, and other programs. Unlike DOS, the shell is a separate program from the operating system, or kernel.

Though powerful, shells are lacking in the ergonomics department: They just don't provide a friendly and intuitive GUI. And no matter how ergonomic the shell, the fact remains it is a shell, and it wants you to type in commands.

Yes, shells are by nature arcane and typing intensive, but they also are powerful. Shells provide many options unavailable to GUI-only systems. When you learn how to use a shell, you won't be able to do without one! Granted, most things are easier to do with a GUI application, but many other things are not. The shell is then the right interface for certain kinds of problems.

If you are accessing an UNIX box remotely, you will more than likely do so through a shell interface. Shells come in different flavors and knowing how to use a shell is a good thing. It is a wise person who is familiar with at least two different shells. It will be of tremendous help if you ever have shell access to a system that doesn't sport your favorite shell.

Most shells in UNIX are programmable, so if you find yourself writing the same commands over and over, it is easy to create a shell program (similar to a .bat file in DOS and Windows) that automates those commands for you. But you can worry about this when the time comes.

Shells are accessible through a terminal program. In KDE, there's an application that provides you with shell access from within the graphic environment. This useful program is called kvt.

Shells are also accessible through a terminal program or a console. Remember when Linux first booted? It had a text interface. That's the console. Linux also provides virtual consoles, which are discussed later in this chapter.

Shell Flavors

There are many shells to choose from. Why? Because people like to do things in different ways, and a number of programmers created new shells to solve some deficiency in a shell they liked. The list shown here is really a multi-species shell evolution tree. The first shell (sh) features have cross-pollinated, helping feature evolution:

➤ sh—In the beginning, this was your only choice. It's called the Bourne shell. Unfortunately it doesn't offer things that you really want in a shell, such as command-line editing.

➤ ksh—The Korn shell. This is a very popular UNIX shell. In the old days, this shell was only available if you had a specific brand of UNIX installed.

➤ csh—The C shell. This shell is similar to the other two when it comes to interactive use (typing on the screen) but very different in its programming grammar. The C shell was the first shell to provide job control (a way to manage running commands) and command history.

➤ tcsh—The tcsh is an enhanced C shell (csh). This shell is similar to the csh but offers command and filename completion and some command-line editing features.

➤ bash—This is the default shell in most Linux distribution. It is called the "Bourne Again Shell," and it is created and distributed by the Free Software Foundation (GNU). It is a very good shell to learn; it has command-line editing and filename completion, and it is compatible with the original Bourne shell.

➤ zsh—This is the newest of all the shells. It is compatible with the Bourne shell.

Graphic Consoles

Even if you are running a graphic terminal, the terminal is just a fancy front end to let you communicate with the shell. KDE provides an application called kvt that you can use to access a shell. You launch a terminal by clicking the kvt icon on the panel. The icon is pictured in the next figure.

Check This Out

Most shells provide a programming language of their own. Many programs that you run under Linux are actually shell scripts written for one of the shells presented here or for other command interpreters, such as Perl and Python.

The kvt button on the panel looks like this.

117

The kvt terminal program offers direct access to the shell through KVT. (Other terminal emulators, such as xterm, as they are called, are also available for you to use.)

Check This Out

If you are working on the console, you can work on multiple consoles at the same time. Each time you switch, you can access virtual consoles by pressing Alt+F*n*, where F*n* is F1–F6. You will be presented with a brand-new virtual console complete with login prompt and everything.

If you are logged into X (KDE), you can still access virtual consoles. You can activate virtual consoles by pressing Ctrl+Alt+F*n*, where F*n* is F2–F6. To return back to your X session running KDE, press Alt+F7. (By default X session runs under terminal 7.)

If you are running X, press Ctrl+Alt+F2 now to get into a console. I want you to get the full experience of working on the command line and forego some of the niceties provided by a graphical environment. It will make your experience more "pure."

Logging in Through a Console

Logging into a console isn't much different than logging into KDE or X Windows. The glaring difference is that instead of using a nice GUI, you get a text interface:

```
Caldera OpenLinux(TM)
Lite
Version 1.2
Copyright 1996-1998 Caldera, Inc.

login: username
Password: mypassword
```

As usual, your password will not be echoed to the screen to protect you and your account. If you entered your login and password correctly, you are ready to go.

118

What Shell Are You Running?

By default, unless your system was configured by someone else, you should be running bash. To check to see what shell you are running, type echo $SHELL.

Words preceded by a dollar sign indicate that the word is really the name of a variable. The echo command will print the value it finds on that $SHELL environment variable. The result should be something similar to what you see here:

```
[alberto@digital alberto]$ echo $SHELL
/bin/bash
```

If for some strange reason you're running something other than bash, type the command bash at the prompt to start using the bash shell for the remainder of the session.

Check This Out

When entering commands to the shell, keep in mind that Linux is case sensitive, so BASH, bash, Bash, and BasH are different commands to the shell. Typically commands you enter will be in all lowercase.

Command Line Program Syntax

Most command line programs use the following syntax:

```
commandname [flags] arg1 arg2 argn
```

The terms are defined as follows:

➤ *commandname* is the name of the command.

➤ *flags* or arguments are options given after the program name that control how the program will behave. Flags are typically differentiated from other types of argument by a leading dash or double dash, as in -h or --help. Other types of arguments can be filenames or some other program-defined keyword. Flags are case sensitive, and tools with many options will use both lowercase and uppercase letters to name their options.

Note

To change your shell permanently, see the section "Changing Your Shell" in Chapter 17, "Command Toolbox: Useful Shell Commands and Shortcuts."

➤ arg1–argn is a list of arguments for the program to work with. Typically this will be a list of files, the name of a directory, or something else required by the program.

Some common commands, such as ls and pwd, are also built into some of the shells to enhance performance. We'll discuss these commands in the next section.

Navigating the File System

The first thing that you need to learn is how to navigate using a shell. You know how to use KFM to move around the file system and access files; doing the same through the shell isn't that much more difficult. However, you'll need to learn a handful of commands:

➤ pwd

➤ ls

➤ cd

Where Are You?: pwd

The first thing you might want to know is where you are in the file system. If you just logged in, you are probably in your home directory. Even though we know this, just for the learning experience, at the prompt enter pwd:

```
[alberto@digital alberto]$ pwd
/home/alberto
```

pwd stands for "print working directory." The shell will respond by listing the absolute path to your current location. An absolute path is one that is specified from the root (/) directory.

Listing Files

The next thing you'll want to do is list the files found in your current directory. This is done with the help of the ls command, which stands for *list*:

```
[alberto@digital alberto]$ ls
Desktop       images       linkToImages   test.txt
Mail          kde          nsmail         test.txt~
html          lg           test.rc        todo.txt
```

As you can see, the plain invocation of ls doesn't provide much distinction between directories (folders) and files.

To tell ls to provide you with more information about the files it finds, you need to specify the -F flag. This option makes ls append a character to the filenames that indicates what it is.

The file type indicators are

➤ * for programs or executable scripts

➤ / for directories

➤ @ for symbolic links

➤ ¦ for pipes

➤ = for sockets

➤ nothing for regular files

```
[alberto@digital alberto]$ ls -F
Desktop/        images/         linkToImages@   test.txt
Mail/           kde/            nsmail/         test.txt~
html/           lg/             test.rc         todo.txt
```

Now you can tell the basic types apart. ls offers many more options. The more useful are listed in the following table.

Useful ls Options

Option	Action
-F	Mark files with characters designating their type
-l	Display long listings
-a	List all files including any hidden files
-s	Print the size of files
-t	Sort listing by file time, with new files first
-R	List files recursively including contents of other directories
-i	List file inode

You can combine multiple flags together, as in ls -Flai. This is the same as saying: ls -F -l -a -i, except that you save a few keystrokes. Here's what that option would list:

```
[alberto@digital alberto]$ ls -Flai
total 9
 157289 drwxrwxr-x   9 alberto   alberto    1024 Sep  1 10:25 ./
 169675 drwxrwxr-x  16 alberto   alberto    1024 Sep  1 10:24 ../
 157290 drwxrwxr-x   2 alberto   alberto    1024 Sep  1 10:24
➥Desktop/
 157291 drwxrwxr-x   2 alberto   alberto    1024 Sep  1 10:24 Mail/
 157292 drwxrwxr-x   2 alberto   alberto    1024 Sep  1 10:24 html/
 157293 drwxrwxr-x   2 alberto   alberto    1024 Sep  1 10:24 images/
 157294 drwxrwxr-x   2 alberto   alberto    1024 Sep  1 10:24 kde/
 157295 drwxrwxr-x   2 alberto   alberto    1024 Sep  1 10:24 lg/
 157296 lrwxrwxrwx   1 alberto   alberto       6 Sep  1 10:24
➥linkToImages -> images/
 157297 drwxrwxr-x   2 alberto   alberto    1024 Sep  1 10:24 nsmail/
 157298 -rw-rw-r--   1 alberto   alberto       0 Sep  1 10:25 test.rc
 157299 -rw-rw-r--   1 alberto   alberto       0 Sep  1 10:25
➥test.txt
 157300 -rw-rw-r--   1 alberto   alberto       0 Sep  1 10:25
➥test.txt~
 157301 -rw-rw-r--   1 alberto   alberto       0 Sep  1 10:25
➥todo.txt
```

Links, Sockets, and Inodes???

➤ What's this link stuff? A *symbolic link* (also called an alias or shortcut in other OSs) is a file that points to another file, and is a commonly used tool. A *hard link* rarely created by the user, is a filename that points to a block of data that has several other filenames as well.

➤ What's this pipe and socket stuff? *Pipes* and *sockets* are special files that programs create to communicate with one another. They are rarely seen, but you might be able to see a socket or two in the /dev directory.

➤ What's this inode stuff? An *inode* is the address of a disk block. When you ask to see inode information through ls, ls prints the address of the first block in the file. You can use this information to tell if two files are really the same file with different names. We'll talk a little more about this when we talk about links.

This listing has a lot of information that I'll cover in bits and pieces throughout this and other chapters. For sake of being complete, the items listed in the listing are as follows (from left to right):

The inode of the file

The permissions for the file

The number of hard links to the file

The owner of the file

The group owning the file

The size of the file

The last modification date for the file

The name of the file

Listing Directories Remotely

You don't need to go to a directory in order to list it. If you provide a pathname to a file or a directory to ls, ls will list the file or directory requested:

```
[alberto@digital alberto]$ ls /opt
bin/        kde/        man/        netscape/
[alberto@digital alberto]$ pwd
/home/alberto
```

ls *in Technicolor*

The version of ls shipped with Linux has the capability to display different file types in different colors. This capability is very useful, as it makes it easy to discern among files, directories, and programs.

To enable this behavior, you can type ls --color, and things will happen. The colors for the most popular file types are listed in the following table.

Typical File Colors (ls --color)

File Type	Color
Regular Files	White
Programs	Green

File Type	Color
Directories	Blue
Links	Aqua

Pretty nifty, eh? It's so nice you might like to have the file types appear in color all the time. Fortunately, you can. Read on to learn how to change the default options of certain shell commands.

Making Shell Options the Default

If you found any of these options useful, more than likely you will want to make them the default. When you run a shell, there are a number of environment variables that control how your shell behaves. For the bash shell, the default shell in Linux, this default information lives on the /etc/profile file.

You can override some of the options by adding entries to the .bashrc file in your home directory. Because this filename starts with a dot, it's invisible by default (and called a *dot file*—and you thought Linux names would be difficult!), but it is there. To make ls work in color by default, add an entry like this to the end of your .bashrc file. (Use KEdit because you don't know how to use a command line editor, yet.) Here are some examples:

```
alias ls='ls --color'
```

To make ls use the -F option, add a line like this:

```
alias ls='ls -F'
```

To make ls use both the -F and --color options, add a line like this:

```
alias ls='ls -F --color'
```

As you can guess, alias associates a name with a command. To make an alias in bash, you use the keyword alias followed the name of the alias followed by an equal (=) sign, followed by the name of the command. If the command is longer than one word (that is, it has arguments), you need to enclose the command and its arguments in apostrophes ('). You can use any name for the alias you like. If the name of the alias is the same as some system command, the alias is the command executed.

Check out your .bashrc to see what aliases have already been defined for you.

Changing Directories: cd

Now that you know how to find out where you are and list the files in a directory, it is time to learn how to go somewhere. To do so, you use the cd command. cd stands for *change directory*. To go somewhere, type the cd command followed by the name of the directory where you want to go:

```
[alberto@digital alberto]$ cd /
[alberto@digital /]$ ls
amd/         dev/        install@      opt/        tmp/
auto/        etc/        lib/          proc/       usr/
bin/         home/       lost+found/   root/       var/
boot/        initrd/     mnt/          sbin/       vmlinuz
```

This example takes you to the root (/) directory.

To return to your home directory, type the cd command without any arguments:

```
[alberto@digital /]$ cd
[alberto@digital alberto]$ ls
Desktop/      images/      linkToImages@  test.txt
Mail/         kde/         nsmail/        test.txt~
html/         lg/          test.rc        todo.txt
```

Relative and Absolute Paths

If you don't provide a leading slash (/) in the path you specify, the path is relative. The shell will append the current working directory to the path you specify, as in the following:

```
[alberto@digital alberto]$ cd images/anotherdir
[alberto@digital anotherdir]$ pwd
/home/alberto/images/anotherdir
```

If the directory images is located in /home/alberto/images, the first line is equivalent to specifying this:

```
cd /home/alberto/images/anotherdir
```

When specifying a relative path, it is useful to know that the current directory can be specified using a period (.) and the parent directory, the directory containing the current directory, as two periods (..), given a directory structure like this:

```
[alberto@digital alberto]$ ls
Desktop/      images/      linkToImages@  test.txt
Mail/         kde/         nsmail/        test.txt~
html/         lg/          test.rc        todo.txt

[alberto@digital alberto]$ cd images (goes down to images)
[alberto@digital images]$ pwd
/home/alberto/images
[alberto@digital images]$ cd ../kde (up one and down kde)
[alberto@digital kde]$ pwd
/home/alberto/kde
```

```
[alberto@digital kde]$ cd .. (up one)
[alberto@digital alberto]$ cd ./kde (down kde in the current dir)
[alberto@digital kde]$ pwd
/home/alberto/kde
```

The PATH Environment Variable

The shell looks for commands and programs in a list of file paths stored in the PATH environment variable. An environment variable stores information in a place where other programs and commands can access it. Environment variables store information such as the shell you are using, your login name, and your current working directory. To see a list of all the environment variables currently defined, type set at the prompt.

When you type a command at the shell prompt, the shell will look for that command's program file in each directory listed in the PATH variable, in order. The first program found matching the command you typed will be run. If the command's program file is not in a directory listed in your PATH environment variable, the shell returns a "command not found" error.

By default, the shell does not look in your current working directory or your home directory for commands. This is really a security mechanism so that you don't execute programs by accident. What if a malicious user put a harmful program called ls in your home directory? If you typed ls and the shell looked for the fake program in your home directory before the real program in the /bin directory, what do you think would happen? If you thought bad things, you are on the right track.

Since your PATH doesn't have the current directory (.) as one of its search places, programs in your current directory must be called with an absolute path or a relative path specified as ./programname.

To see what directories are part of your PATH, enter this command:

echo $PATH

```
[alberto@digital alberto]$ echo $PATH
/bin:/usr/bin:/opt/bin:/usr/local/bin:/usr/X11R6/bin:/opt/kde/bin:
```

125

Filename Expansion: Tab

As I said earlier, shells are not very ergonomic, and most people don't like to type commands or long pathnames very often. Depending on the shell of you use, you might have the ability to have the shell complete filenames and command names for you. The shell will do this whenever the portions of the path you specified cannot be confused for something else.

To activate completion on bash, all you need to do is press Tab after you've typed enough characters. If you wanted a listing of the /usr/local/bin directory, you could type ls /u<Tab>/lo<Tab>/b<Tab>, and the shell will expand each of the paths for you, saving you some keystrokes.

If the shell cannot complete the expansion because multiple completions are possible, hitting Tab again will list everything that could be a match. This is very useful if you have forgotten the name of a command. For example if you type l<Tab><Tab>, the shell will respond with a list of all the programs that begin with an l:

```
[alberto@digital alberto]$ l<Tab><Tab>
laser        lesskey       lkbib         lockfile      lpr
last         let           lmorph        logger        lprm
lastb        lex           ln            login         lptest
lastcomm     lha           lndir         logname       ls
latex        lightning     loadkeys      logout        lsattr
lbxproxy     lintopvf      loadunimap    look          lsdev
ld           lisa          local         lookbib       lynx
ld86         lispmtopgm    locale        lout          lz
ldd          listalias     localedef     lpq
less         listres       locate        lpqall.faces
```

Exiting the Console

To exit a console, issue the logout command. This command will end your session, clear up the screen, and return you to the login prompt. To restart the computer from the console, you can press Ctrl+Alt+Delete.

If you are using a terminal emulator like kvt or xterm, you can simply close the window and exit your system as you did before.

If you leave your system logged in (which might be a fine thing to do on your home machine), remember that anyone will be able to see and edit your files. However, never leave a root session open, as this could lead to fatal security problems or even catastrophic user errors.

Typically, Linux systems are left running permanently and only shut down when required by an upgrade or some sort of software malfunction.

Shutting Down a Linux Box

Shutting down is a bit different from what you might be used to on your PC. Unlike DOS or some other systems, UNIX-like systems need to be shut down gently. Even when no one is logged in, there are a number of processes running. These processes need to be stopped properly, or bad things will happen. Shutting down is accomplished through the shutdown command.

Before you can use the shutdown command, you need to have root privileges. This means that you need to log in as root prior to using the command.

The shutdown command takes a number of *arguments*. These options specify how the system is going to be shut down and when. The required one in this case are -h, which stands for "halt," and the keyword now, which specifies that the system should begin shutdown immediately.

To shut down your system gracefully, on a root console, type the following:

```
[root@digital root]# shutdown -h now
```

Rebooting a Linux Box

Rebooting is just a fancy name for restarting the computer. The shutdown command shown earlier can be used to reboot if you specify the -r option instead of the -h option. The -r option stands for *reboot*:

```
[root@digital root]# shutdown -r now
```

The easiest way to reboot the system is to simultaneously press the Ctrl+Alt+Del keys, taking the system through the reboot sequence. You can perform this action without being logged in the console.

Working with Files on the Shell

In This Chapter

➤ How to Manage and Organize Your Files Using a Shell

➤ How to Read Files

Working with Files and Folders

In Chapter 11, "Shells and Consoles," you learned how to log in and out and how to navigate the file system using a shell. In this chapter you'll continue your exploration of the UNIX shell and learn how to manipulate files and directories using one.

Creating a New Empty File: touch

Most of the time you'll create files as the result of working with some application or shell program. For didactic purposes, I am going to introduce a command that allows you to create empty files here. This ability to generate files as if by magic will make your exploration a little more interesting.

If you need to create an empty file, you can easily do so with the touch command. The purpose of touch is to modify the access and creation times of files, but as a side effect it creates files if they don't already exist.

To create a file, enter the command touch followed by a filename:

```
[alberto@digital alberto]$ touch afile
```

To verify that the file was created, you might want to use the ls command as explained in Chapter 11.

You can provide more than one filename to the command. Filenames can be specified using relative or absolute paths, or a mix thereof. When the command executes, it creates the specified files.

Removing Files: rm

To delete a file, you use the rm command. This command is very dangerous for one reason: Files removed under Linux (or UNIX in general) cannot be recovered unless you have a backup on tape, floppy, or some other medium.

To remove a file, type the following:

```
[alberto@digital alberto]$ rm afile
```

The rm command, because of its inherent danger, provides an option that questions any file that you try to remove. If you supply the -i option, it will question your intentions first:

```
[alberto@digital alberto]$ rm -i afile
rm: remove `afile'? y
```

Command aliases are described in Chapter 11 in the section "Making Shell Options the Default." To see a list of command aliases already active, type alias at the command prompt. A list of all active aliases will be printed for you to inspect.

Check This Out

Oops! I deleted file xrm on tape or another disk, can I get it back?

Is there a backup on tape or another disk?

➤ Yes: yes, you can.

➤ No: nope, the file is gone.

Creating a Directory: mkdir

To create a directory, use the command mkdir and specify the name of the directory (as usual, the name can be a "relative" filename or an absolute path:

```
[alberto@digital alberto]$ mkdir adir
```

If you need to create a entire tree of directories, specify the option -p and the path you need:

```
[alberto@digital alberto]$ mkdir -p
➥adir/anotherdir/yetanother
```

If portions of the path already exist, those portions are preserved and missing portions are added to the path.

Beware the Powers of root!

If you are logged in as root this applies to you: root is a special administrative account that grants unrestricted access to the entire system. This is very valuable when you need to perform system administration type tasks, but it is not an account that you want to use for any other purpose. The root account can perform certain actions that are irreversible, such as erasing *all* files in the disk or some other catastrophic type of thing.

Until you know more about Linux and UNIX in general, I would recommend that you don't use the root account unless it is absolutely necessary, as in the case of adding software or configuring some sort of device.

If you are not logged into your own account, create one right now! See Chapter 18, "Users, Groups, and Passwords," for more information.

Removing an Empty Directory: rmdir

To remove an empty directory, use the rmdir command. The rmdir command is "safe" because it won't remove the directory unless the directory is empty. It looks like this:

```
[alberto@digital alberto]$ mkdir empty
[alberto@digital alberto]$ rmdir empty
```

Removing Files and Directories at the Same Time: rm -R

Usually when you want to erase a directory, you also want to dispose of all files it contains. In UNIX and Linux, this task is accomplished using the rm command that you saw earlier.

To produce that effect, rm needs to recursively delete files that it finds before it can delete a directory. While this is the proper technique, beware: *You can easily erase lots of things before you even realize what's going on. Don't forget, the shell operates very quickly.* Take care when removing files; this is crucial when you are logged in a root, as you could destroy your entire file system with just one command.

Copying Files: cp

To copy of a file, use the cp command. The cp has the following syntax:

```
cp [options] source destination
```

source is the name of the file you want to copy, and *destination* is the name of the copy you create.

If *destination* is a directory (the path didn't specify a filename), the file is copied with its original name into the specified directory.

The *options* argument is shown between brackets to say that *options* are optional. We'll use an option on the cp command in the next section.

Here's an example:

```
[alberto@digital alberto]$ ls -F
Xrootenv.0    afile       anotherlink  helloworld*
adir/         alink@      hello

[alberto@digital alberto]$ cp helloworld /tmp

[alberto@digital alberto]$ ls -F /tmp
fvwmrca00455  helloworld*  install.log   screens/
```

You can copy multiple files to a single directory in a single command by listing several source files separated by spaces. The only requirement is that the last argument (*destination*) be a directory.

Copying Directories

You copy directories in much the same way you copy files. When copying directories you need to tell cp that you want to copy *recursively* all the files and directories contained by the source directory. This is easily done with the -R option. The syntax looks like this:

```
[alberto@digital alberto]$ ls
Xrootenv.0  adir/        afile        alink@       anotherlink
➡helloworld*
[alberto@digital alberto]$ cp -R adir /tmp
[alberto@digital alberto]$ ls /tmp
adir/         install.log
```

Moving Files and Directories: mv

To move a file or directory, you use the mv command. Moving files is similar to copying files. The big difference is that the original file is removed after the new copy is created. The mv command follows this syntax:

```
mv [options] source destination

[alberto@digital alberto]$ ls
Xrootenv.0   adir/       afile        alink@       anotherlink
➥helloworld*
[alberto@digital alberto]$ mv afile file2
[alberto@digital alberto]$ ls
Xrootenv.0   adir/       alink@       anotherlink  file2
➥helloworld*
```

The mv command can also be used to move an entire directory tree.

The mv command provides several options. For more information, refer to its manual page.

Note

To read documentation on a UNIX tool or command, refer to Chapter 15, "Help Please."

Symbolic Links

A *link* is a pointer to a file or folder that is somewhere else in the file system. A link looks and acts like the file or folder it points to. If you are viewing it through KFM, it will have the same icon (with the exception that it will have a little arrow next to it). If you specify the -F flag to the ls command, you'll see an at symbol (@) attached to the end of the link's filename. When you open a link, you see the same file contents of the file the link points to.

Links are very useful as an organizational tool. They allow you to conveniently access files that might be stored deeply in the file system (and therefore have a long and difficult-to-type file path) or even in a different part of the network. Instead of traversing a long path to access a file, you can just access a conveniently located link.

Links can also be used to save disk space. Instead of copying large files to have them handy, you can create links to them where convenient. Links take very little disk space, just a few bytes.

A symbolic link stores the file path of the file it points to. You can move and rename the link without affecting it. However, if the original file—the file that the link points to—is moved, deleted, or renamed, the link breaks. Broken links can be fixed by restoring the original file to its proper location and name. Otherwise they probably should be deleted. Symbolic links *associate* a *file path* with a file.

Hard Links

There's another type of link called a *hard link*. A hard link is similar to a symbolic (or soft) link in that it provides a different name for accessing a file. However, that is where similarities end. Hard links have one advantage: Unlike soft links, which break if you move, delete, or rename the original file, hard links don't.

Hard links don't really point to a file path as the soft links do; instead, they point to the actual data stored on a disk. For this reason, all files have at the very least one link: the name assigned to the file when it was created. When you add another hard link to a file, the file system treats it as if the file had a different name, but the data the link points to is the same as the original file. If you delete the original file, the remaining link still points to the same data on the disk.

As you can see, hard links are tied to the actual disk storage where a file is written. For this reason, hard links cannot cross disk boundaries.

Another small difference is that hard links only reference files—never directories. The only way you can tell a hard link from a file when you use the option -i and -l to ls and ls reports a hard link count greater than one and the inode address printed is the same:

```
[alberto@digital alberto]$ ls -il
  169688 -rwxrwxr-x   2 alberto   alberto      74 Aug 26 12:19 bye.pl
  169972 -rwxrwxrwx   1 alberto   alberto      65 Aug 30 14:49
➥capture.pl
  169688 -rwxrwxr-x   2 alberto   alberto      74 Aug 26 12:19
➥hello.pl
```

In the preceding example, both hello.pl and bye.pl have the same inode: 169688. Notice, too, that both files say they have two hard links. Both files are actually the same file with different names!

Creating Links: ln

Links are created using the ln command. ln is used to create both soft and hard links. The syntax for the command is

> ln **[**options**]** source destination

To create a symbolic (soft) link, you specify the -s option, which stands for *symbolic*. Here's an example for listing a directory:

```
[alberto@digital alberto]$ ls -l
total 2
drwxrwxr-x   3 alberto   alberto       1024 Aug  1 20:41 adir/
-rw-rw-r--   1 alberto   alberto         57 Aug  2 13:12 file
```

Here's an example for creating a hard link:

```
[alberto@digital alberto]$ ln file file2
```

Here's one for creating a soft link:

```
[alberto@digital alberto]$ ln -s file file3
```

Here is the syntax for listing directory again. Notice that file3 points to file:

```
[alberto@digital alberto]$ ls -l
total 3
drwxrwxr-x   3 alberto   alberto       1024 Aug  1 20:41 adir/
-rw-rw-r--   2 alberto   alberto         57 Aug  2 13:12 file
-rw-rw-r--   2 alberto   alberto         57 Aug  2 13:12 file2
lrwxrwxrwx   1 alberto   alberto          4 Aug  2 13:15 file3 -> file
```

Here is the syntax for deleting the original file:

```
[alberto@digital alberto]$ rm file
```

Here is the syntax for listing again. Notice that file3 now points to a file that doesn't exist!

```
[alberto@digital alberto]$ ls -l
total 2
drwxrwxr-x   3 alberto   alberto       1024 Aug  1 20:41 adir/
-rw-rw-r--   1 alberto   alberto         57 Aug  2 13:12 file2
lrwxrwxrwx   1 alberto   alberto          4 Aug  2 13:15 file3 -> file
```

Links are used often in Linux to allow files to be placed in many directories at once. For example, the directory /usr/X11R6 contains files used by X Windows. Some older X Windows programs install into /usr/X11R5 or /usr/X11R4 instead. Through a series of symbolic links, Linux can make files from all three directories appear in a more general X Windows directory, /usr/X11, for easy access. This type of organizing is one of the primary uses for symbolic links.

Reading Files

Being able to move and organize files is an important skill. In the end, computers are primarily for storing and retrieving information. Here are a few commands that you can use for reading files when on a terminal:

➤ cat: Copy the contents of a file to a terminal

➤ less: Page the contents a screen at a time

➤ head: Peek at the first few lines in a file

➤ tail: Peek at the last few lines in a file

Concatenating: cat

The cat command reads one or more files and prints the result to the screen. (It *concatenates* all files to the screen.) cat is a generic command, and it is used very frequently when chaining multiple commands together. When we explore redirection in Chapter 14, "Putting the Shell to Work," I'll show you how the cat is really used.

The basic syntax of cat is

 cat [*options*] *files*

Here's an example of using cat to view the /etc/passwd file (this is the file where information about users is kept):

```
[alberto@digital alberto]$ cat /etc/passwd
root:UGQDnB4s/nDAk:0:0:root:/root:/bin/bash
bin:*:1:1:bin:/bin:
daemon:*:2:2:daemon:/sbin:
adm:*:3:4:adm:/var/adm:
lp:*:4:7:lp:/var/spool/lpd:
sync:*:5:0:sync:/sbin:/bin/sync
shutdown:*:6:0:shutdown:/sbin:/sbin/shutdown
halt:*:7:0:halt:/sbin:/sbin/halt
mail:*:8:12:mail:/var/spool/mail:
news:*:9:13:news:/var/spool/news:
uucp:*:10:14:uucp:/var/spool/uucp:
operator:*:11:0:operator:/root:
games:*:12:100:games:/usr/games:
gopher:*:13:30:gopher:/usr/lib/gopher-data:
ftp:*:14:50:FTP User:/home/ftp:
nobody:*:99:99:Nobody:/:
postgres:!:100:101:PostreSQL Server:/var/lib/pgsql:/bin/bash
alberto:YMMhuMSru1hME:501:501:Alberto Ricart:/home/alberto:/bin/bash
```

As you can see, cat opened the file /etc/passwd and printed every line to the console.

The cat command offers several options; the most useful are listed in Table 12.1.

Table 12.1 cat **Command Options**

Option	Description
-n	Number all lines
-s	Squeeze multiple blank lines into one
-v	Display all characters (invisible characters, too, with the exception of tabs and newlines)
-A	Display all characters (invisible characters, too)

Viewing a Page at a Time: less

When you use cat, you might have already found out that if the size of the file is more than can fit on your screen, the contents scroll much too fast for you to read. One way of handling this is by using a *pager* command.

Pagers allow you to view a screenful (or page) of information at a time. There are two commands that you can use: the original pager called more and the better pager less. In the case of these programs, less is actually more. For example, less allows you to "back up" and scroll up something that more doesn't allow. less also doesn't quit until you tell it to.

When less prints a screenful, it puts at the bottom of the screen a colon (:). This means that there's more information after the current page. While the colon is displayed, you can interact with less and send it commands. Here are some of the more useful:

➤ To scroll forward (or down) another screenful, press the Spacebar

➤ To scroll backward (or up) a screenful, press B

➤ To display the current filename you are viewing and information about where you are in the file, press =

➤ To quit reading, press Q

When you reach the end of the file, less aptly prints "END" at the bottom of the screen; press Q if you would like to exit the program.

Peeking at the First Few Lines: head

Sometimes you don't want to read an entire file, just the first few lines. The command for this is called head, and it prints the first ten lines in a file:

```
[alberto@digital alberto]$ head /etc/passwd
root:x:0:0:root:/root:/bin/bash
bin:x:1:1:bin:/bin:
daemon:x:2:2:daemon:/sbin:
adm:x:3:4:adm:/var/adm:
lp:x:4:7:lp:/var/spool/lpd:
sync:x:5:0:sync:/sbin:/bin/sync
shutdown:x:6:11:shutdown:/sbin:/sbin/shutdown
halt:x:7:0:halt:/sbin:/sbin/halt
mail:x:8:12:mail:/var/spool/mail:
news:x:9:13:news:/var/spool/news:
```

If you pass the -n option, you can control how many lines head prints:

```
[alberto@digital alberto]$ head -n 1 /etc/passwd
root:x:0:0:root:/root:/bin/bash
```

Peeking at the Last Few Lines: tail

The flip side to head is tail. By default it prints the last ten lines. If you supply the -n option, head will print that number of lines from the end of the file:

```
[alberto@digital alberto]$ tail -n 1 /etc/passwd
alberto:x:100:100:Alberto Ricart:/home/alberto:/bin/bash
```

Text Editing under a Shell

In This Chapter

➤ Using the Vim Visual Editor

➤ Working with XEmacs

➤ Running Ispell

Knowing how to use an editor under the command line is a must. The UI for most of these is usually very awkward, especially when you are coming from an environment like Macintosh or Windows. There are literally a hundred different editors available that you can install on your computer. Many have their strengths and disadvantages. In my opinion, there are two command line editors that you should learn. Why two? Because under certain systems only one or the other is going to be available, and you should be able to do your work with either.

The most popular editors are

➤ the Visual Editor (vi)

➤ Emacs

The vi is the most widely available editor on any UNIX-like operating system. For this reason alone it should be one you learn. Knowing that vi can be found in all systems is a comforting thought; you will always be able to edit files no matter what flavor of UNIX you find yourself using tomorrow.

Techno Talk

In general, when you are working with a terminal, you should be able to press the Backspace key and erase the last character. If you press Backspace and get a weird character like **^?**, your terminal is not set up properly.

Typically, this configuration problem will crop up when you are working remotely through a telnet session. Fixing the problem is actually very easy with the aid of the **stty** program. (The **stty** program is actually very complicated, but you don't need to know too many details about how it works—just enough to fix your problem.)

The **stty** program follows this format: stty *command characters*, where *command* is the name of the option, and *characters* is the characters you saw printed when you used them in the shell or the editor.

The frequently used commands are

➤ erase (to associate the backspace key)

➤ kill (to delete characters to the left of the cursor)

➤ intr (to interrupt a program)

➤ susp (to suspend a program)

For my daily work under UNIX, I use Emacs or its cousin, XEmacs. The main difference between the two editors is that vi is about 20 times smaller than Emacs. If you ever (hope you never do) need to do disaster recovery, vi will fit on a floppy; Emacs will not. In terms of features, however, Emacs has them all, and that is not an exaggeration.

An Improved Visual Editor: Vim

Linux distributions come with vi as a link to vim. Vim is an improved version of vi (see the following figure); originally the name was Vi Imitation, but that is no longer true. Vim contributes a slew of features missing from the original program, but the basic commands are the same. So if you learn the newer vim editor, you'll have no trouble with vi, except that you will miss the additional features.

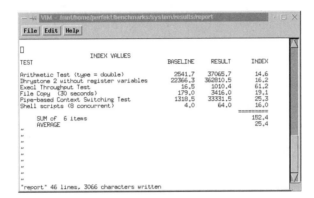

You can see a graphical version of vim here running inside KDE.

Interactive Vim Tutorial

The easiest way to learn vim is to use the online tutorial. In vim's case, this tutorial (a file in your system) is better and more interesting than reading a book because it is, well, an interactive tutorial. Here's how to access it.

To go through the tutorial, you'll first need to copy a file to your home directory. The tutorial is just a text file with instructions on how to use vim.

To install the tutorial, copy /usr/doc/vim-4.5-2/tutor/tutor to your home directory. It is possible that the version number has been upped in your installation,, so copy it this way:

```
cp /usr/doc/vim*/tutor/tutor ~/
```

This process will put the tutorial file, tutor, in your home directory.

To start the tutorial, type the following two commands:

```
 alberto@digital alberto]$ cd
[alberto@digital alberto]$ vim tutor
*~~~~~~~~~~~~~~~~~~~~~~~~~~~~~~~~~~~~~~~~~~~~~~~~~~~~~~~~~~~~~~~~~~
➡~~~~~~~~*
*    W e l c o m e   t o   V I   T u t o r   -   V e r s i o n   1 .
➡2     *
*~~~~~~~~~~~~~~~~~~~~~~~~~~~~~~~~~~~~~~~~~~~~~~~~~~~~~~~~~~~~~~~~~~
➡~~~~~~~~*
```

```
**************
* Lesson 1.0 *
**************

    Vim is a very powerful editor that has many commands, too many to
    explain in a tutor such as this.  This tutor is designed to
    ➥describe
    enough of the commands that you will be able to easily use Vim as
    an all-purpose editor.

    The approximate time required to complete the tutor is 25-30
    ➥minutes,
    depending upon how much time is spent with experimentation.

    It is important to remember that this tutor is set up to teach by
    use.  That means that the student needs to execute the commands
    ➥to
    learn them properly.

    Now, make sure that your Shift-Lock key is NOT depressed and
    ➥press
    the   j   key enough times to move the cursor so that Lesson 1.1
    completely fills the screen.
~~~~~~~~~~~~~~~~~~~~~~~~~~~~~~~~~~~~~~~~~~~~~~~~~~~~~~~~~~~~~~~~~~~~~~~~~~~
    ➥~~~~~~~~
```

As you can see, typing those commands will put you right into a vim session with the tutorial on the screen. Follow the instructions, and you are on your way. The tutorial should take anywhere from 20 to 60 minutes, depending on how many distractions (such as phone calls) occur.

Vim Basics

If you just want to get the hang of it, here's a bare-bones tutorial.

Vim is a modal editor. All this means is that when you are using vim, the program will behave differently depending on whether you are in command mode or editing mode.

Let's go. Create and edit a file with vim. On your command line, issue the following:

```
[alberto@digital alberto]$ vim tutorial
~
~
~
~
"tutorial" [New File]
```

A graphical version of vim can be started from within KDE by issuing the command gvim (graphical vim).

On issuing the command, the editor will take over your terminal. Empty lines are marked by a tilde (~) character. Vim is currently in its command mode. It is waiting for you to tell it what to do.

When in command mode, you can move around the document (assuming there's some text to navigate, which won't be the case in a new document) and issue commands. Table 13.1 is a list of all the cursor moving commands. (As you can see, some are mapped to special keys on your keyboard.)

Table 13.1 Moving Around the Document

Key	Function
l or Right Arrow	Moving forward to the next character
h or Left Arrow	Move back one character
j or Down Arrow	Move down one line
k or Up Arrow	Move up one line
w	Move one word forward
b	Move one word backward

In general, you move your cursor by using the arrow keys (or its hjkl counterparts—I rarely can remember these). To scroll the document, you use the Page Up and Page Down.

The cursor will not wrap or move beyond the beginning or end of a line. When you reach the end, the computer will beep. To go to the next or previous line, use the down or up arrow keys, respectively.

When you begin a new, blank document, you don't have much to do; there's no text to edit or navigate. To add text, you need to get into the insert mode. This mode will allow you to enter text as you normally do in other programs; you are still able to use the arrow keys to move around. (The hjkl keys type a letter when you are in insert mode.) Type i to get into the insert mode. Table 13.2 lists a number of editing commands that you can use while in command mode.

Table 13.2 Vi (Vim) Editing Commands

Command	Description
i	Insert text (begin editing)
x	Delete the character under the cursor (command mode)
dw	Delete characters until the end of the word

d$	Delete text until the end of the line
dd	Delete the current line
u	Undo the last command
U	Undo any changes to the line
Ctrl+R	Redo any undos
Esc	Return to command mode, cancel current action—repeat until vim beeps

To return to the command mode, hold down the Esc key until vim beeps at you. Then you can type a :+*command*. Commands are issued by pressing the colon (:) followed by the name of the command. Table 13.3 lists the basic ones to get you out of vim.

Table 13.3 Vi (Vim) Exiting Commands

Command	Description
:q!	Quit without saving
:wq	Save and quit
:wfilename	Write the buffer to filename

Vim has some editing commands—and the all-important undo. These editing commands work while vim is in command mode.

Command Multipliers: Repeating the Action More Than Once

Commands such as delete can specify a multiplier. If you type a number before the command, the command will be repeated that number of times.

Consider the following text:

```
This is one line of text.
This is another line of text.
```

To delete the words This and is, move the cursor under the T. Make sure you are in command mode by pressing Esc until vim beeps; then type 2dw. To delete both lines of text, put the cursor anywhere on the first line and type 2dd.

Multipliers also work for moving around in the document. To move down five lines, you can type 5, followed by the down arrow.

Accessing the Shell from Vim

You can execute shell commands by preceding them with the exclamation point (!):

```
:!shellcommand
```

When the command finishes executing, you are prompted to hit Enter to return to the editor. To get an interactive shell, enter the name of the shell as the *shellcommand* (bash). When finished working with the shell, type `exit` on the shell prompt, and you'll return to the editor.

Other Stuff

Vim is fairly powerful. It supports multiple documents—or buffers, as they are known—and many other features. The commands covered here are just the bare minimum you need to know to edit files using a terminal. I encourage you to go through the tutorial and to visit vim's home page at `http://www.vim.org`. You'll be happy you did.

XEmacs

XEmacs is the variant of Emacs, the GNU super editor, included with Caldera OpenLinux. XEmacs provides additional enhancements when used under a graphical environment, such as X (KDE)—hence its "X" denomination. Under a terminal, it is almost exactly the same as regular Emacs. Any reference to Emacs applies in terms of usage to XEmacs.

Emacs is the most powerful of editors. It is available for UNIX, Windows, and a slew of other operating systems. It provides features too numerous to cover in 500 pages just dedicated to Emacs alone!

Emacs is an extensible editor. Using a programming language called Lisp, Emacs can be easily extended to do just about anything thinkable.

Many hardcore UNIX people use only one program: Emacs. They start it when they start their work session, and they close it when they exit their system. All their work, with very rare exceptions, is handled through Emacs, including access to the shell.

XEmacs on a console looks like this.

From Emacs you can read, write, and organize your email and calendar, manipulate and organize your files, browse the Web, read news, develop software, transfer FTP files across the network, and much more. No matter what you do under UNIX, it is likely that you can do it through Emacs. Of course, Emacs also edits files. If you get the sense that Emacs is really an environment, you are correct. That is what separates Emacs from other editors.

Here's XEmacs through X—notice all the buttons and menus!

Emacs does everything through modes. A *mode* is just a specialized interface for interacting with a specific program or for working with a specific file format such as text or programming source code. Modes are tailored to the needs of a particular task. If it sounds complicated, it really isn't. The modes are automatically handled by Emacs depending on what you are doing and the file you are editing.

Starting XEmacs and the XEmacs Tutorial

To enter Emacs (XEmacs), just type xemacs at the command prompt. Emacs will greet you with a welcome message and a list of options. Most keystrokes under Emacs work as follows:

 Ctrl+*letter letter*

When you see a command listed as **C-t h**, it means that first you must press Ctrl+t and then h by itself. Yes, Emacs has a lot of command keys, and it requires a little time to get used to it; however, that is time well spent.

To exit Emacs, type Ctrl+c Ctrl+x; this will return you to your shell. Teaching Emacs is beyond the scope of this book, but suffice it to say that it is worth exploring if you are going to do a lot of text editing.

One impressive feature of Emacs is that you can edit files through FTP as if they were local on your disk. For users working on Web-related services, this feature rocks. If your files can be reached through FTP, they can be edited and manipulated just as if they were local files. However, that is an advanced topic for another book.

If you are a programmer, Emacs does source formatting on the fly, so your source code is always formatted in a way that you can read. When reading other people's code, the ability to reformat the code in a way readable to you is invaluable. Emacs also provides an IDE (Integrated Development Environment): You can build your program and debug it right from Emacs.

Emacs also has an online tutorial. To access the tutorial, start Emacs, and in the welcome window type C-h t.

Checking Your Spelling: Ispell

Spell-checking in Linux can be done from the command line with a program called Ispell. Ispell stands for *interactive spell checking*. Ispell enables you to write your document using your editor (which might integrate with ispell directly) and then check it from the shell, like this:

```
ispell filenames
```

Ispell can check multiple files at the same time if you provide them. You can add words to your own private dictionary. If no misspellings are found, the program exits without any messages.

Ispell is very friendly and easy to use. The following figure shows a terminal running ispell.

Word in question

Suggestions—

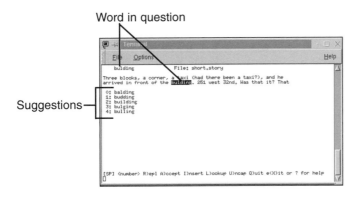

Ispell, and interactive spell checker, is easy to use from the shell.

Ispell highlights the word in question and shows you the context in which it was found. If it finds possible corrections, it will display a list of them. To accept one of the proposed replacements, just type its number. Other actions are as listed at the bottom of the window or screen.

149

Putting the Shell to Work

In This Chapter

➤ Output and Input Redirection

➤ Chaining Commands Together

➤ Regular Expressions

➤ Command History

In Chapters 11–13, you learned a few basics about commands and shells. Although single commands will probably be most of what you do, the real power of shell comes when you are able to string a series of commands together to perform more complex tasks than any single command can accomplish. Shells allow you to do so, and in this chapter you'll learn how to take advantage of this ability, along with a few other nifty command shell tricks.

Using More Than One Command at a Time

You can issue several commands at the same time; just separate each command with a semicolon (;). Here's an example:

```
[alberto@digital alberto]$ pwd; cd ..; pwd; ls -lg
/home/alberto
/home
total 3
drwxr-xr-x  14 alberto  users          1024 Aug 18 19:01 alberto/
```

```
drwxr-xr-x   5 root      root         1024 Aug 14 08:09 ftp/
drwxr-xr-x   7 root      root         1024 Aug 14 08:09 httpd/
[alberto@digital home]$
```

In this example I did a number of things:

I listed the current working directory with pwd, and then I changed directories to the parent (up one) directory by typing two periods (..). I also listed the new current working directory and asked for a long listing of the files there.

When I asked to cd up a directory, it did, and when all commands finished executing, I was left where the last command to affect my current directory stopped (the /home directory—you can tell this if you look at the end of my shell prompt).

Command Groups and Subshells

Command groups allow you to execute a series of commands in a subshell. When you create a command group, Linux fires up a new shell subprocess different from your current shell to execute it. When the command group finishes executing, it returns control to your shell.

You create a command group by enclosing the commands in parentheses, like this:

```
[alberto@digital alberto]$ (pwd; cd ..; pwd; ls -lg)
/home/alberto
/home
total 3
drwxr-xr-x  14 alberto   users        1024 Aug 18 19:01 alberto/
drwxr-xr-x   5 root      root         1024 Aug 14 08:09 ftp/
drwxr-xr-x   7 root      root         1024 Aug 14 08:09 httpd/
[alberto@digital alberto]$
```

If you are really paying attention, you will also notice that when you execute a command group, the current environment is not affected. Note how my starting directory is alberto, and my final directory after the command group ends remained at alberto...yet one of the commands moved up a directory!

The reason for this move is that execution of command groups creates a *subshell*. Subshells have their own environment. (Their initial environment matches your current environment.) When the subshell executed the cd command, it changed the environment of the subshell. However, it did not affect the environment of the parent shell, the shell on which I typed the command.

Redirection

Much of the usefulness of shells comes from the capability to redirect input and output to and from files. Most shell programs are designed to process data using *streams*.

A *stream* is nothing more than data flowing as input or output. For example, a command's input stream usually comes from your keyboard, and its output stream usually goes to your terminal's display. Under UNIX all programs communicate with the ouside world using three streams:

➤ STDOUT—The standard output stream (usually the display)

➤ STDIN—The standard input stream (usually the keyboard)

➤ STDERR—The standard error stream (usually the display

Streams can be interconnected easily or wired in different ways through a shell. Your shell can cause a program to use a file for its input stream and to put results back into a file using the output stream. This is called *redirection*.

STDOUT

Most of the programs you have used so far send their results to the standard output stream, STDOUT, which is usually "wired" to your console. Any time that you see something printed on the console (your screen), more than likely it was sent to the STDOUT stream.

Let's experiment a little with redirecting STDOUT to a file.

Redirecting to a File: >

To redirect output to a file, you use the greater than symbol (>) and provide a filename to receive the output:

```
[alberto@digital alberto]$ ls -l > /tmp/listing
[alberto@digital alberto]$ cat /tmp/listing
total 2
-rw-rw-r--   1 alberto   alberto        388 Jul 29 19:03 Xrootenv.0
-rw-rw-r--   1 alberto   alberto          0 Aug  5 20:16 file
drwxrwsr-x   2 alberto   groupfil      1024 Aug  4 22:13 groupfiles
```

In this example I did just that. I asked for a listing of my files, but instead of getting the listing displayed on my screen, I redirected the output of the ls command to the file /tmp/listing. To prove that it worked, I then sent the contents of the /tmp/listing file to my screen using the cat command you learned in Chapter 12, "Working with Files on the Shell." This technique is useful for creating a list of the files in a directory.

Safety First! Avoiding Clobbered Files: `noclobber`

Redirecting streams has one dangerous side effect: It can kill files. When redirecting output to files, if the file doesn't exist, Linux creates it automatically. This benefit also presents a problem. What happens if the file already exists? The existing file is overwritten automatically. This means that the shell replaces the existing file's data with the new data—without prompting or even notifying you!

Most shells have the capability to set a `noclobber` variable. This variable tells the shell to reject redirections that would result in the destruction of a file and to reject appending to files when they don't exist.

When working with shells, enabling this functionality can be a good idea, because it makes it less likely that the shell will have some side effect you didn't intend.

To enable `noclobber`, type the following on your `bash` shell:

```
noclobber=1
```

If you are using a different shell, like the `C` shell, you might want to try this:

```
set noclobber=1
```

To test if the command took, type the following:

```
[alberto@digital alberto]$ noclobber=1

[alberto@digital alberto]$ touch file

[alberto@digital alberto]$ date > file

bash: file: Cannot clobber existing file
```

If you get the same error, `noclobber` is set properly. I tried to redirect the output of a command called `date` to `file`. Because `file` already existed, such redirection would have caused the contents of `file` to be replaced by whatever `date` printed. Such action is not allowed when you have `noclobber` defined in your environment. (The `date` command is covered in Chapter 17, "Command Toolbox: Useful Shell Commands and Shortcuts.")

Now that you know about redirection, let me show you a neat trick: Let's use the cat command as a minimal text editor. We can do this by issuing the cat command and then redirecting the output to a file, like this:

```
[alberto@digital alberto]$ cat > /tmp/message.txt
This is a test. Until I type a Ctrl+D, I can type all that I want.
I can even enter new lines.

-- Alberto
[alberto@digital alberto]$ cat /tmp/message.txt
This is a test. Until I type a Ctrl+d, I can type all that I want.
I can even enter new lines.

-- Alberto
[alberto@digital alberto]$
```

With redirection, you can use cat as a simple editor. You can edit the current line you are working on, as the shell won't grab the characters until you hit Enter. To finish entering text, just press Ctrl+D.

Appending a File: >>

Redirecting is very useful, but sometimes you don't want to replace the file's previous contents. Instead, you might want to add information to the end of a file. Maybe you want to maintain a list of all your favorite Web sites. In such a case, adding a new entry should not replace the entire file but augment it.

Instead of using a single >, you use a >> to tell the shell to append new output instead of overwriting. If the file doesn't exist, it is created, like this:

```
[alberto@digital alberto]$ cat > /tmp/websites
www.caldera.com
www.redhat.com
[alberto@digital alberto]$ cat >> /tmp/websites
www.mcp.com
[alberto@digital alberto]$ cat /tmp/websites
www.caldera.com
www.redhat.com
www.mcp.com
```

Why couldn't I have used append (>>) for the first cat? Because I enabled the noclobber feature, the >> command would have resulted in an error. Appending to files that don't exist produces an error when noclobber is set. (An alternative would have been to issue a touch /tmp/websites before using cat.)

STDERR

The standard error stream, or STDERR, is where error messages are sent. As you enter more complex commands on a shell, you'll probably want to have diagnostic or warning messages sent to a log file. Redirecting error messages to a new file is especially useful if you are debugging a shell script.

Redirecting Errors

By default, both STDERR and STDOUT point to your console so you can see diagnostic messages. When you redirect STDOUT, STDERR still points to your console, and any errors are still printed there. To redirect errors, you need to specify a file number.

The input, output, and error streams have assigned file numbers in the shell: STDOUT is 0, STDIN is 1, and STDERR is 2. You can combine the file number and the redirection operator. To redirect errors to a different place, you specify the redirection like this:

```
command  > outputfile 2> errorfile
```

Messages printed to the standard error stream, STDERR, will go to errorfile, and standard output to STDOUT will redirect outputfile.

For example, let's say you wanted to create a list of all the files on your system. Depending on your user id, you might not have permission to go into some directories. The following command line will redirect permission access errors to a different file while capturing good output in a separate file:

```
ls -R / > filelist.txt 2> error.txt
```

Command Groups and Redirection

If you wanted to redirect the output of multiple commands, it would seem reasonable to think that you could use a command like this:

```
pwd; cd ..; pwd; ls -l > /tmp/listing
```

However, that command line only redirects the output of the last command. To redirect output for all of the commands, you need to create a command group and redirect standard output for the entire group instead:

```
(pwd; cd ..; pwd; ls -l) > /tmp/listing
```

This places the output of each program in succession into the /tmp/listing file.

Pipes: One Program's Output Is Another's Input

The true power of shells shines when the output from one program becomes the input of another...whose output then becomes the input of yet another, and so on. You can interconnect the input and output of a number of programs in a cascade of useful information. At this point, you might be envisioning a scheme by which you use a series of input and output redirection commands, passing information through a temporary file.

But in a more direct fashion, you can interconnect programs with *pipes*. Pipes are very useful: They allow you to use the output stream of one program as the input stream of another without the need for temporary files.

For example, if you want a list of all users currently logged into the system, you can use the **who** command. The **who** command displays information about each active user, one user per line. If you merely want to know how many users are on the system, but don't need all of the extra information **who** provides, you need to resort to some trickery. UNIX has a command called **wc** that counts the number of words, lines and characters that a file contains. Knowing that **who** outputs information about one user per line, you quickly realize that you'd like **wc** to count the number of lines **who** displays. You can accomplish this by connecting **who** and **wc** together with a pipe:

```
[alberto@digital alberto]$ who ¦ wc
➥-1
        1
```

As you can see, the who and wc commands can be piped by connecting them with a vertical bar (¦). You can tie together as many programs as you want. However, given our limited command vocabulary, there isn't much we can do yet.

Throwing unwanted output away

Sometimes you don't want to see the output from a program on your display, but you also don't want to send it to a file. Maybe you just don't want it at all. For example, when listing all of the files in your system:

```
ls -R / > filelist.txt 2>
➥error.txt
```

You know that this command sends a list of all the files in your computer to filelist.txt, and the access errors it encounters to error.txt. What if you only want to save or know about the errors? Is there any way to throw the long list of files away as the command runs?

UNIX computers all have a special file in the /dev directory called /dev/null, also commonly referred to as the bit-bucket. Any data sent to /dev/null in a stream is thrown away instantly. To throw away the list of files and just keep the errors, you'd type:

```
ls -R / > /dev/null 2>
➥error.txt
```

The errors will still be saved in error.txt, but now you don't have to deal with the long list of files.

One common use of pipes is in conjunction with the **ls** command. If you list a directory that contains many files, such as the /dev directory, the output will scroll past your screen more quickly than you can see it. What do you think the solution is?

If your thought is to make a pipe between ls and a page such as less, you got it! The command you would use to list the /dex directory is this:

```
ls -l /dev ¦ less
```

Getting the Needed Input: Input Redirection

You can redirect input the same way you are able to redirect output. When a program's input stream is redirected from a file, the program uses the characters contained in the file just as if you had typed them on your keyboard.

Input redirection is best illustrated with an example. Pretend that it's your job to prepare memos for circulation. Each time your boss tells you that a memo is ready to be processed, you carry out a complex series of tasks. First, you load the file /incoming/memo.txt into vi. Then, you remove the first ten lines of text which contain some control information, and you save the file. Finally, you copy the file to /outgoing/memo.txt, where your boss retrieves it and sends it to everyone else. Is there a simpler way to do this?

Realizing that you are using the same series of keystrokes over and over again, you decide to simplify your task with input redirection. Using what you learned about vi in Chapter 13, "Text Editing Under a Shell" you create a text file called prepare.txt which looks like this:

```
10dd
:w/outgoing/memo.txt
:q!
```

After creating this file, you try preparing a memo with the following command to the shell:

```
vi /incoming/memo.txt < prepare.txt
```

When you press Enter to execute the command, vi responds:

```
Vim: Warning: Input is not from a terminal
```

This is to tell you that vi will be redirecting its standard input stream from the file you created. A few moments later, your shell prompt returns. After checking the file /outgoing/memo.txt, you confirm that the memo was processed correctly. Using input redirection, a complex task has been made simpler.

Regular Expressions

Although regular expressions are an advanced topic, they can be quite useful if you understand them. So what exactly is a *regular expression*? It's a pattern definition, also called wild cards, that can be used to define what text should look like and allow the shell to find a match. You can use regular expressions on a shell prompt to select groups of files that match the pattern without having to explicitly type the name of each file.

Regular expressions, or REGEXs as they are also called, are used by a variety of programs—including your shell. Sometimes the symbols used to represent the patterns will change a little in meaning, but in general, the basic syntax is the same.

Here's an example of something you might want to do with REGEXs: Suppose that you have a directory with four files—file1.txt, file2.txt, file3.txt, and info.txt—and you want to move them to a different directory. What would you do?

You could execute this command:

```
mv file1.txt file2.txt file3.txt info.txt ../somedir
```

Although no doubt that command would do what you want, it is not something you want to type often, especially if you have 400 files instead of just four! A regular expression can be used to solve this sort of problem. Instead of typing a monstrous command, you could type:

```
mv * ../somedir
```

That looks easier, doesn't it?

The asterisk, or star, is a special character among a group called *metacharacters*. The star defines a pattern that matches everything. Let's take a look at the metacharacters and how you can use them.

Match Anything: *

The star matches any sequence of characters. That's why I can say mv * to move all the files. You can place the star between other letters so that it matches words that might contain other characters. See Table 14.1 for examples of using the star.

Table 14.1 Examples of Using the Star

Examples	Description
*.txt	Matches all files that end with .txt
file*	Matches all files beginning with the word file
file*.txt	Matches all files beginning with the word file and ending with .txt

Match Any Letter: ?

The star is powerful, no doubt about it. Sometimes, in fact, it's too powerful. Because it can stand for any number of characters, it can potentially match things you don't want to match. Luckily, there is a more restrained metacharacter: The ? will match one letter exactly, regardless of what the character at that position is. However, there must be a letter in the position you specify, or there's no match. See Table 14.2 for examples.

Table 14.2 Examples of Using the Question Mark

Example	Description
file?.txt a	Matches all files that begin with file, are followed by a single character, and end in .txt
?	Matches all files that have a one-letter name
??	Matches all files that have a two-letter name

Match in a Range: []

Sometimes you want to match a variety of options. Let's say you wanted to use metacharacters to find file1.txt and file2.txt but not file3.txt. In that case, you need to provide a set of options enclosed by brackets, like this:

```
file[12].txt
```

This pattern will match file1.txt and file2.txt—nothing else.

If you want to find a continuous range of characters—say you wanted to match the numbers 0 through 5—you can specify them as [0-5] instead of [012345].

Negating a Range: !

Sometimes it's easier to specify what you *don't* want matched. For example, if you had files named f11, f12, f13, f14, and f15, and you wanted to move only f12-f15, you could specify the range as I did here. But it might be easier to specify the files you don't want by using f11[!1]. In this case, every file but f11 will be matched.

Command History

Every time you type a command on the shell, the shell remembers it in what is called a *history list*. You can view the history by typing history on the bash prompt. A list of all the commands you have typed will be listed. Each command will have a number associated with it.

You can "recycle" commands that appear in your history to avoid having to retype them. To re-issue a command which appears in your command history, just type an exclamation point (!) followed by the number of the command you want to re-issue:

```
[alberto@digital alberto]$ !138
```

The very last command you entered is special. If you want to repeat it, just enter two exclamation points (!!). For example, you could type this:

```
[alberto@digital alberto]$ !!
```

You can move up through your command history by using the up arrow on your keyboard. Doing so will put the command on your prompt so you have a chance to edit it before you re-execute it.

How many commands your history holds will depend on the setting of the HISTSIZE environment variable. By default, it is set to remember your last 100 commands.

Jobs: Working on Multiple Things Using a Shell

Some command line jobs will take a while to complete. For example, the command `ls -R / > filelist.txt 2> error.txt` could easily take several minutes before it is done. If you have a lot of files and are listing several network drives, expect it to run for half an hour or so.

With Linux being multitasking, you'd probably want to do something else while the command runs. You can do this very easily by running the command concurrently or in the background. To execute the same command in the background, enter the following:

```
ls -R / >filelist.txt 2>error.txt &
```

The key here is the ampersand (&) at the end of the command line. This tells the shell to run the job in the background. After issuing the command, you'll see something like the following:

```
[alberto@digital alberto]$ ls -R / > filelist.txt 2> error.txt &
[1] 872
[alberto@digital alberto]$
```

The job starts and your command line comes back. The number in brackets is the job number or process id assigned to your command. The 872 is the process id for the job in the system-wide process list. The process id for a job is useful in case you need to kill the job (see "Killing a Process: kill" in Chapter 22, "System Monitoring: Keeping an Eye on Your System"). Jobs are a little easier to remember than a process id of 872. When referring to a job number, always precede it with a percent (%) symbol. Both give you a way of controlling the command and to return it back to the front. When the job is completed, you'll see a line like this:

```
[1]-   Done              ls -R / >filelist.txt 2>errors.txt
```

161

This means your job is done running. Note that programs which produce lots of output on the display should not be run in the background unless the output is redirected. Otherwise, your command prompt will be difficult to use, since output from the background command will continue to appear as you type!

Some programs will require interactive input, so every once in a while you'll see this:

```
[1]+  Stopped (tty output)    telnet localhost
```

This means that the job needs input, and has paused to wait for keystrokes from you. To bring the job back to the front and enter the required keystrokes, use the command fg:

```
[alberto@digital alberto]$ fg %1
```

This will bring job number one (%1) back to the foreground. Note that there's a percent symbol (%) before the job number.

To list all jobs started from inside the current shell, use the jobs command, like this:

```
[alberto@digital alberto]$ jobs
[1]+  Stopped (tty output)    telnet localhost
```

Suspending a Job

You can suspend a process that is running in the foreground by hitting Ctrl+Z. This will put the process to sleep:

```
[alberto@digital alberto]$ ls -R / > filelist.txt 2> errors.txt

[1]+  Stopped                 ls -R / >filelist.txt 2>errors.txt
[alberto@digital alberto]$ bg %1
[1]+ ls -R / >filelist.txt 2>errors.txt &
```

In this listing, I started a lengthy process in the foreground. I then put it to sleep (stopped it) by pressing Ctrl+Z and revived it in the background with a bg %1. bg does the opposite of the fg command.

Killing a Job

To kill the current foreground process, you can issue a Ctrl+C. This will terminate the process. To kill a job running in the background, you can use the kill command followed by its job number or its process id:

```
[alberto@digital alberto]$ kill %1
[alberto@digital alberto]$ kill 872
```

As you can see, the shell both is powerful and complex. Even though we have only barely scratched its surface, what you know can help you to get loads of work done!

Help Please

So far, you have been relying on this book for information about Linux. The commands discussed represent only a tiny fraction of what are available. This book doesn't explain how to configure or use many things that you will eventually want to run on your system; for that I would need an additional 400 pages.

Before you despair, remember that this book is intended to get you up to speed with many basic topics related to both Linux and UNIX. In order for you to gain a full understanding, you will have to supplement the information you find here with additional sources. Some of these sources are already in your computer; others are available from other books or from resources freely available over the Internet.

In this chapter, you'll take a short tour on the various resources you can utilize to get up to speed with Linux. This will empower you to find and solve problems on your own. You will learn a great deal by reading and tinkering as your needs require.

One interesting thing about Linux is that it is well documented. Whereas other operating systems (OSs) provide you with detailed information about certain aspects of your system, you will soon realize that Linux provides abundant information on just about everything installed in it. This is mostly due to the open nature of Linux. In a world where the tools are added by a distributed collection of programmers, the only way to bring order is through documentation. Linux has tons of it—if you know where to look.

Linux is a fairly "standard" UNIX as unices go. There are several generic UNIX books that can help you with additional depth and more advanced topics. A list of recommended readings is included at the end of this chapter. Also, if you have access to the Internet, there are several valuable sources of information that you can tap into, including mailing lists and Usenet news groups. Knowing how to use them properly will help you get the answers you need.

UNIX Manual Pages

Your first stop for information is the UNIX man pages. If you are having trouble with a command or some other tool in the system, it is very likely that the tool comes with documentation in the form of a man page. A *man* page is the standard UNIX online documentation format used by the man program.

The UNIX manual is slowly becoming a dinosaur, because better programs exist for reading documentation. The one positive thing about the UNIX manual is that it exists in all unices, Linux or otherwise. For this reason, it's important that you learn how to use it properly.

To read the UNIX manual, you use the man command, and as an argument you give it the name of a program you want to know something about. The following example shows a section of what man prints out if you ask for information about the bash shell:

```
[alberto@digital alberto]$ man bash
BASH(1)                                                          BASH(1)

NAME
       bash - GNU Bourne-Again Shell

SYNOPSIS
       bash [options] [file]

COPYRIGHT
       Bash  is  Copyright (c) 1989,  1991 by the Free Software
       Foundation, Inc.

DESCRIPTION
       Bash is an sh-compatible command language interpreter that
       executes  commands  read from the standard input or from a
```

file. Bash also incorporates useful features from the
Korn and C shells (ksh and csh).

Bash is ultimately intended to be a conformant implementa-
tion of the IEEE Posix Shell and Tools specification (IEEE
Working Group 1003.2).

:

As you can see, the man command provides a formatted version of the online manual.
The colon (:) at the end of the listing indicates that there's more information. Man
information is passed through a pager program called less. You may recall that less
displays information one screenful at a time. Here are a few things you can do with
less:

➤ Press the Spacebar to view the next page.

➤ Type /*word* where *word* is a term that you are looking for. This will search the
 document for the word you specify and stop the pager at word's first occurrence.

➤ Type q to return to the command prompt.

Try the man command to read some information about the man command (man man).

Searching for a Tool: apropos

Man is very useful if you know the name of the command you're interested in. You
can do a man *commandname*, and you are on your way. But what if you don't know the
name of the command you are looking for?

That is where the apropos command comes in: It allows you to search for keywords
instead. As a result, it displays a list of documents that might be related to your ques-
tion.

Great! There's only one small hang-up: the database that apropos searches, called the
whatis Database, does not exist until you create it. (You'll learn how to do this in the
section "Building the whatis Database: makewhatis.") After you build it, you can
query the database with the apropos command, for example, to find out about com-
mands related to your tape drive:

```
[alberto@digital alberto]$ apropos tape
mt (1)                   - control magnetic tape drive operation
smbtar (1)               - shell script for backing up SMB shares directly
to UNIX tape drive
st (4)                   - SCSI tape device
```

From this information, you know that there are at least three manual pages (use the
man command) that relate to your tape drive. The numbers you see in parenthesis
indicate a manual section.

165

The UNIX manual is organized into several sections. Each section is organized by topic. Table 15.1 provides a list of the sections.

Table 15.1 Sections of the UNIX Man Pages Under Linux

Section Number	Topic
1	User commands, programs, and applications
2	System calls and kernel error codes
3	Library function calls
4	Special files (things in /dev directory)
5	Standard file formats
6	Games and other funny-type programs
7	Miscellaneous things that don't fit elsewhere
8	System administration commands, programs, and applications

Building the whatis Database: makewhatis

To build the **whatis** database, you'll need to use the makewhatis command. To start building the database, enter this command:

```
/usr/sbin/makewhatis
```

Note that you must be root (you can also be su and execute the command) in order for this program to work properly. After a few moments, the database will be built. If you have an older computer, this action could take a while.

If you don't specify a section, man will search sections that cover commands first; typically, the order will be sections 1, 8, and 6.

It is possible that a command is described in more than one section of the manual. To view a document specific section, specify the man command like this:

```
man section command
```

In the preceding example, the man command is listed twice: in sections 1 and 7. To read the information on section 7, enter this command:

```
man 7 man
```

Getting a Brief Command Description: whatis

Sometimes you don't care to read five paragraphs of the UNIX manual just to find out what a command does. In those cases, the whatis tool can also be used to obtain a brief description of the command. To operate in this mode, you provide the name of the tool as an argument.

whatis will print out a one-line description of what a command does. I have found that whatis is a great exploration tool. If you go into a program directory such as

/sbin, you can quickly learn what the commands there do by issuing this command:

cd *directory*; whatis *

This will take you to the directory you specify under *directory* and issue a whatis on all the files that it finds there. The * is a regular expression that specifies all files it finds in that directory:

```
[alberto@localhost alberto]$ cd /sbin; whatis *
adjtimex (2)          - tune kernel clock
adjtimex (8)          - display or set the kernel time variables
arp (8)               - manipulate the system ARP cache
(And more...)
```

Searching Standard Locations: whereis

Sometimes the help you need is in locating the file or program you're looking for. As explained earlier, your shell finds commands by looking into your environment variable. When you issue the name of a command, the directories listed in the PATH environment variable are searched for a matching command. If found, the command is executed; otherwise, you get the dreaded "command not found" response.

Because some directories holding tools are not included in the default user path, your shell will not see them. In those cases, you can use the whereis tool to find the actual path to the tool you want to use.

Not only does whereis locate a binary, but it will also locate source and manual pages having the name you provide. The format for the command is this:

whereis *command*

Note

For more information on regular expressions, take a look at Chapter 14, "Putting the Shell to Work."

In the following example, I search for the command passwd:

```
[alberto@digital alberto]$ whereis passwd
passwd: /usr/bin/passwd /etc/passwd /etc/passwd.OLD
/usr/man/man1/passwd.1 /usr/man/man5/passwd.5
```

Built-in Command Information

Most recent commands store basic usage information right in the program. Under Linux, you can always try the command name with a --help or -h argument. Typically, the information listed will span more than one screen, so remember to pipe the output through less:

commandname --help ¦ less

If the command you are using is a "smart" UNIX command, it will respond in a reasonable way even if it does not understand the `--help` flag. Typically, when a program encounters an unknown argument, it reverts to spewing its usage information. The usage information will tell you the basic format of the command along with the flags that it supports. Obviously, this won't tell you what the program does (unless you already know), but some information is better than none at all. If man failed, you might need to surf the Web to find some information. I have found that searching the command name in an engine such as Yahoo usually points me in the right direction.

Online Help via /usr/doc

Linux stores many documentation and supplemental information files in /usr/doc. This directory is littered with a series of directories named after the program or tool to which they belong. Inside each you will typically find a README file containing some last-minute information about the program and frequently asked questions (FAQs) to features or issues with the program. This information is in addition to any documentation that you might find through man or other documentation readers.

The online help the in /usr/doc directory also contains some of the most important general Linux information on your computer:

➤ The Linux Installation and Getting Started Guide—This is a "getting started" manual for Linux beginners created by the Linux Documentation Project. The Linux Documentation Project is an initiative to create a complete set of online manuals for Linux computers.

➤ The Linux System Administrator's Guide—This manual is about UNIX system administration and was created by the Linux Documentation Project.

➤ The Linux Network Administrator's Guide—This manual describes how to use Linux in network environments and how to administer large, Linux-based networks. This manual was also created by the Linux Documentation Project.

➤ Other feature texts created by authors at the Linux Documentation Project.

➤ HOWTO documents—These feature guides on how to accomplish certain advanced tasks, such as configuring software or some interesting networking tool.

These documents are located in /usr/doc/html, but they are stored in HTML format, which means that you won't want to read them with a pager like less. You can access them in two ways, depending on whether you are in a KDE (X) session or a console. In a KDE session, launch Netscape Navigator to view the online manuals. The actual URL is file:/usr/doc/html/index.html; as shipped, Navigator is configured to open a link to this page by default. If you are working from a console, start the text-based Lynx browser by typing "lynx" at the command line. Lynx is also configured to go to this page by default.

In addition to using Navigator and Lynx, if you are in KDE, you can type the URL into KFM's URL location field, and KFM will display the documentation for you.

More about HOWTO documents

Most standard Linux distributions include HOWTO documents. These documents explain how to do many things, like how to set up a DNS server in your box and how to configure a sound card. Most of these documents are written by fellow users or the developer of a tool as a help to the Linux community.

Many of these documents are invaluable. However, most are too long (the average document is about 60 pages long!) and tend to include a lot of peripheral information. This could present some difficulty to users who are new to Linux; their background level is not the same as that of a hacker. But this is what you get. In a free OS, it's not too easy to come by a good technical writer who can distill what you need to know from what is nice to know.

The HOWTO documents on OpenLinux 1.3 systems can be found by visiting the online documentation URL in /usr/doc, as we discussed in the previous section.

Mini HOWTOs

The mini HOWTO is similar in spirit to a HOWTO document; however, mini HOWTOs tend to be more free-form and shorter. HOWTO documents follow certain formatting standards that don't bind mini-HOWTOs.

Mini HOWTOs can be found in the HOWTO index page on your OpenLinux 1.3 computer, and are designated by the word "Mini" somewhere in the title.

LDP—Linux Documentation Project

The LDP is probably the most useful and most helpful online information about Linux. The LDP's goal is to create reliable documentation for Linux, covering installation, kernel development, kernel information, network administration, system administration, and user guides. The authors at the LDP make sure that the documentation distributed with Linux is accurate and up-to-date.

Some of the manuals developed by LDP are available online in your system, as we've already discussed. Others are available through the Internet. If you have Internet access, you can view the latest documentation at http://sunsite.unc.edu/LDP.

In addition to providing online manuals and HOWTO documents, the LDP is responsible for maintaining a number of FAQ (Frequently Asked Questions) documents about Linux. These can be found at the LDP homepage on the Internet.

Reading Compressed Documentation: zless

Occasionally, you may encounter compressed documents in /usr/doc or other help areas on you Linux computer. Compressed documents can be identified because they end with one of the following filename extensions: .qz, .z, or .Z.

When you encounter a compressed document on you Linux computer, you will either need to decompress it before reading it or use a special utility that can peek into compressed documents.

zless is a tool that allows you to view compressed text files (filenames ending in a .gz, .z, or .Z) with the less pager. If the zless command is not available, you can achieve the same by using zcat and less in a pipe:

```
zcat filename ¦ less
```

Info Pages

A lot of developers are starting to use GNU's info to write documentation. The GNU info system uses hypertext to relate different pieces of information. The goal of info is to make reading a documentation page easier by proving a way to jump between different sections of the documentation.

The concept is similar to using a Web browser. To read documentation, you use the info command followed by the name of the tool you are interested in. If you don't provide a tool name, info will show you a list of all the commands it knows about and some entry points to the info documentation itself. The following figure shows a screen in info.

The info program.

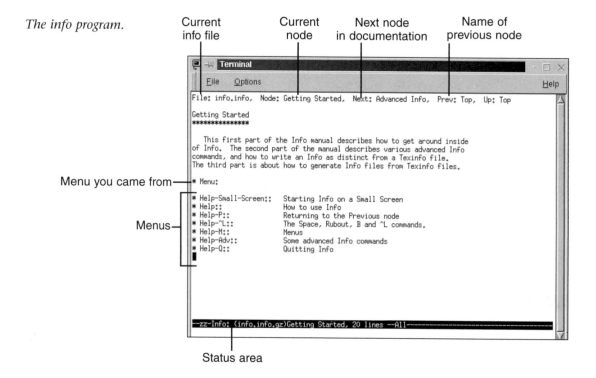

170

The basic commands for moving in info are listed in Table 15.2.

Table 15.2 Info Commands

Key	Description
Space	Page down
Backspace	Page up
b	Beginning of the page
?	Help
n	Next node
u	Previous node
l	Last node
u	Up
m	Menu (type menu name or ? for a list of options)
Ctrl+g	Cancel current operation (or menu)
f	Cross reference (type cross reference name or ? for a list of options)
d	Show a directory of all the documents info knows about

Each page in an info document is called a *node*. A node can contain menus and cross-references. Menus are related nodes within the same document. Cross-references are nodes typically located in a different document.

The easiest way to learn how to use info is to go through its interactive tutorial. To access the tutorial, enter info at the command prompt, and type h to follow instructions. On Emacs you can enter info by typing Ctrl+h i.

Usenet: Internet Newsgroups

If you have access to the Internet and newsgroups, there are many places where you can find information about Linux. The groups are organized according to topics. People all over the Internet post questions and answers to groups that fancy their interests.

There are thousands of newsgroups for all topics and interests. But with the aid of a good reader such as Netscape Communicator's Colabra, included with OpenLinux 1.3, you can cruise through several postings until you find what you want. (Do a man -k news to find console-capable news tools installed in your system.)

Some newsgroups are moderated. A moderated group has a posting reviewed by the group's maintainer, who then decides if your post merits distribution.

Usenet newsgroups are full of noise, because a lot of users post blindly without doing their own research into the problem. If you have looked at all the resources

171

mentioned in this chapter and you still don't have a solution to the problem, it probably is a valid question.

When posting a question, it is always a good idea to put the version and distribution of your software, and then the tool that you are having a problem with (include version information). Sometimes different software versions can determine what the correct answer is to your question. Be brief but descriptive, and only ask one question per message.

Some of the Linux groups follow:

➤ `comp.os.linux.advocacy`—A newsgroup dedicated to flame on why Linux is better than other OSs.

➤ `comp.os.linux.announce`—This is a moderated group for announcements about Linux developments, bug fixes, software releases, and so on. This is probably the most "informational" of all the groups regarding what is going on in the Linux world.

➤ `comp.os.linux.development.apps`—This group is for programmers interested in porting applications to Linux.

➤ `comp.os.linux.development.system`—This group is for programmers interested in developing kernel and system software.

➤ `comp.os.linux.hardware`—This one is for hardware questions, support, and why Linux won't work on hardware x.

➤ `comp.os.linux.misc`—This is a group for all topics that don't fit anywhere else.

➤ `comp.os.linux.networking`—This group is about networking and networking hardware.

➤ `comp.os.linux.setup`—This one is for installing Linux, how to get service X running, and so on.

➤ `comp.os.linux.x`—This group is dedicated to installing, configuring, and running X under Linux.

➤ `alt.os.linux.caldera`—This group is for Caldera OpenLinux specific issues.

Cross-posting (sending the same question to multiple groups) is not cool. Ask your question only in groups that are specifically related by subject to your query; you are more likely to receive an answer.

Useful Books

Finally, there's a ton of commercial literature for Linux and UNIX. Your mileage will vary in quality and variety of information. Your choice of book will depend on what you are wanting to do with UNIX. The best way to find a book to suit your needs is to visit an online bookstore such as Amazon.com, BarnesAndNoble.com, or Borders.com and search for the words "linux" and "unix."

PLEASE, OH PLEASE, OH PLEASE, PLEASE...

Permissions: Protecting and Sharing Your Work

In This Chapter

➤ Working with Permissions

➤ User Categories

➤ Assigning Permissions by Numbers

➤ Assigning Permissions by Symbols

As you know, Linux is a multi-user system. This means that many people can access and work on the same computer at the same time. Because of this, there's a need to provide a mechanism that allows users to share and protect files as necessary to make collaboration and security work properly. The mechanism for accomplishing this is the permissions mechanism built into the file system.

This chapter explains permissions and strategies for sharing files with other users. If your system has more than one user, you might need to protect your files. If your system is a standalone machine that only you have access to, this chapter provides an informative overview.

How Does Permissions Work?

When you add a user to the system, several things happen, including the following:

➤ You create a home directory for the user's files

➤ The system adds entries on one of the its databases so that files the user creates are marked as being owned by that user

➤ The user is added to at least one default user group Adding users and groups is covered in Chapter 17, "Users, Groups, and Passwords."

All these steps serve one purpose: to give you a mechanism for protecting private or group-owned files from public view or use. Under Linux, given the appropriate hardware resources, you could easily sustain thousands of users comfortably in one machine. I know of a place where two little Pentium boxes with 128MB of RAM and several gigabytes of storage serve more than 400 users, plus 200 different Internet services—each running under its own virtual domain name and serving a large number of users! (Each machine can actually handle the entire load plus a lot more, but for safety reasons the services are available from two machines.)

Now just imagine 400 strangers snooping through your files! You have two solutions:

1. Don't keep or author any sensitive materials you don't want others to read—a drastic but very secure option.

2. Utilize the UNIX permissions mechanism to avoid most unwanted eyes from prying at your secrets.

We'll explore the second option. Every user is assigned a certain level of access when his or her account is created. The level of access is indicated by the group memberships of the user. The system's administrator (root) can change these memberships at any time. When a user logs in, the system associates the user with a particular identity. Using this identity and the file permissions system, Linux decides what the user is allowed to do and which files the user is allowed to read or manipulate.

At the most basic level, the permissions system is actually quite simple. Each file in the system is owned by exactly one user and related to exactly one group. Every file also has a set of nine switches that control who can read, write, or execute the file. (There are more switches, but I'll talk about them in the next section, "The Effective User ID.")

Any given user fits into one or more roles in relation to a given file:

➤ The *owner* or *user* role: The user in question is the owner of this file (typically its creator). The owners can assign permissions to the file as he or she sees fit.

➤ The *group* role: The user in question is a member of the group related to the file. Groups are designed to help control access to files in a multi-user collaboration.

By relating a file to a group of people, access to a file can be controlled for many people at once. Any user can belong to any number of groups, but a file is related to exactly one group at a time.

➤ The *other* role: This user is not the owner of this file, nor is the user a member of the group related to this file.

For each file in a Linux system, three permission "switches" exist for each of these roles (for a total of nine switches):

➤ Read (R)—This switch grants permission to look at the file's contents.

➤ Write (W)—This switch grants permission to change the file's contents or delete the file.

➤ Execute (X)—This switch grants permission to run the file as a program. In the case of directories, this level also means permission to **cd** into the directory.

By default, even if not purposefully assigned, files will have some permissions already set. Thinking of permissions as a table like that shown in the following figure is very useful.

Owner			Group			Others		
R	W	X	R	W	X	R	W	X
✓	✓	✓	✓	–	✓	–	–	–

A checkmark indicates granted permissions, and a dash means the lack of such permission.

So according to the table, owners are allowed to read, write, and execute the file.

Group members are only allowed read and execute permissions. Anyone not an owner or member of a group cannot read, write, or execute a program; if the file in question was a directory, such a user could not traverse it, either.

Let's look at an example to demonstrate the way permissions are usually represented. You can display permission information for a file by using the ls command with the -l option:

```
[root@digital alberto]# ls -l
total 2
-rw-rw-r--   1 alberto   alberto      388 Jul 29 19:03 readme.txt
drwxrwxr-x   4 alberto   alberto     1024 Aug  2 14:39 stuff
```

Permissions are displayed as a series of ten dashes and/or letters at the beginning of each line.

➤ The first character position tells you about the file's type. Regular files such as reme.txt show a dash (-) in this space. Directories such as "stuff" in the previous example show a d. Links display an l, and other special files—such as devices, sockets, and pipes—display c or b, s, and =, respectively.

➤ The next nine positions represent the nine permission switches. The first three switches apply to the file's owner, the middle three to members of the file's group, and the last three to "other" users. Each group of three switches contains a read switch, a write switch, and an execute switch, in that order. When a switch is on (permission granted), a letter appears: r for read, w for write, and x for execute. When a switch is off (permission denied), a dash (-) appears. In the case of readme.txt, above, you can see that the owner has permission to read and write, the group has permission to read and write, and others only have read permission. In the case of the above directory called stuff, all users have read and execute permission (which means that all users can cd into the directory). However, only the owner and group have write permission and will be allowed to create files in the stuff directory.

The Effective User Id

Access to files and processes will depend on your current username and current group affiliations. I say "current" because during a session it is possible for you to assume the id of a different user (that is, if you know that user's password).

To see a list of your effective user id and group affiliations, you can use the id tool. The id command prints information about your current username, current group, and a list of all the groups that you belong to. This information can also be obtained using the commands whoami and groups. However, the id command provides more information and can be used for other purposes as well.

To see what groups you belong to, in a shell, type id:

```
[alberto@digital alberto]$ id
uid=501(alberto) gid=501(alberto) groups=501(alberto)
```

As you can see by issuing this command, my username, alberto, has been assigned a user id (UID) of 501 and a group id (GID) of 501. The operating system keeps track of your username and group affiliations by number. This system is more efficient and can keep track of about 65,536 different UIDs!

Running the same command as the superuser (root) yields different information:

```
[root@digital alberto]# id
uid=0(root) gid=0(root) groups=0(root)
```

As you can see, root has both a UID and GID of 0. The root user on any UNIX system is UID 0 and will always belong to at least one group, whose ID is also 0. It is possible for root also to belong to many more groups.

Substitute User: su

Often while working with and configuring software, it is necessary to become the root user—or any other user, for that matter. Instead of logging out and logging in again as a different user, a better alternative might be to issue the su command. This

command effectively substitutes your current UID and GID with those of the user you want to become and grants you all the permissions of the user you su'ed to. Here's an example:

```
[alberto@digital alberto]$ su root
Password:
[root@digital alberto]# cd
[root@digital /root]# exit
exit
[alberto@digital alberto]$
```

In this example, I issued the su command. As an argument I provided the name of the user that I wanted to become. In this case I specified root; note that su used alone assumes "su root" by default.

Notice that su will require the password of the user you are su'ing into. To return to my regular user account, I issued an exit command (you can also hit Ctrl+D). This action terminated the root shell and returned me to my original session. Always remember to return to your user account after you are finished with the task that required the su.

Beware of the Powers of Root!

Root is a special administrative account that grants unrestricted access to the entire system. This power is very valuable when you need to perform system administration-type tasks, but it is not an account that you want to use for any other purpose. The root account can perform certain actions that are irreversible, such as erasing all files on the disk or some other catastrophic type of thing!

Until you know more about Linux and UNIX in general, I would recommend that you don't use the root account unless it is absolutely necessary. Examples include adding software or configuring some aspect of your system that specifically requires you to log on as root.

Changing Groups: newgrp

Whenever you create a file, your default group is the one assigned to the group ownership of the file. If you are a member of multiple groups, you can change your effective GID by using the newgrp tool. The newgrp tool is analogous to su in that you provide the name of the group you want to use as a default for the session. If you are not a member of the group in question, you are not allowed to change your effective GID.

Special Users

Your Linux system already comes with several accounts created.

Many of these accounts (`bin`, `adm`, `lp`, `sync`, `halt`, `mail`, and so on) exist for the benefit of a program or some other system functionality. These *pseudouser* accounts, as they are called, are important for the system to be able to perform certain tasks while still upholding the permissions mechanism.

Home Directories

Each username has its own home directory. By default, Linux puts home accounts inside of the `/home` directory. The one glaring exception are accounts of pseudousers. (You should not try to change the location of those accounts.)

Traditionally, UNIX-like operating systems have not arrived so thoroughly configured out of the box. Rather, system administrators have had to explicitly organize home directories by themselves. Standard Linux systems, however, keep user accounts in `/home`.

Changing File Permissions

If you are a file's owner or the superuser, you can change permissions on a file. For this purpose, you use the `chmod` command.

The `chmod` command offers a symbolic mode in which you add or subtract permissions and a numeric mode in which you specify the permissions you want for the file. Before using the `chmod` command, you need to know how to use its numeric and symbolic modes.

Permissions by the Numbers: 4, 2, 1, and 0

Permissions can be set as numbers. Although this method might seem a little complicated to the uninitiated, it really isn't. For one thing, there are only four numbers that you need to worry about:

➤ The number 4 specifies read permissions

➤ The number 2 specifies write permissions

➤ The number 1 specifies execute permissions

➤ The number 0 specifies no permissions of any kind

If you wanted to enable read and write permissions, you add the values: 4+2=6, so you assign the number 6.

If you wanted to enable read and execute permissions, you add the values again: because 4+1=5, you use the value 5.

If you wanted to enable read, write, and execute, you would add 4+2+1 to get 7, the value you should assign. The values for the individual permissions are designed so they form unique values in various combinations.

Easy? I think it is. However, the one thing that might complicate matters is that you need to specify permissions for all three roles at the same time: owner, group, and others. To do so, string a sequence of three of these permissions together. The result is a number called a *mode*.

To give a file's owner and group read and write permission, but only read permission to all other users, specify the mode as 664: (4+2) for the owner, (4+2) for the group, and (4) for others.

Permissions Using Symbols: u, g, o, r, w, and x

It is sometimes useful to set permissions using symbols because they allow you to set permissions one role at a time or one permission at a time. For example, you can grant group read permission to a file without needing to know the owner or other users' permissions for the file.

In order to set permissions using symbols, you must remember the letters which go with certain words: user or owner (u), group (g), others (o), read (r), write (w), and execute (x).

A symbol-based permission string follows one of two formats:

➤ identity-permissions to deny permission(s)
➤ identity+permissions to grant permission(s)

Here are a few sample permission strings; their meanings should become increasingly clear.

Table 16.1 Granting Permissions Using Symbols

string	Permissions	Granted to
ugo+rwx	read, write, execute	owner, group, and others
ug+w	write	owner and group
g+rx	read and execute	group

Table 16.2 Denying Permissions Using Symbols

string	Permissions	Denied to
ugo-rwx	read, write, execute	owner, group, and others
o-rw	read and write	others
go-x	execute	group and others

Note that the string "ugo" can be replaced with "a" for "all." For example, "ugo+w" and "a+w" both grant write permission to everyone.

Using chmod *to Change Permissions*

To change the permissions on a file, you take the mode you calculated or the symbols you need and use the chmod command. The syntax is chmod [options] *mode file-name* [*filename...*]

Let's try this on the computer. Let's create the following:

➤ Two regular files called fileone and filetwo

➤ One directory called adir

➤ A symbolic link named filethree

```
[alberto@digital alberto]$ touch fileone filetwo
[alberto@digital alberto]$ mkdir adir
[alberto@digital alberto]$ ln -s fileone filethree
[alberto@digital alberto]$ ls -l
total 2
-rw-rw-r--   1 alberto   alberto         388 Jul 29 19:03 Xrootenv.0
drwxrwxr-x   2 alberto   alberto        1024 Aug  4 18:05 adir
-rw-rw-r--   1 alberto   alberto           0 Aug  4 18:05 fileone
lrwxrwxrwx   1 alberto   alberto           7 Aug  4 18:05 filethree ->
fileone
-rw-rw-r--   1 alberto   alberto           0 Aug  4 18:05 filetwo
```

Now let's change filetwo and filethree to mode 644. We'll also deny (remove) all write permisstions to adir.

```
[alberto@digital alberto]$ chmod 644 filetwo filethree
[alberto@digital alberto]$ chmod ugo-w adir
```

Now let's list the results:

```
[alberto@digital alberto]$ ls -l
total 2
-rw-rw-r--   1 alberto   alberto         388 Jul 29 19:03 Xrootenv.0
dr-xr-xr-x   2 alberto   alberto        1024 Aug  4 18:05 adir
-rw-r--r--   1 alberto   alberto           0 Aug  4 18:05 fileone
lrwxrwxrwx   1 alberto   alberto           7 Aug  4 18:05 filethree ->
fileone
-rw-r--r--   1 alberto   alberto           0 Aug  4 18:05 filetwo
```

What happened? Both filetwo and adir show changed permissions as expected, but filethree's modes remain as they were. The reason for this odd occurrence is that chmod does not change the mode of a symbolic link—permissions of a symbolic link are never used. What it did instead was to change the mode of the file the link pointed to—fileone! So fileone and filetwo have a mode of 644 (4+2)(4)(4), or rw for

180

owner, r for group and other. All of the w, or write switches have been turned off for adir.

Setuid, Setgid, and Sticky Bits

In addition to the permission bits described in the section "Permission by the Numbers: 4, 2, 1, and 0," UNIX provides three other bits that are used for other purposes. The *setuid* bit sets the user id of the running program to the user id of the owner of the program. This way, the program can run with permissions that the user of the program doesn't necessarily have. The program, when running effectively, has the same user id as the owner of the file. Similarly, the *setgid* bit runs a program with the group id of the group that owns the program. This assignment allows programs to access files and processes that the user running the program would not normally have.

The setgid bit under Linux also has a special use. When set on a directory, it sets the group ownership of files added to the directory. This way, even though the default group for a particular user is different than that of the group, it is assigned to the project directory—ensuring that files created there will be accessible to members of the group.

The sticky bit is used in conjunction with directories to protect files the directory contains, although it was originally designed for a different purpose. When set, it only allows the owner of the directory, the owner of the file, or the superuser to delete files that the directory contains. The sticky bit's presence is how directories like /tmp that are shared by many users have a little more privacy than they would have using the standard permission settings.

The setuid, setgid, and sticky bits have the values of 4000, 2000, and 1000, respectively, and are set using the chmod command. To use them, just add the file mode to the values (or combinations you want) to them. To grant or deny setuid/setgid or sticky permissions using symbolic mode, use s for setuid and setgid and t for sticky.

For example, if a directory has a mode of 777 (which means RWX permissions for all users), you can set the sticky bit by changing its mode to 1777. To set the setgid, you would change the mode of the same directory to 2777. Using symbols, to set the suid bit on a file, you would use "u+s". To set the setgid bit, use "g+s". To set the sticky bit, use "a+t."

The Default File Mode: umask

All files are created with a default mode, depending on the file type (a regular file or a directory). Wouldn't it be cool if you could somehow define the settings that you want when you create files? Well, you can!

This process involves using the umask command. The numbers you provide to the umask command are similar to the ones for the modes, except that they have had

their bits inverted. This means they are not as straightforward to work with. Don't ask me why there isn't a less strange way of setting these bits; that's just the way it is.

To view your current umask, type umask at the shell:

```
[alberto@digital alberto]$ umask
022
```

To make it easy for you, I'm providing a table with reasonable umask values that you can set (see Table 16.3). If you don't see the values you need in the table, you can set those permissions on the fly by using the chmod command. (That's what I do when the umask command requires too much thought.)

Table 16.3 Common umask Values

umask	User	Group	Other
000	rwx	rwx	rwx
002	rwx	rwx	r-x
007	rwx	rwx	---
022	rwx	r-x	r-x
037	rwx	r-x	---
077	rwx	---	---

Now all you need to do is type the umask command followed by the value you want to set. From then on all files you create during the current session will have those properties.

So what umask should you use? It depends on your need to share files with others.

Your default umask will depend on whether your administrator added a User Private Group (see "Group Ownership and User Private Groups"). If your account has a UPG, the default umask is 002; otherwise it is 022.

Group Ownership and User Private Groups

Sometimes you'll want to collaborate with different users on a project. This situation probably means that you will want to edit files others create, and they will want to edit files you create. To make this collaboration work while protecting the work from other users, you need to work with groups.

Typically, a group is created for a project, and users are added to the group. Files for the group collaboration will be put in a "neutral" directory in the system. This directory will allow read, write, and execution privileges to members of the group. To ensure that files created in the directory belong to the group, the setgid bit mentioned in the section "Setuid, Setgid, and Sticky Bits" is set on directory. (Creating

groups is discussed in Chapter 18, "Users, Groups, and Passwords.")

The only problem with this approach is that the permission of files will be set according to the user's umask and, in turn, will depend on whether the user has a User Private Group (UPG).

When UPGs are used, instead of users belonging to the generic group "users," Linux creates a UPG for the user when the account is added. The user is (and should be) the only member of his or her own group. This exclusiveness allows the user to have an umask of 002 without compromising the security of any personal files. By default, a umask of 002 allows full control of the file to the owner and the group associated with the file. In the case of the UPG, the group linked to the file is also the owner, so things are safe.

If the UPG mechanism is not used, members of the group will have to be systematic about the umask they use when creating project files. Given human nature, the result is that a series of files will be editable by the owner only, requiring the owner to do a chmod on the file to allow other members of the group to modify the files. The UPG mechanism provides a solution to this problem—and for this reason it is very cool.

Command Toolbox: Useful Shell Commands and Shortcuts

In This Chapter

➤ User Utilities

➤ Finding Files

➤ Text and File Utilities

➤ Splitting Files into Smaller Files: `split`

➤ Accessing a Computer Through the Network: `telnet`

➤ Working on the Console: `setfont`

➤ UNIX Printing Primer

➤ UNIX Text Processing

This chapter introduces a number of basic tools and command line programs that you can use while working on the shell. There are many more tools available, but these are some of the more basic ones. You have already learned a few in each category. Although this chapter is not comprehensive, it will give you an idea of what you will find. Many more tools are available—so many, in fact, that it could be the topic for an entire book.

User Utilities

Every once in a while during the course of your work, you will want to change your password, change your shell, find files, search files, and so on. Here are some commands to help you.

Changing Your Password: `passwd`

Use the `passwd` command to change your password. Because the command is interactive, it will ask you for your current password (to ensure that some other user doesn't change your password while you are away from your computer) and then for a new password. After successful confirmation of your password, it is accepted by the system. Note that passwords are never echoed to the screen to avoid being spied by nearby eyes, as in the following code:

```
[alberto@digital alberto]$ passwd
Changing password for alberto
(current) UNIX password: ********
Enter new UNIX password: ********
Retype new UNIX password: ********
passwd: all authentication tokens updated successfully
```

The superuser (root) can use the same `passwd` command to change any password in the system. When the superuser provides a username as an option to the command, he or she can change the password for any user in the system. The superuser does not need to authenticate the user's password. Changing a user's password as the superuser would look like this:

```
[root@digital /root]# passwd alberto
Enter new UNIX password: ********
Retype new UNIX password: ********
passwd: all authentication tokens updated successfully
```

Changing Your Shell: `chsh`

If you don't like your shell, you can use the `chsh` command to change it. Only shells listed in `/etc/shells` are acceptable for use. It can be used interactively, like this:

```
alberto@digital alberto]$ more /etc/shells
/bin/bash
/bin/sh
/bin/ksh
/bin/csh
/bin/tcsh
[alberto@digital alberto]$ chsh
Changing shell for alberto.
Password: ********
New shell [/bin/tcsh]: /bin/bash
Shell changed.
```

If the shell you like is not listed, add an entry to the /etc/shells file, and then you'll be able to set it.

Changing Personal Information: chfn

The chfn (change finger name) command changes additional information about yourself, such as your full name, office address, and office and home phone numbers. This information is accessible using the finger command (which is typically disabled in most systems because it poses certain security risks). It is used by some programs to determine your full name and other information. The chfn command, like the passwd command, is interactive:

```
[alberto@digital alberto]$ chfn
Changing finger information for alberto.
Password: **********
Name [Caldera OpenLinux User]: Alberto Ricart
Office []: Rm. 3210 Left Wing
Office Phone []: 800 555 1212 ext 800
Home Phone []: not listed

Finger information changed.
```

Who's on the System: who and w

The who and w commands can be used to see who is logged into the system. The w tells you who is logged on and what they are doing:

```
[alberto@digital /etc]$ w
 17:17:07 up   5:42,  2 users,  load average: 0.05, 0.13, 0.09
USER      TTY      FROM            LOGIN@  IDLE   JCPU   PCPU  WHAT
alberto  tty1                     11:51am 5:25m 33.95s  0.13s xinit
➥/etc/X11/
alberto  ttyp0    192.168.0.10     5:07pm 1.00s  0.50s  0.08s w
```

The who command simply tells you who is logged into the system:

```
[alberto@digital /etc]$ who
alberto   tty1     Sep 20 11:51
alberto   ttyp0    Sep 20 17:07 (192.168.0.10)
```

Both these commands point out who is logged in through a remote terminal. The FROM column in the w command (the first example in the previous section) lists the IP address of remote users. The who command also displays the address of remote users between parentheses.

Viewing and Setting the Date and Time: date

The date command allows you to read the current date and time as well as to set the time for your system (if you runt it as root). It provides a multitude of options that allow you to use a variety of formats for the date and time.

By default, if you enter the date command, it prints the current date and time. To format the date, provide the + argument followed by a formatting string. The various options for the formatting strings (shown in Table 17.1) are preceded by a percent (%) symbol.

Table 17.1 Date Options

Option	Description
%H	Print hour in 24-hour format with leading zeros (00..23)
%I	Print hour in 12-hour format with leading zeros (01..12)
%k	Print hour in 24-hour format (0..23)
%l	Print hour in 12-hour format (1..12)
%M	Print minutes (00..59)
%p	Print AM or PM
%r	Print time in 12-hour format with AM/PM (hh:mm:ss AM)
%s	Print the number of seconds since 1/1/70
%S	Print second (00..61)
%T	Print time in 24-hour format (hh:mm:ss)
%X	Print time in locale's time representation (%H:%M:%S)
%Z	Print time zone (e.g., CST)
%a	Print locale's abbreviated weekday name (Sun)
%A	Print locale's full weekday name, variable length (Sunday)
%b	Print locale's abbreviated month name (Jan)
%B	Print locale's full month name (January)
%d	Print day of month (01..31)
%D	Print date as mm/dd/yy
%j	Print the number of the day in the year (001..366)
%m	Print the month (01..12)
%U	Print week number of year (00..53)
%w	Print day of week (0..6), with 0 corresponding to Sunday

Option	Description
%W	Print week number of year with Monday as first day of week (00..53)
%x	Print locale's date representation (mm/dd/yy)
%y	Print last two digits of year (00..99)
%Y	Print the year using 4 digits (1970...)

For example, to print the date in long format, you would type this:

```
[alberto@digital alberto]$ date +"%A %B %d %Y"
Sunday September 20 1998
```

Note that the format string, %A %B %d %Y, is enclosed by quotation marks ("). (Enclosing the string in quotes is necessary so that the shell doesn't think it is receiving four separate arguments.) When you enclose the string in quotes, you can then add any text as separators inside of the string. For example, to add a comma after the day, you would type this:

```
[alberto@digital alberto]$ date +"%A, %B %d %Y"
Sunday, September 20 1998
```

To print the date as a number using the pattern YYYYMMDD, do this:

```
[alberto@digital alberto]$ date +%Y%m%d
19980920
```

To set the system clock, you would provide a date in the following format:

date *MMDDhhmmYYYY*

MM is a two-digit number for the month (01–12)

DD is a two-digit number for the day (01–31)

hh is a two-digit hour (in the 24-hour format, 00 is midnight, 23 is 11 PM)

mm is a two-digit minute (00–59)

YYYY is a four-digit year (1998)

Getting a Calendar: cal

The cal command prints a calendar. By default, it prints a calendar for the current month:

```
[alberto@digital alberto]$ cal
    September 1998
Su Mo Tu We Th Fr Sa
       1  2  3  4  5
 6  7  8  9 10 11 12
13 14 15 16 17 18 19
20 21 22 23 24 25 26
27 28 29 30
```

189

If you provide a single argument, it is assumed to be a year:

```
[alberto@digital alberto]$ cal 1998
                        1998
```

```
            January                   February                    March
   Su Mo Tu We Th Fr Sa       Su Mo Tu We Th Fr Sa       Su Mo Tu We Th Fr Sa
                1  2  3        1  2  3  4  5  6  7        1  2  3  4  5  6  7
    4  5  6  7  8  9 10        8  9 10 11 12 13 14        8  9 10 11 12 13 14
   11 12 13 14 15 16 17       15 16 17 18 19 20 21       15 16 17 18 19 20 21
   18 19 20 21 22 23 24       22 23 24 25 26 27 28       22 23 24 25 26 27 28
   25 26 27 28 29 30 31                                  29 30 31

             April                      May                       June
   Su Mo Tu We Th Fr Sa       Su Mo Tu We Th Fr Sa       Su Mo Tu We Th Fr Sa
                1  2  3  4                    1  2        1  2  3  4  5  6
    5  6  7  8  9 10 11        3  4  5  6  7  8  9        7  8  9 10 11 12 13
   12 13 14 15 16 17 18       10 11 12 13 14 15 16       14 15 16 17 18 19 20
   19 20 21 22 23 24 25       17 18 19 20 21 22 23       21 22 23 24 25 26 27
   26 27 28 29 30             24 25 26 27 28 29 30       28 29 30
                              31

             July                     August                    September
   Su Mo Tu We Th Fr Sa       Su Mo Tu We Th Fr Sa       Su Mo Tu We Th Fr Sa
                1  2  3  4                          1              1  2  3  4  5
    5  6  7  8  9 10 11        2  3  4  5  6  7  8        6  7  8  9 10 11 12
   12 13 14 15 16 17 18        9 10 11 12 13 14 15       13 14 15 16 17 18 19
   19 20 21 22 23 24 25       16 17 18 19 20 21 22       20 21 22 23 24 25 26
   26 27 28 29 30 31          23 24 25 26 27 28 29       27 28 29 30
                              30 31

            October                  November                   December
   Su Mo Tu We Th Fr Sa       Su Mo Tu We Th Fr Sa       Su Mo Tu We Th Fr Sa
                   1  2  3        1  2  3  4  5  6  7              1  2  3  4  5
    4  5  6  7  8  9 10        8  9 10 11 12 13 14        6  7  8  9 10 11 12
   11 12 13 14 15 16 17       15 16 17 18 19 20 21       13 14 15 16 17 18 19
   18 19 20 21 22 23 24       22 23 24 25 26 27 28       20 21 22 23 24 25 26
   25 26 27 28 29 30 31       29 30                      27 28 29 30 31
```

Note that cal 98 and cal 1998 will print very different calendars, as 98 and 1998 are very different years.

To display a particular month in a year, provide two arguments. The first is taken as the month, the second as the year:

```
[alberto@digital alberto]$ cal 12 1998
      December 1998
Su Mo Tu We Th Fr Sa
        1  2  3  4  5
 6  7  8  9 10 11 12
13 14 15 16 17 18 19
20 21 22 23 24 25 26
27 28 29 30 31
```

Finding Files

In Chapter 15, "Help Please," you learn about the commands whereis and which, which can be used to find programs and other system-related files in specific locations. UNIX also provides other tools so that you can search files with more discrete criteria.

In this section, you'll learn how to use the find and locate commands.

Finding Files by Name: find

The UNIX find command is a hard one to master. It provides a zillion options that can intimidate many users. However, with a little instruction, you can learn how to use find for 90% of your needs. The basic syntax for the find command is

```
find paths expression
```

The find command searches the paths provided for a file that matches expression. You can search multiple paths for a file, because the expression list doesn't start until find locates an argument that begins with a dash (-).

The most basic of options is –name. It tells find that this is the name of the file you are searching for. This option is much more powerful if you use wildcards (*, ?, and []) to specify the name. (See the section "Regular Expressions" in Chapter 14, "Putting the Shell to Work.")

The -print option tells find to print any matches to the terminal. This is optional under Linux, but some versions of find in other UNIX systems require it because by default, find does not print any results. Here's a simple example:

```
[alberto@digital alberto]$ find /home/alberto /tmp -name "*.txt" -
print
/home/alberto/intro.txt
/home/alberto/Desktop/Trash/intro.txt
/home/alberto/.netscape/cache/0F/cache3603EFAF0010427.txt
/home/alberto/intro2.txt
/home/alberto/kdetools.txt
/home/alberto/Hello World.txt
```

191

```
/home/alberto/test/test.txt
/home/alberto/test/todo.txt
/home/alberto/file.txt
/home/alberto/file3.txt
/home/alberto/file1.txt
/home/alberto/file2.txt
/home/alberto/afile.txt
find: /tmp/.XF86Setup5909: Permission denied
find: /tmp/kfm-cache-0: Permission denied
find: /tmp/kfm-cache-100: Permission denied
find: /tmp/.XF86Setup6565: Permission denied
find: /tmp/otherMail: Permission denied
find: /tmp/.XF86Setup514: Permission denied
/tmp/file.txt
```

In this example, I want to find all files inside /home/alberto or /tmp that have a name ending with .txt. Note that I enclosed the expression in quotation marks to avoid having the shell glob (interpret) and expand the star itself. Notice that in the results, find was not able to search the directories to which I didn't have privileges.

Although the regular expression helps in finding matches, it is still case sensitive; files with a .TXT extension are not found. Replacing the -name option with -iname makes the search case insensitive, so files ending in both .txt and .TXT are found:

```
[alberto@digital alberto]$ find /home/alberto /tmp -iname "*.txt" -
➡print
/home/alberto/intro.txt
/home/alberto/Desktop/Trash/intro.txt
/home/alberto/FILE.TXT
/home/alberto/.netscape/cache/0F/cache3603EFAF0010427.txt
/home/alberto/intro2.txt
/home/alberto/kdetools.txt
/home/alberto/Hello World.txt
/home/alberto/test/test.txt
/home/alberto/test/todo.txt
/home/alberto/file.txt
/home/alberto/file3.txt
...
```

The find command provides a myriad of options, including the capability to search for files by modification and access date. In addition, find is able to execute commands using the files found as arguments to a command. This is done with the -exec. option. Here's an example:

```
[alberto@digital alberto]$ find /home/alberto -iname "*.txt" -exec wc
➡{} \;
     22      329     1896 /home/alberto/intro.txt
     22      329     1896 /home/alberto/Desktop/Trash/intro.txt
```

```
    0        0        0 /home/alberto/FILE.TXT
   10       50      785
➥/home/alberto/.netscape/cache/0F/cache3603EFAF0010427.txt
   44      329     1894 /home/alberto/intro2.txt
  197      330     2403 /home/alberto/kdetools.txt
    1        1        8 /home/alberto/Hello World.txt
    0        0        0 /home/alberto/test/test.txt
    0        0        0 /home/alberto/test/todo.txt
    0        0        0 /home/alberto/file.txt
    0        0        0 /home/alberto/file3.txt
    0        0        0 /home/alberto/file1.txt
    0        0        0 /home/alberto/file2.txt
    0        0        0 /home/alberto/afile.txt
```

Notice in this example that after calling the wc command, there are a pair of braces ({}). These braces are replaced by the name of the file matching the search—which then becomes the argument to the wc command. Also note that at the end there's a semicolon (;). It tells find that the -exec option is completed. To avoid having the shell interpret the semicolon as a command group, the semicolon is followed with a backslash (\).

Locating Files: locate

As you can tell, finding files takes a long time. The find command needs to search the disk for the files you specify. If you are doing a search on a filename, there's a better and faster way: locate.

The locate command gains its speed by prebuilding a database of all known filenames. Instead of scanning the disk for a match, it uses sophisticated database techniques to find the file instantaneously—or close enough to instantaneously. The drawback of this feature is that if the file you are searching for was created after the database was updated, the database won't have an entry for it, and therefore locate won't be able to find it. Typically, this is not an issue because locate updates its database every morning at 5:55 AM or so. What, your computer isn't on at that time? Well, you can run the command manually, too.

Building the locate Database: updatedb

To create the locate database, you must be root and issue the command /usr/bin/updatedb. The program will take a while to complete its run, but after it does it, you are in business.

Finding a File: `locate`

To search for a file, just type its name or a portion of its name (no wildcards), and any file path matching your search will be printed. Here's an example:

```
[root@digital alberto]# locate telnet
/mnt/cdrom/col/install/RPMS/netkit-telnet-0.12-1.i386.rpm
/usr/bin/telnet
/usr/include/arpa/telnet.h
/usr/lib/xemacs-19.16/etc/w3/telnet.xbm
/usr/lib/xemacs-19.16/lisp/comint/telnet.elc
/usr/man/man1/telnet.1.gz
/usr/man/man8/in.telnetd.8.gz
/usr/man/man8/telnetd.8.gz
/usr/sbin/in.telnetd
/var/lib/LST/contents/netkit-telnet
/var/lib/LST/installed/netkit-telnet
```

All that is left is for you to decide what file you want! Not bad. The same command could have probably taken 10 minutes to complete using the `find` command.

Finding Files that Contain a Word or Pattern: `grep`

Whereas the `find` command looks for matches according to file system attributes (name of the file, modification time, and so on), the `grep` command searches for patterns inside of a file. For example, if you wanted to find files that contain the word *command*, you could do this with `grep`:

```
[alberto@digital alberto]$ grep command *.txt
intro.txt: Through a command line interface
intro.txt:The UNIX shell is not going away anytime soon. For this
reason it is a lso covered in detail. In order for you to gain
expertise an facility using Linux you have to be as comfortable in a
command line environment as you are in a graphical one.
intro2.txt: Through a command line interface
intro2.txt:using Linux you have to be as comfortable in a command line
```

Notice that `grep` prints the line of text where it found a match. If the file has more than one match, they are all printed. A special option `-c` prints the number of times the word was matched in the file:

```
[alberto@digital alberto]$ grep command -c *.txt

Hello World.txt:0
afile.txt:0
file.txt:0
file1.txt:0
file2.txt:0
```

```
file3.txt:0
intro.txt:2
intro2.txt:2
kdetools.txt:0
```

The grep command can also be used in a pipe to filter output you get from other programs. For example, to see a list of users on the system who are coming from the IP beginning with 192.168, you should type the following:

```
[alberto@digital alberto]$ w ¦ grep 192.168
alberto   ttyp0     192.168.0.10      5:07pm  4:53    1.17s  1.03s  -bash
alberto   ttyp1     192.168.0.10      5:54pm  0.00s   0.64s  0.09s  w
```

The grep command is very powerful, and you can combine it with regular expressions for your searches. See the man page for more information.

Text and File Utilities

Here are some utilities for working with textual information. Many of these utilities can be used creatively for purposes very different from text processing.

Counting Lines, Words, and Characters: wc

The word count (wc) utility is useful in many ways—it allows you to count the words, lines, and characters that appear in one or more files. Its syntax is simple:

```
wc [options] files
```

The options provided by wc are

-c	Print only the number of bytes (characters)
-w	Print only the number of words
-l	Print only the number of lines

If you supply more than one file, wc is happy to also provide you with a summary report for all the files. If you don't supply an option, it prints all the information, lines, words, and characters—in that order. Here's an example of using this command with the /etc/passwd and /etc/group files:

```
[alberto@digital alberto]$ wc /etc/passwd /etc/group
    21      28    770 /etc/passwd
    26      26    346 /etc/group
    47      54   1116 total
```

195

Although at simple inspection you might think you don't need this command (and you might be right), there are a number of situations in which creative use of the wc command can give you the information you need.

Sorting Lines of Text: sort

The sort command allows you to order lines in a file according to numeric value, alphabetic order, or phone book order. The sort command makes use of the notion of "fields," in which a line of text represents various bits (fields) of data and each line in the file represents a record. Fields are typically separated by a special character, such as a colon, tab, comma, or any other character that the developer of the file thought of.

The more frequent options to sort are

-t	To specify a field separator
-n	To specify numeric sorting
-k	To specify the fields where the sort will take place (default is first character on the line)
-f	To ignore case (the letters "B" and "b" are treated as equal)
-r	To reverse result

If you wanted to sort the /etc/password file according to username, you could type this:

```
[alberto@digital alberto]$ sort /etc/passwd
adm:x:3:4:adm:/var/adm:
alberto:x:501:501:Caldera OpenLinux User:/home/alberto:/bin/bash
bin:x:1:1:bin:/bin:
...
shutdown:x:6:11:shutdown:/sbin:/sbin/shutdown
sync:x:5:0:sync:/sbin:/bin/sync
uucp:x:10:14:uucp:/var/spool/uucp:
```

To sort the file numerically according to UID (the user id for the user is the third field), use the following command. Note that in the /etc/passwd file, fields are separated by colons:

```
[alberto@digital alberto]$ sort -t : -k 3 -n /etc/passwd
root:x:0:0:root:/root:/bin/bash
bin:x:1:1:bin:/bin:
daemon:x:2:2:daemon:/sbin:
adm:x:3:4:adm:/var/adm:
...
nobody:x:65534:65534:Nobody:/:/bin/false
```

Formatting Text: fmt

If you write a file using a console-based editor, the editor might not word-wrap your text into lines. If you were to print the file, the text will probably not be wrapped for you. Most users like to have files with lines that are around 75 characters wide, because that is the amount of text that fits into a text terminal. You can apply word-wrap to any file by using the fmt command. Here's an example:

```
[alberto@digital alberto]$ cat intro.txt
What This Book Is About (Paraphrasing Randal L. Schwartz in Learning
➥Perl)

Among other things, this book is about 300 pages (and then some). This
book is a
lso a gentle introduction to Linux. By the time you've gone through
this book, y
ou'll have touched on the majority of the most common operations found
in Linux.

This book is not intended as a comprehensive guide to Linux - on the
contrary, i
n order to keep the book from being yet another comprehensive
reference guide, I
've been selective about covering the things you are most likely to
use early in
 your Linux hacking career. For more information, check out the
voluminous and r
eadily available Linux and UNIX reference material.
...
```

If you look at the output, you'll notice that words are broken at the wrong places. Using the fmt command, I can easily reformat this file for printing and reading better on the screen:

```
[alberto@digital alberto]$ fmt -w 68 intro.txt
What This Book Is About (Paraphrasing Randal L. Schwartz in
Learning Perl)

Among other things, this book is about 300 pages (and then
some). This book is also a gentle introduction to Linux. By the
time you've gone through this book, you'll have touched on the
majority of the most common operations found in Linux.

This book is not intended as a comprehensive guide to Linux -
on the contrary, in order to keep the book from being yet another
comprehensive reference guide, I've been selective about covering
the things you are most likely to use early in your Linux hacking
career. For more information, check out the voluminous and readily
available Linux and UNIX reference material.
```

Much better! The fmt command has many options; however, the -w and -s options are the most important. The -w option tells fmt how wide to make the line. If you don't provide a -w option, fmt reverts to using 75 characters as the width of a line. The -s option tells fmt to only split lines. If you had some sample text that was shorter, the default behavior is for fmt to join lines and then split them according to its internal rules.

Check This Out

Compression is discussed in Chapter 20, "Installing Programs and Applications," in the section "UNIX Compressed Archives: Gzip and Compress."

Splitting Files into Smaller Files: *split*

Say you wanted to copy a file to a floppy disk, but the file was much larger (even compressed) than could fit on a single disk. How do you deal with this? One way is to use the split command. The split command has this syntax:

```
split [option] size file outfilename
```

The options are -l for splitting text files by line count and -b for splitting a file by byte count. After the option, you specify the size. When using the byte option, you can add a b for bytes, k for kilobytes, or m for megabytes. *File* is the name of the file you want to split, and *outfilename* is the base name the command will use to name all the chunks. Different filenames are generated by appending an extension to the file.

To split a large file into 1395K chunks so that each chunk will fit onto a standard floppy disk:

```
[alberto@digital splitter]$ ls -l
total 5801
-rw-r--r--  1 alberto  alberto   5915554 Sep 20 11:51 book.zip
[alberto@digital splitter]$ split -b 1395k book.zip book.zip.
[alberto@digital splitter]$ ls -l
total 11607
-rw-r--r--  1 alberto  alberto   5915554 Sep 20 11:51 book.zip
-rw-rw-r--  1 alberto  alberto   1428480 Sep 20 18:39 book.zip.aa
-rw-rw-r--  1 alberto  alberto   1428480 Sep 20 18:39 book.zip.ab
-rw-rw-r--  1 alberto  alberto   1428480 Sep 20 18:39 book.zip.ac
-rw-rw-r--  1 alberto  alberto   1428480 Sep 20 18:39 book.zip.ad
-rw-rw-r--  1 alberto  alberto    201634 Sep 20 18:39 book.zip.ae
```

There's no join command, so to join the file into one large file, use a command you already know, cat:

```
cat book.zip.?? > book.zip
```

The files will be catenated (copied) together into one big file. The expression ?? matches any two characters (aa through ae in the previous example). This works because the shell orders the files alphabetically, so ab is guaranteed to follow aa.

Accessing a Computer Through the Network: *telnet*

The telnet command allows you to log in to a remote computer using a shell. For all practical purposes, you are working on a console on the remote computer, and you can use any command just as though you were physically at the keyboard of the computer in question. The telnet command is very easy to use: Just type telnet followed by the host name of the system with which you want to work. This will present you with a login prompt much the same as the ones you have been using in the past few sections.

One thing with telnet sessions is that sometimes your keyboard won't behave the way that it ought to. To fix this problem, see the sidebar discussion on the stty command in Chapter 13, "Text Editing Under a Shell."

To exit from a telnet session, type exit or press Ctrl+D at your prompt.

Working on the Console: *setfont*

If you are working using a text interface on a EGA/VGA console, you might wonder why you cannot see more than 24 lines of text. Well, there's a way of fixing that: the setfont command.

The setfont command changes the font used by the console to a different size. Changing the size of the font also changes the maximum line width and the number of lines you can see; therefore, the font you select will determine your visible working space.

A number of fonts are installed in the /usr/lib/kbd/consolefonts directory. The font files are named using a type; typically, you'll want to pick one whose name starts with default (as the type of characters will change depending on the fonts) and a size. Standard VGA font size is 16 (16 pixels tall), so using a smaller font will make a huge difference. The font type/size combination also affects readability quite a bit, and different fonts of the same size will look very different on the screen. Some font files contain all three sizes: 8, 14, and 16. To specify the correct size, just provide a dash (-) followed by the size (setfont will prompt you when it's needed). If your screen goes nuts, just enter setfont again to return to your default setting.

To change a font, specify the name of the font file (you don't need to give the full path):

```
setfont fontname
```

199

One of the more popular fonts which will increase your display size considerably is selected using:

```
Setfont /usr/lib/kbd/consolefonts/alt-8x8
```

Experiment with different types and sizes until you find one that feels most readable to you.

UNIX Printing Primer

In this book, I sort of neglected telling you how to print files, partly because if you are using a word processor such as StarOffice, WordPerfect, or Applix, these programs already know how to print without going through this fuss (StarOffice is included on the CD that comes with this book.)

If you want to do UNIX text processing from the command line (as contrasted with word processing in a GUI), there are a few things you need to know that will affect the final presentation of the document you print. Printing under Linux and UNIX is radically different from printing under Windows or the Macintosh. Printing from the command line involves three steps:

1. Create a document with a text editor, adding any formatting commands to it as you need. These formatting commands, or macros, will depend on the formatting program you use. However, the idea of text markup (text processing, as UNIX folks like to call it) is the same.

2. Run your document through one or more filters (some filters might be as basic as the `fmt` command I talked about earlier); the final filter will typically produce a file that contains all the necessary printer control codes to render your document. Sometimes, the filter can send this output directly to the printer.

3. Send your filtered file to the printer using a program called `lpr`.

If you only need to print a plain text file, you'll have to do several things. The program you use will depend on the type of printer you have. Typically, printers are separated into two camps: those that have PostScript and those that don't.

If your printer has PostScript support, you'll probably use a program called `enscript`. If not, you'll use a program called `pr`. At the surface level, these programs are equivalent—save that `enscript` harnesses features available to PostScript so it has a lot more of them. These programs at the basic level allow you to specify margins, headers, and length of a line of text. Not fancy, but they provide the basic formatting capabilities you need to generate a reasonably plain-looking document.

Here's an example. If you wanted to print a text file called `intro.txt`, you would send it to pr:

```
pr intro.txt
```

The same file sent to a PostScript printer would be done like this:

```
enscript intro.txt
```

Both `pr` and `enscript` can send the output to the printer, and that is what they will do by default. That aside, these basic invocations will hardly produce the output you expect. What are the page margins? Where do the lines fold? You get the idea. You need to set up all these options on `pr` or `enscript`, or your document will use your printer's default settings. Your defaults will be something like left and top margins 1/2" from the edge of the paper, line length of about 72 characters wide, and Courier (typewriter) typeface—more than likely not what you want. So what are you to do?

The first thing you need to do is read the `man` page and figure out the default settings you want for `pr` or `enscript`. In addition to those, you might have to use another formatting command such as `fmt`. When you figure out the various settings, you just use them over and over.

My typical `enscript` session goes something like this:

```
[alberto@digital alberto]$ fmt -w 65 intro.txt ¦ enscript --
margins=100:100:100:100 -h -B
[ 1 pages * 1 copy ] sent to printer
```

I use `fmt` to create lines that are about 65 characters wide and then pipe the output to `enscript`. I set the options for the margins at 100 pixels (72 pixels = 1"), and with the `-h` option, I suppress the printing of the banner page (a page that tells who printed the file and wastes paper). The `-B` option suppresses the printing of the header line that usually shows the document title, the last time it was saved, and the page number.

I could produce similar output using `pr` like this:

```
fmt -w 65 intro.txt ¦ pr -o 15
```

The `-o` option specifies the number of characters for the left margin; 15 characters is about 1.5".

UNIX Text Processing

To produce fancier output, such as bold text, different typefaces, and so on, you need to use one of UNIX's formatters such as `groff` (GNU's version of the traditional `troff` formatting program). If you look at the source of a `man` page, you'll see the formatting codes that you use with `groff`. (To see the source, use `zless` on any document inside of /usr/man/man1/). Here's an example of what you'll see:

```
.TH man 1 "September 2, 1995"
.LO 1
.SH NAME
man \- format and display the on-line manual pages
```

```
.br
manpath \- determine user's search path for man pages
.SH SYNOPSIS
man [\-acdfhkKtwW] [\-m system] [\-p string] [\-C config_file] [\-M
➥path]
[\-P pager] [\-S section_list] [section] name ...
.SH DESCRIPTION
.B man
formats and displays the on-line manual pages.  This version knows
about the
.B MANPATH
and
.B (MAN)PAGER
environment variables, so you can have
your own set(s) of personal man pages and choose whatever program you
like to display the formatted pages.  If
.I section
is specified,
.B man
only looks in that section of the manual.
You may also specify the order to search the sections for entries
```

As you can see from this source text, groff (troff!) formatted files don't have any blank lines. Formatting commands (macros) must begin at the left margin. The name of the macro usually begins with a dot (.) or an apostrophe ('). Formatting continues until another macro overrides it.

The macros you use will depend on the type of document you are designing. The macros in the preceding listing are designed for formatting UNIX manual pages. Man, for example, defines macros such as .B for bold and .I for italics and more complex macros for defining headers, descriptions, and so on. If you have ever composed an HTML page using a text editor, formatting text from the UNIX command line is not all that different (conceptually anyway), except for the markup tags. Markup tags will change depending on the macro package you use. For example, another package called ms provides formatting for papers.

As you might have figured out, what you can do in reality depends on the macros you have. Besides the man macros mentioned earlier, other libraries such as ms, mm, and me are used to format other types of documents (see groff_ms, groff_mm, man, and me in section 7 of the UNIX manual; to get there, type man 7 *keyword*). The codes and how they format the document differ from package to package.

When your text is formatted in this (somewhat perverse) way, you can generate text, PostScript, HTML, output for LaserJet printers and other formats using the groff command. The resulting file is what you then send to the lpr command to print it. The lpr command takes whatever you give it and spools it to the printer. The syntax looks like this:

```
nroff -Tps -macropackage filename ¦ lpr
```

Substitute *macropackage* with the name of the macros (man for man pages, ms, me, mm, and so on) and *filename* with the name of your file.

As you can tell, there's quite a bit that you need to know in order to produce a simply formatted document. UNIX text processing doesn't end with groff. Other more sophisticated typesetting systems such as TeX and LaTeX can produce professionally formatted documents. Many printed technical publications are developed and printed using TeX and LaTeX.

So why all the complication? The intent of the UNIX command-line printing system is to produce files with any text editor that can display and print properly to a wide range of devices, including the screen. So you can generate man pages, print them on paper, generate HTML pages, and generate pdf (Adobe Acrobat) files, all from the same formatted file. If you want simply to use word processing or desktop publishing, stick to a GUI word processor such as the one included in StarOffice. It will save you time when all you need is a nice-looking document printed on paper.

Part 3

Essential System Tasks Under Linux

You've checked out KDE, and you've gotten down and dirty with the command line. What's left to do? With Linux, just as with everything else in life, there are those things you just have to do. Don't worry, it's not nearly as bad as it sounds—you've got the information in Part 3 to help you along the way. These chapters walk you through backing up your box, installing software, monitoring your system, and you even get to meet LISA. There's even a chapter for the truly adventurous on how to customize your Linux system. There's your heads up, now let's get cracking!

HOW WAS
YOUR DAY?

Users, Groups, and Passwords

In This Chapter

➤ Adding Users

➤ Modifying Users: usermod

➤ Deleting Users: userdel

➤ Adding, Modifying, and Removing Groups

➤ Users and Passwords

➤ Linux and Shadow Passwords

If you have a standalone system, you probably don't have to worry much about managing multiple users and accounts. It's also a strong possibility that you'll continue to use the same account you created when you installed the system.

If you are in a networked environment, however, you might want to grant access to other users to your system. Therefore, the topics in this chapter are of moderate importance to you. If you are administering a system with multiple accounts, you should make certain to read this chapter and understand what this is all about. For further help, be certain to refer to the Linux System Administrator's Guide, discussed in Chapter 15, "Help Please."

The entire reason for logins and passwords is for security's sake. In UNIX, we want to protect our work from others. And unlike a Windows 95/98/NT–based PC, UNIX systems can support a great number of concurrent users. In other words, multiple users can work on and make use of your computer and its services at the same time you are working on it through the network or some other attached terminal. If you haven't read Chapter 16, "Permissions: Protecting and Sharing your Work," it is probably a good time for you to do this.

Adding, removing, and managing users is an administration chore. Luckily, nowadays this chore is fairly automated, as the tools are more flexible and are able to take care of some of the many steps. In the earlier days, you had to add, remove, and manage users by hand, maybe with the help of a custom script that you developed yourself.

Although the tools automate the process somewhat, it is useful to know what goes on behind the scenes. At the center of these activities are /etc/passwd, /etc/shadow, and /etc/group. These files are really system databases that contain user and group information. The /etc/passwd file stores the following:

➤ A list of usernames (logins)

➤ A User ID (UID) number to represent the login

➤ A Group ID (GID) that represents the default group membership for a login

➤ Optional information about the user such as phone number, office, and so on

➤ The location of the home directories

➤ The user's default shell

The group database, /etc/group, stores the following:

➤ A list of user groups

➤ A password for the group (group names could be enabled to work as an account, although public use accounts of this type are usually a really bad idea)

➤ The GID number

➤ A list of all the usernames that belong to the group separated by commas

The shadow passwords file, /etc/shadow, readable only by root, stores an encrypted password for each login

Let's take a look at what you would need to do if you weren't using tools. When you add a user, you need to enter the appropriate information into the /etc/passwd and /etc/group files. You also have to create the user's home directory, copy all the necessary initialization files to the new home directory ("rc" files like .bashrc, .login, .logout, and .profile), create a mailbox for the user, and, if the user belongs to some sort of email alias, add the alias. It is crucial that you keep your UIDs and GIDs straight and that they are not duplicated. After building all this, you have to verify

that directories you create for the user, like the user's home directory, have the appropriate permissions and so on. In the end, it is a lot of tedious work, especially if you need to add more than a few users!

Luckily, nowadays UNIX tools manage most of this tedium. Some tools do a better job than others. Which one you use for your administration will depend on your choice and on the number of users that you need to manage. Some of the tools, such as useradd, are mediocre, whereas some, such as adduser, are fantastic!

The useradd and adduser tools are installed in the /usr/sbin directory. Your shell should be able to see these programs if you are logged in as root. Managing user accounts is a privileged role for the superuser.

Adding Users

So you need to add a user. What do you do? Your choices are to use adduser and useradd.

adduser

adduser is a command line tool for adding user accounts. It is interesting because it manages both /etc/passwd and /etc/group to implement User Private Groups (UPGs; see Chapter 16), a strategy in which each user is made a member of a group that only he or she belongs to. Using UPGs simplifies the process of sharing files between users, and for this reason alone, adduser should be the program you use for adding accounts to your system. If you installed OpenLinux using the standard install option as you were instructed, adduser should already be on your system. If it is not, you can install it from your CD.

To add a new user, just type adduser *username*, like this:

```
[root@digital alberto]# adduser flower

Looking for first available UID... 502
Looking for first available GID... 502

Adding login: flower...done.
Creating home directory: /home/flower...done.
Creating mailbox: /var/spool/mail/flower...done.

Don't forget to set the password.
```

This command swiftly found the next available UID and GID and created entries for them in /etc/passwd and /etc/group. It created the home directory /home/flower,

copied all the startup files from /etc/skel, and then created a mailbox.

Although this is the bulk of the work, optional details about the user, such as the user's real name, were not set. To set those details, you can use the chfn command. See the section "Changing Your Personal Information: chfn" in Chapter 17, "Command Toolbox: Useful Shell Commands and Shortcuts."

A more important detail that is not set by default is the account password. To set a password for the account, see the section "Changing Your Password: passwd" in Chapter 17.

Something to keep in mind when adding users is that the username should be kept at eight or fewer characters. Longer usernames are not handled properly by the system and/or other programs.

Useradd

Useradd is similar to adduser; the only problem is that it doesn't manage the groups database, nor does it implement the UPG scheme, which can simplify much of what you do in the long run. To add an account through useradd, just type the following:

```
useradd -m username
```

The -m option creates the home directory. The password for the account still must be set, as must the real name for the user and other user information.

Modifying Users: usermod

As time goes by, some users will need certain changes made to their accounts. The easy way to make changes is to use usermod, because it offers various options that you can set.

Moving a Home Directory

To move a home directory, use this syntax:

```
usermod -d newdirpath -m login
 [root@digital root]# usermod -d /home/newflower -m flower
```

This option modifies the location of the home directory specified by the /etc/passwd file to point to the directory specified by the -d option. It also creates the home directory if it doesn't exist. The -m option moves the contents from the old home directory into the new one.

If you are changing the name of the home directory, you'll probably also want to change the login name for the user. This option only changes the home directory name; the login name remains as it was.

Changing a Login Name

To change a login name, type the following:

```
usermod -l newlogin currentlogin
[root@digital root]# usermod -l newflower flower
```

This option changes the login name for the user. All other information remains the same. Typically, when you change a login name, you'll also want to change or move a home directory, as explained in the preceding section. In the example shown here, the login name flower is changed to newflower.

Changing Secondary Group Memberships

To change secondary group memberships, type this:

```
usermod -d newdirpath -m login
usermod -d /home/newflower -m flower
[root@digital root]# groups flower
flower : flower users
[root@digital root]# usermod -G wheel,database flower
[root@digital root]# groups flower
flower : flower wheel database
```

The groups command prints a list of all the current group affiliations for a user. If you don't provide a login name, it operates on the assumption that you want to know the group affiliations for the current user.

To change all secondary group affiliations (not the default group), provide a list of the group names separated by commas but with no spaces between them. If a group is omitted, that membership is removed. The sole exception is the primary group for the user.

Deleting Users: `userdel`

To delete a user from the system, you can use the userdel command. Userdel takes as an argument the login of the user. This will remove the named user from the /etc/passwd file. However, the user's home account, mailbox, UPG, and other group affiliations will still be left behind. The syntax looks like this:

```
[root@digital root]# userdel newflower
```

Typically, before you remove the user, you should back up the corresponding account and mailbox or ask the user to do so prior to removing the account. After you have taken the necessary precautions, use userdel to remove the user. Then use groupdel to remove the user's UPG entry. You'll also have to use a text editor to eliminate the removed login from all other entries in the /etc/group file.

211

If you are using UPGs and the default group for the user is the corresponding UPG, you can reduce the number of steps by typing the following:

```
usermod -G username username
```

This will remove all group affiliations for the user except the UPG (the default group). The default group is provided as an argument to -G because usermod requires it. After you have completed the previous step, you can type the following:

```
userdel username
```

This deletes the user from the /etc/passwd file. You can finish the task by removing the UPG from the /etc/group. Finalize the removal by deleting the user's home directory and his or her mailbox (make sure you backed them up first!), like this:

```
rm -R /home/username /usr/spool/mail/username
```

Adding, Modifying, and Removing Groups

Managing groups is similar to managing accounts. Note that some of the functionality provided by these commands can also be attained through programs like usermod. Your choice of which one to use will depend on what you are doing at that moment.

Groupadd

Before you can work with a group, you need to create it. Creating a group is easy; just use the groupadd command:

```
groupadd -g GID groupname
[root@digital alberto]# groupadd -g 600 weirdgroup
```

The one catch with groupadd is that you need to supply a GID that your /etc/group file is not currently using. To make numbering easy on you, you might want to designate custom groups to start with a GID of 30000 or some other large number less than 65536 (the maximum number).

Managing Group Memberships: gpasswd

The gpasswd program is used to manage the group file. The basic functionality for adding and removing users is straightforward. The -a flag is used to add users (note that the group must already exist), like this:

```
gpasswd -a username groupname
[root@digital alberto]# gpasswd -a flower users
```

The -d flag is used to delete users, like this:

```
gpasswd -d username groupname
```

Users and Passwords

UNIX (and Linux) security begins with proper password selection. Therefore, it is a good idea to use passwords that cannot be easily guessed. Using simple scripts and available programs, a deviant hacker can test several thousand passwords in a few seconds.

Password Don'ts

➤ Do not use birthdays, social security numbers, or phone numbers.

➤ Do not use names of relatives or pets.

➤ Do not use words that appear in a dictionary.

➤ Do not give your password to anyone—not even to a system administrator. If this person is really an administrator, he or she doesn't need your password!

Password Do's

➤ Mix upper- and lower-case.

➤ Add numbers and punctuation marks to make it harder to guess. Your final password should probably be random letters and numbers.

➤ Change your password every two months or any time that you think your password might have become compromised.

➤ Good passwords should roll out of your fingers and be easy to type. Many people are very adept at telling what you type from the motion of your fingers. If you have to think about it, it is probably not a good password for you.

Linux and Shadow Passwords

If you are managing a computer that is connected to the Internet and that supports several users, you should consider enabling shadow passwords in your system. Shadow passwords are installed by default as a part of the standard installation. To see if shadow passwords are currently installed on your system, try this:

```
$ ls /etc/shadow
/etc/shadow
$
```

You should have received the same response. If ls responds instead like this, you should install shadow password support immediately:

```
ls: /etc/shadow: No such file or directory
```

Shadow passwords protect system passwords by making the file that actually contains passwords (/etc/shadow) readable only by root. The /etc/passwd file will contain

stars (*) where the encrypted password was previously found. This is because even though passwords are encrypted in the /etc/passwd file, low-end computers have become very fast and able to decrypt them in a short amount of time. In the late 1980s, it probably would have taken days or weeks to decrypt this information. With today's technology, however, it can take only a few minutes. By making the password file readable only by root, this establishes yet another security layer around this information.

For more information on shadow passwords and how to enable them, you should take a look at your man documentation for shadow (section 5 of the UNIX manual, man 5 shadow), pwconv, and pwuncov.

Backups: Safeguarding Your Work

Without a doubt the most important maintenance task that you can perform on any computer is a backup. Backups can be tedious tasks, but it's usually when you have neglected to do it that you most need it! Having a backup for your data can mean the difference between an inconvenience and a catastrophe. Without a backup, you'll have a dé já vu experience recreating the work you lose. As you might already know, that is no fun. Restoring your system from a backup can be an inconvenience, and maybe a few hours of work will be lost, but it is much different than losing work you've created throughout past weeks, months, or even years!

A backup might be required even for simple user errors such as deleting important files. Unlike Windows or other operating systems, under UNIX/Linux there's no "undelete" program, Norton Undelete, or any other tool to restore deleted files. If the file is deleted, it is gone. The reason these utilities don't exist for UNIX/Linux is the

way that disk space is allocated: When you delete a file and release its storage space, this space will probably be written over next. So even if such tools existed, it is likely that they would be useless. Your only guarantee of getting a file back is to have a backup.

Although backing up is not difficult, it can be tedious and time-consuming. However, you should consider it an essential task and time investment. To put it in perspective, some backup is better than none at all. How often you should do it will depend on many issues. The answer is that *it depends*. A server that constantly has new information on it needs to be backed up more often than a standalone user workstation that rarely changes. If your system acts as a file server on which users or other programs store data, all bets are off. You don't have the luxury of determining what is a good interval; you should back it up daily.

On a multiuser system such as Linux, proper backup is even more important. A crashing disk could take away the work of many, potentially hundreds of, users. Losing other people's work is a good way to have a lot of people mad at you! Regardless of the type of system you have, you'll need to back up the data. Linux can make it easier than you thought, provided you have the right equipment.

Your backup hardware needs might be as simple as floppy disks or tape media, or as complicated as requiring specialized hardware that maintains redundant systems in which a secondary disk is ready and waiting to transparently take the place of the failed one. This chapter covers simple backups. Specialized hardware is better administered by an experienced administrator. In terms of media, you can use floppies, although in the long run tapes are much more reliable, and in turn some optical media might be more reliable than a tape. How reliable information is will depend on the length of time that you'll need to keep data around.

To see a list of compatible tape drives, see Appendix B, "OpenLinux Compatibility Guide."

Media Are Just Devices

The programs you can use for backing up under UNIX/Linux have been around for a long time and are very stable. None of these programs rely on a particular piece of hardware to perform their function and can all work equally well outputting their data to a floppy, a tape, any kind of disk, or a file. The file used for a backup is often just the device (/dev) file where you point your backup to go.

How you handle your backup strategy is really a matter of personal preference. If you establish policies, such as describing what you back up, it becomes easier to do many system administration tasks. Also, it is important to have the right hardware for making backups. By "right hardware" I mean that the disks you back up must fit onto a convenient backup medium; otherwise, you'll have more tapes or disks than you'll know what to do with. If you can afford it, buy a tape drive. This medium is inexpensive and can hold a lot of data. Other backup solutions might also work on your network, depending on how much data you need to back up.

Backup Media

There is an incredible array of choices for backup media these days:

➤ Floppy disks

➤ Floptical disks

➤ Magneto-optical (MO) disks

➤ Quarter-inch cartridge tapes (QIC)

➤ Minicartridge QIC and Travan tapes

➤ Write-once CD-ROMs (CD-Rs)

➤ Rewritable CD-ROMs (CD-RWs)

➤ Iomega Jaz and Zip drives

➤ Nine-track magnetic tapes

➤ 4mm Digital Audio Tapes (DATs)

➤ 8mm cartridge tapes

➤ DLT cartridge tapes

These media are described in the following sections.

Floppy Disks

Floppy disks are the most convenient backup medium available because your system likely has a built-in floppy disk drive. The standard capacity is 1.44MB. Some 2.88MB drives made it into the market a few years back, but they never caught on. The drawback of floppy disks is that they are slow, fairly expensive (about 30–60 cents per disk), and not very useful for backing up anything that requires more than a couple of disks. The one advantage is that most computers are equipped with one.

Floptical Disks

These higher-capacity disks take advantage of optical tracking technology to improve head positioning and therefore maximize the amount of data that can be packed onto the surface of a disk. Floptical drives can read standard 1.44MB and 720KB floppy disks. Density of information can be anywhere from a few megabytes to 200MB per disk.

Magneto-Optical Disks

Magneto-optical disks have a plastic or glass substrate coated with a compound that, when heated, allows a magnetic source to realign the polarity of the material. When the material cools, its polarity is frozen. The material can be rewritten by a subsequent write operation.

Data is read by a lower-intensity beam, and the polarization pattern is interpreted as a byte stream. A wide variety of these devices are commercially available, ranging in format from 5 1/2 inches to 3 1/2 inches. These devices can store information ranging in size from 128MB to more than 2GB.

Read speed on MO disks is as fast as that on a hard disk. Write operations usually take a little longer but are still faster than write operations on a slow hard disk or a standard floppy disk. Medium reliability is very high.

Quarter-Inch Cartridge Tapes

QIC tapes get their name from the fact that the tape's width is 0.25, or one quarter, of an inch. Many PC users are familiar with minicartridge QIC drives, but these are discussed in the next session, alongside Travan tapes.

QIC drives originally shipped as standard equipment on a number of older UNIX workstations and were the primary means for booting an "empty" system and for data interchange. The original QIC drives stored very small amounts (20-60 megabytes), but QIC-SCSI drives in the range of 250MB-525MB are currently popular. The largest QIC-SCSI drives shipping at the moment store 26GB (gigabytes) and store data at around 60MB per minute.

True QIC drives are exceedingly reliable and are favorites of many UNIX workstation users. The cartridges themselves are built like (heavy) tanks and can be read thousands of times.

Travan Tapes

A minicartridge QIC tape is a low-end, PC-market backup storage solution that uses the same .25-inch tape width found in true QIC drives. Some vendors are pushing the minicartridge format to store up to 1600MB by using a .315-inch format, resulting in Travan tapes.

Standard QIC tapes can hold anywhere from 11MB to 150MB and are usually designated as QIC-11 or QIC-24, depending on the amount of storage space they provide. Storage space in megabytes is indicated by the number following the QIC portion of the designation.

Sometimes tapes created on one vendor's drive are not readable by another vendor's drive. This is due to byte ordering and other special formatting issues. Within a vendor, tapes are usually backward compatible, meaning that you might be able to read lower-density tapes on a higher-density drive; however, you should verify this before you upgrade to a new drive in the same product line and discard your old one.

Travan tapes are similar in size to minicartridge QIC tapes but store 120–8000MB per tape depending on the type of tape drive mechanism used. Travan tapes are compatible with the minicartridge QIC tape formats, making them attractive if you have legacy minicartridge QIC tapes. Its price, capacity, and performance make this system a very attractive option.

218

Write-Once CD-ROMs

New technology and price drops have made the CD-R a popular choice with multimedia enthusiasts. The CD-Rs use a technology similar to a regular CD, but instead of being "pressed," they are burned using a process similar to MO disks. CDs created by CD-Rs are not as rugged as pressed CDs, but they will last far into the future if you take care of the disk. These disks are compatible with any desktop system that has a CD-ROM, which has helped in making this a popular write once-read many (WORM) format. Current capacity is about 600MB. Recording speed is slow—typically 2–8X speed, whereas most CD-ROMs can read at speeds up to 32X. New formats for CD-ROMs that are currently in the works will yield 17GB of storage, making them a very interesting solution to backup and archival tasks.

Rewritable CD-ROMs

The popularity of CD-Rs helped pave the way for a newer medium to emerge: the CD-RW. Based on the same technology for the CD-R, CD-RWs are a medium that can be reused, much like a floppy disk. The material the medium is made from and the drives used with CD-RWs is different from the standard CD-R, but the process is basically the same concept.

Iomega Jaz and Zip Drives

Zip is a popular removable disk drive. They are very inexpensive: around $150 for the drive and $10–$15 per disk. Each disk holds about 100MB. They are available in SCSI(small computer systems interface—pronounced "skuzzy"), parallel, and combination flavors.

The SCSI drives require a SCSI interface (a special type of disk controller, or host adapter as they are called, that uses standardized commands for accessing the hardware).

Jaz drives are a higher-performance, higher-capacity version of the Zip drives. Jaz drives are a bit more expensive, about $350, and require a SCSI interface. Disks cost more than $99 and pack 1GB+ of fast storage space. This is a hot product.

Nine-Track Magnetic Tapes

This is an old format of tape written at 800, 1600, or 6250BPI (bits per inch) density. This format is not in great use today except by old mainframes. Some programs such as dump, a backup program, use this format as a basis for their tape capacity calculations.

4mm Digital Audio Tapes

The DAT, which stores 1.3GB of information on a 60-meter tape (1.95GB on a 90m and 2.6GB on a 120m), was originally designed for the audio market. Digital data storage (DDS), the computer version of DAT, provides the smallest storage solution of all. Its capacity is typically more than doubled by the use of compression. Drives with

hardware compression can store up to 8GB. The preferred tape backup system is DDS for most UNIX users. These drives, many of which can be had for about $400, require a SCSI interface. This is the type of tape drive that I have on my own setup, and it is great!

8mm Cartridge Tapes

8mm cartridges (also known as "Exabytes," for the only company that manufactures them) are the same size as their video counterparts. Many administrators purchase high-quality "video grade" tapes instead of the premium data versions. Drives can store 2–5GB, and current versions can pack up to 40GB into a single tape at a blazing 360MB per minute write speed. Because fewer tapes are needed, this is a very convenient format, especially for server systems. 8mm drives are commonly found in multidrive libraries for storage capapcity exceeding 300GB.

DLT Cartridge Tapes

DLT, or digital linear tape, was originally pioneered by Digital Equipment Corporation, and was used for ages on large VAX servers. The first DLT drives stored 40-60MB, but were proven to be some of the most reliable magnetic storage media ever, in part thanks to their .50 in (half-inch) tape width and linear data path.

Current DLT tape drives store up to 70GB compressed at a rate of 300MB per minute. Like 8mm drives, DLT drives are often found in ultra-high capacity storage libraries. Desktop models are available for the prestige-conscious desktop user, however.

What to Back Up

Typically, you don't need to back up the entire system, as a good amount of the stuff on your disk (at least initially) you already have as part of your installation CD. This provides you with a twofold benefit: Your backups will be smaller (because there is less stuff to back up), and they will go faster (again as a result of the reduced data). Linux offers good organization of important configuration files that are typically kept in a common place. As you configure and change your system, you should maintain a log (a simple account to which you can send an email message can make a simple but effective way of documenting changes you perform to your system) and use it to drive your backup strategy. At the very least, you should back up these directories:

➤ /etc

➤ /usr/lib

➤ /usr/X11R6/lib/X11 (if you use X Windows)

➤ /usr/src/linux (if you have modified your kernel sources)

➤ /home

➤ /var/spool/mail

It's important to back up these directories because they contain system configuration files, user files, and user mail spool directories. Given the low cost of tape drives today, you probably ought to invest in one. The capacity should match the size of the hard disk you have. Although spawning a backup onto multiple tapes is a very common thing, there's nothing worse than a missing tape or a tape gone bad. By putting all your data onto one tape, you know you have it, and you don't have to worry about partial backup issues.

Simple Backups

A *simple backup* is one in which you copy your files onto another medium. There isn't a strategy, so it is simple to do—provided you know what you want to save. You can use the cp command to copy the files, or you can use an archiving tool such as tar, which I describe next.

Tape Archive: tar

The simplest of backup utilities is tar. Its functionality is fairly simple: It creates a file that archives other files. It is common in UNIX to distribute programs in a tar file. (tar files are analogous to zip files found in the PC world.) Modern versions of tar can not only archive but also compress data, making the tar file smaller. Note that compressing tar files on tape is not recommended because tar is then unable to recover from tape errors.

The tar program has many options. I would recommend that you read its man page to see what it has to offer (see Chapter 15, "Help Please," for information on accessing man pages). In the following section, you'll learn the least you need to know to make use of tar.

Making a tar File

The format of the tar command follows this pattern:

```
tar options destination source
```

To back up my home directory in /home/alberto to the file /tmp/bkup.tar, I would type the following:

```
tar cvf archiveName pathsToArchive
```

```
tar cvf /tmp/bkup.tar /home/alberto
```

In `tar`, the arguments are typically given without a dash. The order of the options (cvf) and the arguments that follow are important. In our case, the cvf options tell tar to

➤ Create an archive (c option)

➤ Be verbose and list all it does (v option)

➤ Put the archive on a file or device (f option)

The f option expects the next argument to be the filename or device where the tar file will be created. In our case, it is a regular file in the /tmp directory called bkup.tar: /tmp/bkup.tar. This file can be replaced by the name of your backup device where you want the file written. (I'll examine this later in this section.)

The f command will back up all the files in my home directory into a file that I called bkup.tar. One important thing about tar is that if I give it a path to back up, that path is preserved. So when I "untar" the files (we'll see this later, in the section "Extracting Files from the tar Archive"), it will create a home/alberto directory if it doesn't already exist. Note that the leading forward slash (/) is removed.

All paths and files specified after the file argument are diligently copied. In my case, I only provided /home/alberto, but I could as easily have typed this:

```
tar cvf /tmp/bkup.tar /home/alberto /var/spool/mail/alberto
```

This command would have backed up my home directory and my mailbox into the same archive.

Extracting Files from a `tar` Archive

There's no "untar" command. To extract files, you use the tar command and provide different options. To extract the files in the tar file I created in the preceding section, I would type this:

```
tar xvf archive destination_or_name_of_file_to_extract
tar xvf /tmp/bkup.tar /
```

The first argument contains the options to the tar command. In this case, the xvt options tell tar to

➤ Extract files (x option)

➤ Be verbose and list what it does (v option)

➤ Read from the file archive provided (f option)

The second argument specifies the name of the archive (/tmp/bkup.tar).

The final argument (/) is optional and specifies the path where I want to put the files I extract from my archive. If I don't provide this option, the archive is extracted wherever my shell happens to be. Remember that when I created the file, I specified

/home/alberto. When tar created the archive, it removed the leading / so that the archive could be extracted into any directory. By choice, I am extracting the archive back into /, which will put all my files into /home/alberto, effectively replacing any files that have the same name.

If the path you provide is neither absolute nor relative, it is taken to mean a particular file in the archive to extract, and tar will try to extract this file only. The only caveat is that you need to know the path to the file in the archive. If I know that I want to restore /home/alberto/nsmail, I could type this:

```
tar xvf bkup.tar home/alberto/nsmail
```

Tar would only extract the path home/alberto/nsmail, putting it into the current directory (remember that tar, by default, strips the leading slash [/] on any path you provide).

Extracting a File into a Device

Although creating a tar file is easy, it is not what tar is about. What's more important is that you can extract directly into a device. The device (typically a tape drive) won't have a file system, so it cannot be mounted or accessed in the same way that you access your disks. However, it will store the data as if it were a file. So, if you tar into a tape or floppy, the entire tape or floppy is taken to be one large tar file. (Multiple tar files can be put in a tape; I'll talk about that in a little bit.) In the case of a floppy, you won't be able to mount it because it won't have a file system where you can store files. (Remember that we discussed mounting in Chapter 7, "Working with Disks.")

Taring into a device

Taring into a device is the same as *taring* into a file. The only difference is that the destination of the archive is the path to the device representing your backup hardware. The basic devices that you'll want to work with are floppies and tape drives.

Floppy Devices

To create a tar file on a floppy, you use the /dev/fd*x* device, where *x* is the number of your floppy drive. Typically, this will be 0 if you've got only one floppy, or 0 or 1 if you've got two floppies:

```
tar cvf /dev/fd0 /etc /home/alberto/nsmail
```

This command will tar /etc and /home/alberto/nsmail into the floppy drive. It should all fit onto the backup medium; if it doesn't, you'll get an error. I'll show you how to span multiple disks or tapes later in this chapter, in the section "Spanning Multiple Disks or Tapes."

Tape Devices

Tape drives are typically hung from two different devices (your hardware might specify something else):

➤ st

➤ rft

Techno Talk

If you are using a floppy tape device, you might need to rebuild your kernel to provide support for it. If your tape drive seems to be unsupported, check out Chapter 24, "Customizing Your Linux Kernel" for information on how to do this.

The st devices correspond to SCSI tape drives. The rft devices correspond to tape drives that use the floppy controller or "floppy-tape" devices. (Inexpensive PC tape drives, such as QIC type drives, usually use this option.) As with other devices, there might be more than one, so the devices are differentiated from each other by the drive number they use.

The standard device files for SCSI tapes are, therefore, /dev/st0 and /dev/st1. The standard device files for the floppy-tape drives are /dev/rft0 and /dev/rft1.

So, to backup to my tape device (a SCSI drive), I enter this:

```
tar cvf /dev/st0 /etc/alberto/nsmail
```

The default behavior of these tape devices is to rewind the tape when the write operation is finished. If your tape drive is capable of storing a few gigabytes, this could be rather wasteful, as most of the tape could remain empty. For this reason, there are nonrewinding versions of these devices that allow you to place multiple files onto one tape.

The nonrewinding tape devices are /dev/nst0 and /dev/nst1 for SCSI devices and /dev/nrft0 and /dev/nrft1 for floppy-tape devices. When you use these devices to write to the tape, the tape is not rewound, allowing you to write another archive to it. Between each file, you write to the tape so there will be a marker. You can rewind and forward the tape to your desired archive by using the mt command.

The mt Command

The mt command allows you to perform many things with a tape, including wind and rewind the tape by files (by archives it contains) using the nonrewinding device interface.

To rewind the tape, use this syntax:

```
mt /dev/nst0 rewind
```

To wind the tape forward over the two next archives on the tape, type this:

```
mt /dev/nst0 fsf 2
```

One trick to this command is to realize that mt has no concept of the current archive,

so you'll need to make sure that you have a list of the archives that you have on tape. Also, as a sanity check, you'll want to make sure you are starting your count from the beginning of the tape by issuing a rewind prior to winding the tape forward.

Similarly, it is important to remember that the tape drive writes markers between different archives. This is the information that mt uses to detect different archives. After you extract data in one archive, in order to work with the other, you'll need to forward the tape to the next archive by issuing this command:

```
mt /dev/nst0 fsf 1
```

Whatever you do, don't replace archives on a tape, unless you are replacing the entire contents of the tape. The one thing that you don't want to do is overwrite the beginning of one archive by replacing a short archive with a longer one.

Extracting from a Device

Extracting from a device is done much the same way as from a file:

```
tar xvf device path
```

If you don't provide a destination, all files are extracted to the current directory while preserving their path organization. If you provide an absolute or relative path, files will be put there. If the path you provide is neither absolute nor relative, it is taken to mean a file in the archive to extract.

When extracting from a multiarchive tape, remember to use the nonrewinding interface and mt to forward the tape.

Spanning Multiple Disks or Tapes

If the file you are trying to archive doesn't fit onto a single floppy or tape, you'll need to specify the M option to tar. The M option tells the device to span multiple disks or tapes. Each tape or disk is a complete and standalone archive (with the sole exception that the last file on any disk or tape might be split between disks or tapes). This means that you can extract and work with each disk or tape as if it were its own archive.

To back up my nsmail directory onto multiple floppies, I type this:

```
tar cMvf /dev/fd0 /home/alberto/nsmail
```

When the first floppy disk gets full, it will ask you to insert a new one. It is important that you number each floppy or tape in the order they were written so that when you extract them, data won't be corrupted.

To extract a multivolume archive, enter the following:

```
tar xMvf /dev/fd0
```

Tar will ask for each of the volumes (in this case, floppies) in order. Make sure you have all of them.

The one drawback with tar is that it doesn't keep track of files that need backing up. In order to use tar, you need to decide which files you want to back up and provide a list of these files to the program. Although it offers some facilities to address this limitation, there are better programs for this task. If you want to do incremental backups and have a program keep track of files that need to be backed up, you'll need to use dump.

A Backup Strategy

Doing incremental backups under UNIX/Linux means using the dump utility. This utility is powerful. It can handle backups that span multiple tapes and can create incremental backups. If you can fit your entire backup onto a single tape, you'll be able to automate your backups. Just start up the backup, and let it run. Because dump actually keeps track of what was dumped before and only backs up things that have changed, there are a couple of tricks that you can use to back up only those items that you have added and modified since you installed your system (not including the "unconfigured" operating system).

My strategy is to back up at well-defined times:

➤ Right after the system software is installed but before anything is configured

➤ After the system software is installed and configured

➤ Any time additional software is installed and configured

Using this strategy, the order of things is to back up your system right after installing it. This is done to a special device file called /dev/null, which simply discards any data that you send to it. Because dump will keep track of the date it last dumped, subsequent backups will only store things that have been modified after that date. This is a neat trick because your backup set won't include your system's software distribution. This will set the beginning of time for the dump utility to operate. The backup level for this dump should be at level 0; it must include everything in the newly installed system.

Dump uses the concept of levels to determine what to back up. Level 0 (zero) backs up everything. Level 1 backs up everything modified after the level 0 dump. Level 2 dumps only backup items that have changed since the last lower-level dump, and so on.

Subsequent backups should be performed at level 8 or 9. This will effectively back up everything that has been modified in the machine since the first backup was made.

To restore files stored in a tape created with the dump utility, use the restore program described later in this chapter, in the section "The restore Command."

The dump **Command**

The dump utility is not installed by default on your system, but it is included on your CD. In the col/install/rpms directory, it should be named something like dump-x.i386.rpm, where *x* will be some numbers related to the version of the program. To install the program, visit the col/install/rpms directory on the CD. As root, issue the following command:

```
rpm -i dump*.rpm
```

The dump command uses the following syntax:

```
/usr/etc/dump [options [argument ...]
filesystem]
```

The dump command tracks the scope of a backup by assigning each backup a level. Levels range from 0 to 9. Level 0 copies the entire file system. Subsequent dump levels copy only files that have changed since the most recent dump with a lower-level number.

The typical strategy is to begin with a level 0 dump and then make incremental backups at regular intervals. Level 0 dumps should be performed with extreme care; they should be run with the machine in single-user mode, and fsck (the file system consistency checker) should run before the dump to verify that the file system is consistent. This is important, because most of the files you restore will come from dump level 0 tapes if you don't plan to substitute your CD for a level 0 backup! For more information, see the fsck and dump man pages.

Booting in Single-User Mode

Linux can be booted into single-user mode. This setting skips all system configuration and, after asking your root password, starts you in a root shell. This mode should only be used for special maintenance tasks, such as doing a dump at level 0 or some other emergency-type task. To start your system in single-user mode, at the boot prompt, type the name of the Linux image (tab to see a list of available images) followed by the word single.

A running system can also be "brought down" to single user mode using the shutdown command without the –r (for reboot) or the –h (for halt) options by issuing the following command at the command prompt:

shutdown now

After a few moments, you'll be asked for the root password, and then you'll be "dropped" into single-user mode.

One disadvantage worth noting is that dump is unable to back up single directories or files; it can only be used to back up an entire file system. To back up individual files or directories, use tar or cpio. For information on how to use these programs, refer to your Linux documentation.

Note that tapes created under one hardware/software configuration are not usually portable to other operating systems or drives. In some environments, even tapes created with older versions of the dump program are unreadable by newer versions of the

restore program. So test your backups when you do an upgrade, and keep old versions of the program close by.

Tape Capacity

The one issue with dump is that it doesn't calculate how much data your tape can hold for you. Therefore, you'll need to figure capacity by yourself in order to make correct use of your tape.

This might seem easy enough—but it isn't. Each tape system has a different density (the amount of data that can be written to one inch of tape). Tapes are of different lengths, and dump calculates all these settings based on a nine-track tape running at 1600 bytes/inch and with a default tape length of 2300 feet. Sound confusing? Don't give up.

The basic math for calculating your tape drive's capacity is as follows:

1. Write the tape capacity in GB (make sure you *don't* use the compressed capacity for this purpose, because that "maximum" capacity will depend on the compressability of your data! If your tape capacity is expressed in terms of megabytes, divide that capacity by 1024.

2. Convert your tape length to inches. If the length of your tape is in meters, multiply it by 39.37 to obtain the number of inches. If your tape length is in feet, multiply this number by 12.

3. Multiply your tape capacity from step 1 by 1,073,741,824 to obtain the capacity of your tape in bytes.

4. Divide your calculation from step 3 by the number you calculated in step 2. This is your tape density.

5. Divide the number from step 3 by 32,768. This is the number of 32K blocks your tape is able to hold.

6. Multiply the number calculated in step 5 by 21.18. This is the size of your tape based on 1600 bytes/inch.

7. Divide the number from step 6 by 12 and drop any fractions. This is the tape length you should specify for dump.

Here's an example for a 90m 1.95GB DDS tape:

1. Tape capacity in GB: 1.95GB
2. Tape length in inches: 90m × 39.37 = 3,543
3. Tape capacity in bytes: 1.95 × 1,073,741,824 = 2,093,796,556
4. Tape density: 2,093,796,556 / 3,543 = 590,967
5. Tape capacity in 32K blocks: 2,093,796,556 / 32,768 = 63,897
6. Tape size in 1600 bytes/inch terms: 63,897 × 21.18 = 1,353,338
7. Adjusted tape length in feet: 1,353,338 / 12 = 112,778

Whew! In a world where tape density could be figured out automatically by querying the device, it seems silly to have to do this. But heck, this program was originally done eons ago, and given the different types of tape devices (SCSI or otherwise), that could be a challenging task to develop, too! Also, remember to check your manufacturer's Web site. It is possible that it posts information on how to use its hardware with dump.

Whatever you do, remember to write this number down and stick it in a note to the bottom of your drive. That way you won't have to figure it out again. If you don't have a calculator handy, remember that KDE has one that should work just fine.

dump *Examples*

The following command will create a level 0 dump (indicated by the 0) on the device specified by the -f flag (in this case /dev/nst0) of the specified disk /dev/hda1 (see /etc/fstab for the name of your disk devices):

```
dump -0u -f /dev/nst0 -s 112778 /dev/hda1
```

Replace *nst0* with the appropriate name for your tape device and *hda1* with the device used by your root partition. This dump will include all the files found on the device. If you have additional disks, you'll have to run dump again for each. If you specify the u option and the backup finishes successfully, dump will remember the date, time, and level of this backup. This effectively sets a starting point that can be used to evaluate which files need to be dumped next time.

To create an incremental backup that includes only files modified since the last backup of a lower level, in this case 0, use a higher level dump:

By default, dump writes its output to the default tape unit; you need to remember to specify the -f option followed by the device for your tape drive.

You can redirect the backup to a file using the -f option:

```
dump -9uf /tmp/backup /dev/hda1
```

The preceding command will create a file called backup in the /tmp directory. To redirect the output of dump to STDOUT (standard output), specify a dash (-) instead of a filename:

```
dump -9uf - /dev/hda1 ¦ gzip > /dev/st0
```

In the preceding example, output from dump was sent to STDOUT and piped to the gzip (see Chapter 20, "Installing Programs and Applications") program to be compressed. If your tape doesn't provide hardware compression, using the preceding command can be an effective way of increasing tape capacity.

For complete information on the myriad of options that dump provides, read your system's documentation.

The restore *Command*

To extract files backed up with dump, use restore. The restore copies files stored in a dump tape or file to the current directory. It's important to note that using restore can, and will, clobber existing files with matching names. Restore will also create any directories or directory trees that it needs before extracting a file. This feature is powerful if you know what you are doing. When in doubt, extract files using restore to an empty directory and move the files by hand. Restore has the following syntax:

```
restore [options [argument ...]]
```

To specify the device holding your backup, use the -f option and follow it by the location of your dump.

The restore command has an easy-to-use interactive shell-like interface that allows you to navigate through the dump tape as if you were in a file system. The interactive session is started by using the -i option:

restore -f /dev/nst0 -i

When restore loads, you can use commands such as cd and ls to move around the tape catalog. These commands are built into restore and are not the same ones you use on a shell.

To add a file to a list of files you wish to extract (restore), type add *filename*, where *filename* is the name of the file you want to extract. If you add a directory, all files and directories it contains are added. To remove files from a list, type del *filename.* This command doesn't delete the file from the tape; it just removes it from the extract list. To extract the files, just type extract. At the end of the extraction, you will be asked if you want to set the owner/mode for '.'?[yn] You should respond no, as this could change the owner and mode of the directory where restore is going to extract files from.

Here's a sample session:

```
 1: [root@digital /tmp]# restore -i -f /dev/nst0
 2: restore > ls
 3: .:
 4: auto/ dev/  etc/  home/ root/ tmp/  var/
 5: restore > add home
 6: restore > ls
 7: .:
 8:  auto/  dev/   etc/   *home/  root/   tmp/    var/
 9:
10: restore > del home
11: restore > ls
12: .:
13: auto/ dev/  etc/  home/ root/ tmp/  var/
```

```
14:
15: restore > cd home/alberto/test
16: restore > ls
17: ./home/alberto/test:
18: afile
19:
20: restore > add afile
21: restore > extract
22: You have not read any tapes yet.
23: Unless you know which volume your file(s) are on you should start
24: with the last volume and work towards the first.
25: Specify next volume #: 1
26: restore > quit
27: [root@digital /tmp]# ls
28: home
29: [root@digital /tmp]# cd home/alberto/test
30: [root@digital test]# ls
31: afile
```

The version of restore shipped with my version of Linux has a problem. If you try to add a file, it will give you an error message. The workaround is to add a directory such as home (see line 5 of the previous listing). Note that when you add a file or a directory, restore marks it by placing a star (*) next to it (see line 8). After adding this directory, delete it (see line 10). Then you can go ahead and add files as you want. Parent directories will be automatically added. When you are done making your file selection, type extract (see line 21). Dump will ask you to read a tape. If your dump only spans one tape, type 1; otherwise, type the number of the last tape you used for this dump. To get information on a dump, type what. To get help on an interactive restore, type help or ?, which will print the following information:

```
restore > ?
Available commands are:
        ls [arg] - list directory
        cd arg - change directory
        pwd - print current directory
        add [arg] - add `arg' to list of files to be extracted
        delete [arg] - delete `arg' from list of files to be extracted
        extract - extract requested files
        setmodes - set modes of requested directories
        quit - immediately exit program
        what - list dump header information
        verbose - toggle verbose flag (useful with ``ls'')
        help or `?' - print this list
If no `arg' is supplied, the current directory is used
```

restore *Examples*

Restoring interactively is easier than using the command line. However, you can do this too. To restore a particular file, specify the -x option and provide a path relative of root, like this:

```
restore -x home/alberto/file.rtf -f /dev/nst0
```

The preceding command will extract (-x) the file specified (/home/alberto/file.rtf) from the tape to the current directory. If the directory path doesn't exist, restore will create them. It's a good idea to change directory to /tmp so that recovered files go to a safe place and existing files are not overwritten. After the file has been recovered, you can move the file to its final destination.

To create a catalog from files on a dump tape, use the -t option. Unless you know that your tape drive supports read-behind-write verification, it is always a good idea to create a catalog from your tape. This will ensure that the backup tape you made contains the correct information and that the tape is readable.

To create a catalog, enter the following:

```
restore -t -f /dev/nts0 > tapecat.txt
```

This will create a file called tapecat.txt with the listing of the files on your tape.

Graphical Backup Programs

There are a couple of graphical backup programs available: BRU2000, included on your CD, and KDat, a KDE backup application (go to http://www.kde.org for more information on KDat).

BRU2000

Currently, OpenLinux is including a license to BRU2000, a program that can be used both through the command line and a graphical interface to perform dump-like backups of your system. The big advantage over dump is in using its graphical user interface, so it is easy to use. Not having to worry about tape sizes and other insidious details could be well worth it. Using the program is self-explanatory. You first select your backup device (/dev/nst0 or whatever applies to you). To create your backup device, just use the New Device command under the File menu. After you've selected your backup device, you'll need to pick your backup options from the Backup command under the options menu. A dialog box will require various settings. Then click the backup button. This will prompt you for the files you want to back up. From there, click the Start Backup button, and you are on your way.

Like dump, BRU supports incremental backups, so you can implement the backup strategy discussed in the section "A Backup Strategy."

Here are some screen shots of the program:

The BRU2000 program.

BRU's backup window.

Installing Programs and Applications

In This Chapter

➤ RPM: The Red Hat Package Manager

➤ Installing, Upgrading, Downgrading, and Removing Software

➤ Verifying Your System

➤ Graphical Front Ends to RPM

➤ Non-RPM Packages

Software installation on Linux is fairly sophisticated through the use of RPM. Although you can install software that has been archived by tar and other programs, most of the time you'll want to install RPM packages. It goes without saying that when you have a choice on what package format to install, pick the RPM version. RPM packages provide a multitude of benefits, and that's why we'll cover it in great detail.

RPM: The Red Hat Package Manager

RPM is an open software and source packaging system. It was initially developed for Linux but has since made available for anyone to use under the GPL.

RPM is a great packaging system because it not only deals with installing software as other systems have done for years but also maintains a database of installed software and their interdependencies. This database is searchable, so you can find what package a file belongs to, and allows you to even check to see if the file has been modified,

accidentally corrupted, or deleted since its initial installation. In terms of dependencies, RPM makes sure that you install any required packages that might be necessary for the operation of other software you are installing.

RPM can work through FTP, so you don't need to download software in order to install it; RPM can do both at the same time. It also keeps a handle on configuration files, so when you upgrade the software or your system, those customizations are maintained. This is something that has been a problem for all operating systems and software installs since the beginning of upgrades.

For developers and programmers, RPM allows the packaging of binaries (programs) and source code for users. If a developer modifies the source code to a program, these "patches," as they are called, are maintained separate from the "pristine" or virgin sources. This makes it easy to upgrade the base source and reapply patches to new versions.

For administrators, RPM allows them to upgrade a system, without reinstalling everything and then going through the configuration pains. RPM can efficiently upgrade only those packages that have changed without losing your customizations.

For up-to-date information on RPM, see `http://www.rpm.org` on the Web.

Installing, Upgrading, Downgrading, and Removing Software

Just the fact that you can install, upgrade, and downgrade software on your system, and remove it from your system, without having to do so manually is a good enough reason to install rpm software.

Installing

It is extremely easy to install a package. Here is the syntax:

```
rpm -i mypackage-1.0-2.i386.rpm
```

Typically, you might need to have root privileges in order to install a package. RPM takes care of installing everything—software and documentation—putting everything in its right place.

There are some errors you can get while installing. If RPM detects that the new package will overwrite a file belonging to another package, it will inform you of a conflict. To override, you can supply the --replacefiles option:

```
rpm -i --replacefiles mypackage-1.0-2.i386.rpm
```

If a package depends on another, you will see an error telling you that the package requires another. You should obtain the required package and then retry the installation of your software. You can also override this warning with the --nodeps option; however, doing so is setting yourself up for a problem.

If the software is already installed, you'll get an error telling you that the package has already been installed. To install over the package, you should provide the --repalcepkgs option, like this:

```
rpm -i --replacepkgs mypackage-1.0-2.i386.rpm
```

Upgrading

Upgrading an application is just as simple as installing one. Instead of specifying the -i option, you specify the -U option, like this:

```
rpm -U mypackage-1.0-4.i386.rpm
```

It's important to keep in mind that upgrading a package actually uninstalls the previous installation. If the configuration files for the upgraded version are not compatible, you'll see a message telling you so. RPM will save your original configuration file for you to reconcile with the new one.

Downgrading

Sometimes upgrading is really upgrading to new undesirable bugs. To downgrade back to the software you had before you acquired the bugs, just upgrade to the old package and provide the --oldpackage option.

```
rpm –U --oldpackage myoldpackage-1.0-1.i386.rpm
```

Uninstalling

If you figure out that you don't want the software you've installed, use the -e (Erase) flag. This time, only provide the base name for the package. For a package named mypackage-1.0-4.i386.rpm, just type the following:

```
rpm -e mypackage
```

A Database of Installed Software

The most interesting feature in RPM is the capability to query information about files and packages installed on your system. This feature is killer as you can query RPM to search its list of installed software for a number of things. Querying (searching) takes place using the -q option.

Finding Information About the Package

To find information about a package file, do an `rpm` query for information about the package. You would type the following:

```
rpm -qip packagefile
[alberto@digital alberto]$ rpm -qip DUMP-0_4.RPM
Name        : dump                    Distribution: OpenLinux 1.2
Version     : 0.4b4                         Vendor: Caldera, Inc.
Release     : 1                         Build Date: Wed Jan 07
➥01:15:34 1998
Install date: (not installed)          Build Host:
➥buildmeister.caldera.com
Group       : Administration/Archiving Source RPM: dump-0.4b4-
➥1.src.rpm
Size        : 295767
Packager    : Raymund Will <ray@lst.de>
Summary     : BSD dump/restore backup system (BETA).
Description :
dump and restore, as known from BSD/SunOS/..., is a quite
reliable method for backup, because 'dump' gets all needed
information directly from the storage media -- not via
the high-level filesystem-interface (as tar, cpio, etc. do).

Additionally the output format of dump is readable on
other platforms (like SunOS, BSD) and vice versa.

But BEWARE, this software is still under development (BETA)!!!
Don't rely too much on it -- but without testing, there would be
no further improvement! Interleave with another backup method
would be a good idea.
```

Finding the Package that Owns a File

If you want to find out what package a file came from, type this:

```
rpm -q -f filepath
[alberto@digital alberto]$ rpm -q -f /sbin/restore
dump-0.4b4-1
```

Finding Files that are Owned by a Package

To see all the files owned by a package, just enter the following:

```
rpm -q -l packagename
[alberto@digital alberto]$ rpm -q -l dump
/etc/dumpdates
```

```
/etc/rmt
/sbin/dump
/sbin/rdump
/sbin/restore
/sbin/rmt
/sbin/rrestore
/usr/doc/dump-0.4b4-1
/usr/doc/dump-0.4b4-1/CHANGES
/usr/doc/dump-0.4b4-1/COPYRIGHT
/usr/doc/dump-0.4b4-1/KNOWNBUGS
/usr/doc/dump-0.4b4-1/THANKS
/usr/doc/dump-0.4b4-1/TODO
/usr/doc/dump-0.4b4-1/dump-0.4b1.announce
/usr/doc/dump-0.4b4-1/dump.lsm
/usr/man/man8/dump.8.gz
/usr/man/man8/rdump.8.gz
/usr/man/man8/restore.8.gz
/usr/man/man8/rmt.8.gz
/usr/man/man8/rrestore.8.gz
```

Finding Documentation Related to a Package

Say you want to learn all sources of documentation that were installed with a particular package. RPM can help here too. Just type the following:

```
rpm -q -d packagename
[alberto@digital alberto]$ rpm -q -d dump
/usr/doc/dump-0.4b4-1
/usr/doc/dump-0.4b4-1/CHANGES
/usr/doc/dump-0.4b4-1/COPYRIGHT
/usr/doc/dump-0.4b4-1/KNOWNBUGS
/usr/doc/dump-0.4b4-1/THANKS
/usr/doc/dump-0.4b4-1/TODO
/usr/doc/dump-0.4b4-1/dump-0.4b1.announce
/usr/doc/dump-0.4b4-1/dump.lsm
/usr/man/man8/dump.8.gz
/usr/man/man8/rdump.8.gz
/usr/man/man8/restore.8.gz
/usr/man/man8/rmt.8.gz
/usr/man/man8/rrestore.8.gz
```

Now you know what to read for your package!

Verifying Your System

Many times you might need the ability to check a file or an application, or even your entire system for signs of corruption. RPM keeps track of a *checksum* (a fancy calculation yielding a unique number that can be used to determine if a file's contents change). By issuing a simple command (rpm -Va) you can verify your entire system!

If RPM prints something, more than likely that package needs to be reinstalled. If you don't see any messages, the verification process succeeded. Specifying rpm -Vf will verify just a single file. Note that some configuration files you modify will be listed, but this is normal.

To compare an installed package against a package file, you would type rpm -Vp *fullpackagename*, as in the following example

```
rpm -Vp mypackage-1.0-4.i386.rpm
```

Graphical Front Ends to RPM

A couple of graphical front ends to RPM are available: One is part of the KDE environment and is called kpackage (kpackage-0.9.02-1.i386.rpm; see the next figure), the other is called glint (glint-2.3-3.rpm). Although having a UI version of the program is a step in the right direction, the command line tool provides many features that are not accessible through the UI. For this reason, I am covering the command line version of the program instead.

Here's a screenshot of the kpackage tool. It provides a nice front end for installing RPM packages; however, it lacks many of the powerful querying facilities that the RPM program offers.

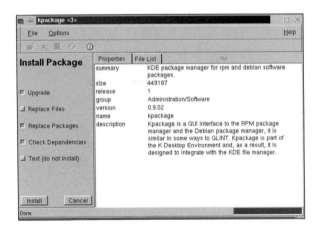

Non-RPM Packages

Although RPM is great, there are times that the software you are to install won't be in the form of an RPM package. FTP sites like http://sunsite.unc.edu/pub/Linux/ distributions/redhat/contrib/i386/ have tons of programs already packaged in

RPM, so you should check there to see if what you need is already available in package format.

If it is not, more than likely it will be supplied in a tar or compressed tar file. Working with the tar program for backups is discussed in great detail in Chapter 19, "Backups: Safeguarding Your Work." If you need to install a program that doesn't come packaged in RPM format, it is a good idea to install this program into its own directory in the /opt directory. The /opt directory contains mostly third-party software, such as KDE, Netscape, and so on. To make the program visible to the shell, you can create a link for its executable file in the /opt/bin directory. If this directory doesn't exist, you should create it and add it to your PATH environment variable.

Tar

To extract files from a tar file, follow these steps:

1. Create a directory where you are going to put the files from the archive. It is possible that the tar file will scatter a number of files to the current directory, so it is always a good idea to create a new directory to receive the files.

2. Move the tar archive to the destination directory.

3. Put the Cd into the directory.

4. Extract the file using tar: tar xvf *afile*.tar.

If the maker of the tar file was conscientious enough to place all the files into a directory, you are set. Sometimes the tar file will contain a file called install.sh or some other installation script. Follow instructions as per any readme files (view them with a page such as less).

UNIX Compressed Archives: Gzip and Compress

Many times tar files will be distributed in compressed format; the typical extensions for compressed files are .gz (gnu zip, or gzip), .Z for the compress program, and .zip for Windows zip compressed archives. If the file has a name like *file*.tar.gz, that file is a gnu zip compressed tar file. To extract it, you'll have to specify the z option to tar:

```
[alberto@digital /tmp]$ tar -xzvf file.tar.gz
nsmail/
nsmail/Drafts
nsmail/.Drafts.summary
nsmail/Trash
nsmail/.Trash.summary
nsmail/Sent
nsmail/.Sent.summary
nsmail/Unsent Messages
nsmail/.Unsent Messages.summary
```

```
nsmail/Inbox
nsmail/.Inbox.summary
```

Another way of accomplishing the same task is to use pipes using the gzcat program (similar to cat). This program reads information in the compressed archive, decompresses it, and copies it out to the STDOUT. Here's an example of how to use gzcat and tar together:

gzcat *file***.tar.gz ¦ tar -xf -**

In this example, gzcat pipes the resulting output, a tar file, to the tar program. The tar program looks for data in its STDIN stream because the dash (-) is provided to the f option as an argument.

Another way is to decompress the gzip file and then use tar normally. This is more inefficient, and if you are short on disk space, it could cause you to run out of space:

gunzip *file***.tar.gz; tar -xf** *file***.tar**

The gunzip, gzcat, and the z option to tar can handle files with the .gz or Z extension. If you find a really old archive, you might find it with a .z extension; this is also a gzip compressed file.

If the file is not compressed with tar, it just sports a .gz extension. You can use gunzip to decompress it, like this:

gunzip file.gz

Windows Compressed Archives: Zip

The zip archive format (.zip) originally developed for DOS by Phil Katz is in use by virtually every Windows computer. Linux users can also extract and create this file format using the unzip and zip tools.

To unzip a file, just use the unzip command:

```
[alberto@digital /tmp]$ unzip file.zip
Archive:  file.zip
   creating: nsmail/
 extracting: nsmail/Drafts
  inflating: nsmail/.Drafts.summary
  inflating: nsmail/Trash
  inflating: nsmail/.Trash.summary
  inflating: nsmail/Sent
  inflating: nsmail/.Sent.summary
 extracting: nsmail/Unsent Messages
  inflating: nsmail/.Unsent Messages.summary
  inflating: nsmail/Inbox
  inflating: nsmail/.Inbox.summary
```

LISA: Linux Installation and System Administration Utility

In This Chapter

➤ Basic Functions of LISA

➤ Verbose System Analysis

➤ Software Package Administration

➤ System Configuration

➤ Network Configuration Area

Caldera OpenLinux includes an administration and configuration tool called LISA. LISA provides an interface to user management, package installation, and system configuration. Some of these tasks are described in other sections because it is faster and more powerful to use the host programs directly rather than use them through LISA. LISA is not freely distributed software, so it is not a common part of other Linux distributions. For simple networks, it provides access to all the common aspects of system and software configuration.

To use LISA, you must be logged in as root. LISA provides a UI through a console; therefore, system configuration can be done even if you are not using the X Window system. Navigation and operation are done using the arrow keys to select command options. The Enter key is used to choose selected commands, and the Esc key is used to go up a level or to exit the program. On screens that display controls, you can use the Spacebar to mark a highlighted option.

Basic Functions of LISA

LISA groups its functionality into three categories:

➤ System Analysis

➤ Software Package Administration

➤ System Configuration

The utility also provides a help system that discusses several topics of interest for system administrators. You should browse this section for additional information and help resources.

Here's the main screen it presents when you start it up.

The main LISA screen. Use your arrow keys to highlight a category and press Enter to go there. Press Esc to exit the program. For viewing online help about using LISA, press F1. Detailed information about the current selection can be obtained by pressing F2.

Verbose System Analysis

The system analysis area can give you information about your hardware and configuration settings. This information is useful to assess your current hardware and configuration settings.

The system analysis area is subdivided into several other areas:

➤ **Automatic System Analysis**: This area displays basic system information, such as when the system was last started, the current load, the host name, and the IP address of your computer.

➤ **Automatic Kernel Analysis**: The kernel analysis displays information on the kernel currently in use on your system. It includes information such as kernel version, who built it, the compiler used for building it, the file systems that it supports, and current devices.

➤ **Automatic Hardware Analysis**: The hardware area displays the more detailed information about your hardware, such as the type of processor installed, the amount of RAM, the size of the swap disk, information about your graphics card, disk drives, PCMCIA, and other hardware devices.

➤ **Automatic Partition Analysis**: This area displays information on the disk partitions in your computer. It lists the partitions by their device names and provides the size and type for each of the partitions.

➤ **Automatic Network Analysis**: The network area provides information about your network devices and configuration. It displays information on the traffic handled by your Ethernet devices and detailed configuration information (IP, netmask, broadcast address, and so on). In addition, it displays the current routing table. (This information shows how packets are forwarded from your computer to other networks.)

➤ **Display Boot Process Messages**: This area displays the boot messages from the last boot. Checking this area after installing a new kernel can tell you if your hardware was recognized properly. When your computer boots, it is very hard to follow these messages because they scroll by so quickly. This information is also available from /var/log/messages, but that file includes every boot plus other running information. The Boot Process area is more succinct.

➤ **Display Script Configuration File**: This area displays the /etc/lst.cnf file. This file contains information that packages use to find out information about your system. You should not edit this file by hand. It makes for interesting (or boring) reading, depending on your interests.

➤ **Display System Configuration File**: This area displays another configuration file, /etc/system.cnf, used by the system to configure itself. You should not change this file by hand.

Software Package Administration

This area is a front end to RPM (discussed in Chapter 20, "Installing Programs and Applications"). You can use LISA to perform tasks similar to what you can do with RPM. For novice users, this could be an easier way to perform those tasks.

The Software Package Administration area subdivides into four sections:

➤ **Select installation source:** This allows you to select the source for the RPM packages. You can install packages using a path or a specific CD-ROM on the local hard disk or available through the Network via NFS. At the time of this writing Caldera has a public NFS server available at IP 207.179.39.2; the path is /OpenLinux-1.3. You can use this method to upgrade and install new packages provided you have the bandwidth. This method for installation relies on fast network access, so PPP connection via a modem is probably not fast enough for this.

➤ **Information about the available software packages:** This area displays a screen listing all the installed packages. Select one to see the details. This is similar to going into RPM and issuing rpm -qi *packagename*.

➤ **Installation of additional software packages:** You can install additional packages using this area if you provide an installation path (CD-ROM or NFS) volume. This is an installation interface to RPM.

➤ **Remove software packages that have already been installed:** This is a de-installation interface to RPM.

System Configuration

The system configuration area provides a simplified interface to configuring your system. This is much easier than mucking with configuration files directly. As usual, you should understand what you are doing, or you could make your system unbootable.

The System Configuration area subdivides into four major areas:

➤ Hardware Configuration Area

➤ System Configuration Area

➤ Network Configuration Area

➤ Boot Manager Configuration

Hardware Configuration Area

The hardware configuration area provides other configuration screens for configuring your disks, keyboard, modem, mouse, printer, tape drives, and the X11 Server:

➤ **Diskette drives:** Provides options for specifying the drives you have installed.

➤ **Hard disks:** Provides options for configuring a disk, changing partition information, and formatting new disks.

➤ **Keyboard map:** Allows you to pick your keyboard locale map.

➤ **Modem:** Allows you to select your modem type and configuration.

➤ **Mouse:** Select and configure your mouse.

➤ **Printer:** You can easily add a printer to your system in this area. Printer drivers are provided for the more popular printers. If yours is not listed, don't despair. Choosing a similar model from your manufacturer might do the trick. Also, check http://www.caldera.com for additional printer configuration tips and instructions.

➤ **CD-ROM:** Provides a list of CD-ROMs that you can use and configure with Linux.

➤ **Streamer:** Allows you to configure your tape backup drive.

➤ **X11 Server:** Allows you to select the X11 server appropriate for your video card and create a customized configuration file.

246

System Configuration Area

The system configuration area provides an interface for the following:

➤ **User Administration:** You can add, delete, and manage users and groups, as well as set default values for users added through LISA. This interface is very serviceable for novice users. The LISA user administration area doesn't currently take advantage of UPG schemes, which simplify user collaboration. For more information, see Chapter 18, "Users, Groups, and Passwords."

➤ **Configuring the Mount Table:** This provides you with an interface to modify the /etc/fstab file for adding network mounts.

➤ **Configure the Swap Area:** This area allows you to format a partition designated as a swap partition and add it to the list of swap areas. Linux supports multiple swap partitions.

➤ **Set Hostname:** Provides you with an interface to assign the host name of the machine. The information you enter here is propagated at boot time through scripts. This is the preferred way to set the name and domain of your computer. Use a fully qualified domain name such as host.domain.dom.

➤ **Configure Timezone:** Allows you to configure how the hardware clock on your computer should be read. If you have a dual boot computer, more than likely your other operating system (OS) sets the clock to the local time. UNIX and UNIX-like systems typically have their clock set to GMT (Greenwich Mean Time) and then calculate your local time based on your time zone. With this control, you can tell Linux how to read your clock so that you can share it with other OSs.

➤ **Configure daemons/server autostart:** This screen allows you to enable and disable services that start when your computer boots. If you are not using a service, it is best to leave it off, saving your resources. You should only disable things that you know are not necessary for the proper use of your computer, or some failures will occur.

➤ **Kernel module administration:** This area displays information about modules available to your kernel. From here you can add and remove modules. The names of the modules displayed are cryptic, so some familiarity with the modules is helpful. You should take a look at Chapter 24, "Customizing Your Linux Kernel." Familiarity with the kernel configuration programs might be helpful.

Network Configuration Area

This area configures various network options, from your network card to services that you need to collaborate on a network. The basic subareas follow:

➤ Add a computer to the host table

➤ Configure network access

➤ Configure General Network Services

247

Host Table Configuration

This option allows you to view and manipulate the /etc/hosts file via an interface. It has commands to

➤ Display the current /etc/hosts file

➤ Add a new entry to the /etc/hosts file

➤ Delete an entry from the /etc/hosts file

The /etc/hosts file keeps track of computers on your network so that users can reference them by name instead of by their IP address. If your network is large, you will not use /etc/hosts; you will use a Domain Name System (DNS) system to provide the name-to-IP and IP-to-name translations. Without a translation service like that provided by the /etc/hosts file or DNS, you will need to know the IP address of every machine with which you want to communicate.

If you have a small network (a tiny area network, or TAN) for several PCs at home, you can use /etc/hosts to provide the name translation that your Linux box will need to be able to reach your other computers via TCP/IP. (Note that TAN is not a technical term, but I vote that it should be. Many homes are starting to have multiple computers wired together.)

Network Access Configuration

The Network Access Configuration area allows you to configure your Ethernet card and to enter router information.

It provides two options:

➤ Configure Network Card

➤ Enter Router

Information about your network should be added or modified using this component.

General Network Services Configuration

The General Network Services area allows you to configure your network cards, basic network services like DNS, NIS, and email.

It has three subareas:

➤ **Configure Domain Name Service:** This area allows you to define your DNS server.

➤ **Configure NIS:** This allows you to configure your workstation to use NIS (Network Information Services) as a client or as a server.

➤ **Select a Mail Transfer Agent:** This area allows you to configure your preferred mail transfer agent. Currently it only provides one option: sendmail.

Boot Manager Configuration

This area displays information about lilo (the Linux Loader). On systems with multiple partitions, this will allow you to configure the boot partition and other settings. You will learn about lilo in Chapter 24.

System Monitoring: Keeping an Eye on Your System

In This Chapter

➤ Monitoring Memory

➤ Monitoring Processes

➤ Monitoring Your Disk

➤ Log Files

Many processes run on your system. In this chapter, you will get an overview on how you can monitor and control what your system is doing. For the most part, you won't need to use any of these commands unless you suspect a problem or are trying to figure out how to fine-tune your system. Nevertheless, it's very cool to know that you can look at different things to determine problems with performance or security, or just to keep an eye on what's going on.

In terms of performance, Linux is fairly lean and mean as far as operating systems (OSs) go. In fact, it puts many other expensive OSs to shame. Although additional CPU speed will no doubt make your computer faster, additional RAM is likely to make more of an impact in terms of how fast you think things are happening. The single thing that can slow your computer the most is not having enough RAM for the programs you typically run at the same time. Linux makes do when it doesn't have enough RAM by *swapping*.

Swapping copies data and programs currently in your computer's memory (RAM) to disk is known as *virtual memory*. This makes room in the computer's real memory (RAM) for another process to do whatever it needs to. When the swapped task needs to execute again, the Linux kernel puts it back in RAM, swapping out some other process. The amount of processes and tasks you can run depends on the amount of space you have assigned to your swap disk (virtual memory) and the amount of RAM you have installed. It is possible for you to run out of space on your swap disk, and at such a point, some programs will stop working. As you can tell, swapping doesn't sound like something you want happening on your computer. Swapping can slow your computer to a crawl; you can tell when this is happening if you hear your hard disk thrashing (making noise all the time). The more RAM you have on your computer, the more programs you can run at the same time without swapping.

Monitoring Memory

There are several programs that can tell you what is going on with your computer's memory.

How Much Memory: free

The simplest of these programs is called free. It displays how much memory you have available both in real RAM and as virtual memory, as in the following code:

```
[alberto@digital alberto]$ free
                total        used        free      shared     buffers
➥cached
Mem:            38956       10196       28760        8468         836
➥5292
-/+ buffers/cache:          4068       34888
Swap:           39276           0       39276
```

Procinfo

Procinfo displays similar information as free, plus a bunch more. Information displayed by procinfo is collected by the kernel in the /proc directory. Here's a screen dump of what is displayed by my lightly loaded Linux laptop:

```
[alberto@digital alberto]$ procinfo
Linux 2.0.33 (root@buildmeister.caldera.com) (gcc 2.7.2.3) #1
➥[digital]

Memory:        Total        Used        Free      Shared     Buffers
➥Cached
Mem:           38956       10316       28640        8540         836
➥5356

Swap:          39276           0       39276
```

```
Bootup: Sat Oct 03 09:46:52 1998    Load average: 0.00 0.01 0.00 2/32
➥544

user  :        0:00:07.88   0.2%  page in :      5623  disk 1:      1563r
➥633w
nice  :        0:00:00.00   0.0%  page out:       787
system:        0:00:11.74   0.2%  swap in :         1
idle  :        1:23:49.60  99.6%  swap out:         0
uptime:        1:24:09.21         context :     31137

irq  0:    504922 timer           irq  8:          0
irq  1:         2 keyboard        irq  9:          1
irq  2:         0 cascade [4]     irq 10:          1
irq  3:      1872 smc91c92_cs     irq 11:          1 i82365
irq  4:         1                 irq 12:          0
irq  5:         1                 irq 13:          1 math error
irq  6:         2                 irq 14:      12829 ide0+
irq  7:         1                 irq 15:          0
```

In addition to your current memory usage, it tells you when your system was last booted and its load average for the last 1, 5, and 15 minutes (0.00, 0.01, and 0.00). This information is followed by the number of runnable processes, total number of processes (2/32 on the listing), and the last process to run (544).

Next, procinfo displays information about the time the system has spent in user code, system code, or idle. *Nice time* is user code that is running with a lower priority. It also gives you the total time the machine has been up.

The next column displays information about virtual memory and disk activity. Page in and page out indicate amount of data that has moved in or out of a disk and into memory. One page is equal to 1K of data. Swap in and swap out indicate the number of pages swapped from disk to memory and from memory to disk. Context, as you can see in the preceding screen dump, is the number of context switches that have taken place. The disk column (it display more disks if you have more than one) will show the number of reads (1564r) and the number of writes (633w) since the system was booted.

This is followed by information on activity of devices connected to IRQ, such as keyboard or serial ports. Procinfo should also be able to display additional information on modules (kernel packages that are not loaded until needed) and activity for other devices if you supply the -a flag. At the time this book was written, the version of procinfo shipped with COL 1.3 was broken and didn't display this information.

Monitoring Processes

Your system is continuously running processes. To get an idea of what is going on with your system, there are a number of programs that you can use.

Listing the Current Top Processes: *top*

Top gives you a real-time look into what your computer is doing. After you start it up, it will refresh once per second, displaying information about the principal processes on the computer.

Here's a sample screen:

```
20:33:53 up  2:05,  2 users,  load average: 0.17, 0.07, 0.02
35 processes: 34 sleeping, 1 running, 0 zombie, 0 stopped
CPU states:  4.6% user,  6.9% system,  0.0% nice, 88.6% idle
Mem:   38956K av,  12376K used,  26580K free,  10640K shrd,    1156K
➥buff
Swap:  39276K av,      0K used,  39276K free                    5908K
➥cached

    PID USER     PRI  NI  SIZE  RSS SHARE STAT  LIB %CPU %MEM   TIME
➥COMMAND
    655 alberto   20   0   612  612   452 S       0  9.7  1.5   0:10 top
    656 root       8   0   592  592   436 R       0  1.7  1.5   0:00 top
      1 root       0   0   340  340   268 S       0  0.0  0.8   0:02
➥init
      2 root       0   0     0    0     0 SW      0  0.0  0.0   0:00
➥kflushd
      3 root     -12 -12     0    0     0 SW<     0  0.0  0.0   0:00
➥kswapd
    444 alberto    0   0   696  696   404 S       0  0.0  1.7   0:00
➥login
    363 root       0   0   344  344   272 S       0  0.0  0.8   0:00
➥getty
    177 root       0   0   304  304   240 S       0  0.0  0.7   0:00
➥rpc.rstatd
     19 root       0   0     0    0     0 SW      0  0.0  0.0   0:00
➥nfsiod
     20 root       0   0     0    0     0 SW      0  0.0  0.0   0:00
➥nfsiod
     21 root       0   0     0    0     0 SW      0  0.0  0.0   0:00
➥nfsiod
     22 root       0   0     0    0     0 SW      0  0.0  0.0   0:00
➥nfsiod
    107 root       0   0   328  328   260 S       0  0.0  0.8   0:00
➥inetd
```

```
      57 root      0   0   260  260   208 S      0  0.0  0.6   0:00
   ➥update
     109 bin       0   0   312  312   244 S      0  0.0  0.8   0:00
   ➥rpc.portmap
     116 root      0   0   356  356   276 S      0  0.0  0.9   0:00
   ➥syslogd
     119 root      0   0   476  476   276 S      0  0.0  1.2   0:00
   ➥klogd
```

At the beginning of the listing, top displays general information about the system. The first line displays the current time, amount of time the system has been up, number of users, and load average for the last 1, 5, and 15 minutes.

The second line displays the total number of processes running in the system and what they are doing: sleeping processes, those that are not currently doing anything; zombie processes, those that are processes that should be dead but for some reason are still around; and stopped processes.

The third line displays the various CPU states, such as how much time your computer has spent executing user or system code, or nice time. Nice time represents time spent by processes that are executing with a lower priority. These processes are represented by a positive priority because they are nice to other processes (typical priority is 0). Negative priority processes are allocated more CPU so they have a higher priority and get additional chances to run.

On the fourth and fifth lines, you see information regarding real and virtual memory. Virtual memory is the one that uses the swap disk to accommodate more processes than you can run given your RAM.

Following the general information area is a listing of all the main processes, including the ID for the process (PID) owner and priority and resource consumption for CPU and memory.

When top is running, there are a number of options you can specify to customize the information it displays. Some of the more useful are shown in Table 22.1.

Table 22.1 Top **Options**

Interactive Commands	Description
Space	Updates display
Ctrl+L	Redraws the screen
?	Prints help
i	Toggles display of idle processes
c	Toggles display of command name/line

continues

Table 22.1 Continued

Interactive Commands	Description
l	Toggles display of load average
m	Toggles display of memory information
t	Toggles display of summary information
k	Kills a task (with any signal)
r	"Renices" a task (change its current priority)
P	Sorts by CPU usage
M	Sorts by resident memory usage
T	Sorts by time/cumulative time
n	Sets the number of processes to show
s	Sets refresh rate
q	Quits

Process Status: ps

The ps (process status) command also displays similar information to what the top command offers about processes. The ps command is useful for finding the PID of a process so that you can kill or renice it. (*Renicing* a process changes its current priority. I'll talk more about renicing later in the setion "Nicing a Process: nice and renice.) To display a list of all processes running on your system, enter the following:

ps aux

This command will list all processes (including other users), using user format and including processes not associated with a terminal, like this:

```
[alberto@digital /]$ ps aux
USER      PID %CPU %MEM  SIZE   RSS TTY STAT START   TIME COMMAND
alberto   371  0.0  1.8  1072   712 p0 S   10:56   0:00 /bin/login -
➡h 192.168
alberto   372  0.0  1.6  1152   624 p0 S   10:56   0:00 -bash
alberto   566  0.0  1.8  1072   716 p1 S   11:23   0:00 /bin/login -
➡h 192.168
alberto   567  0.0  1.5  1152   620 p1 S   11:24   0:00 -bash
alberto   630  0.0  1.0   904   392 p1 S   11:41   0:00 man 7 signal
alberto   641  0.0  1.2  1124   480 p1 S   11:41   0:00 sh -c
➡/bin/gunzip -c
alberto   643  0.0  1.2  1148   500 p1 S   11:41   0:00
➡/usr/bin/less -is
alberto   657  0.0  0.9   856   372 p0 R   11:43   0:00 ps aux
alberto   658  0.0  1.0  1084   420 p0 R   11:43   0:00 more
```

```
bin         108  0.0  0.8   836   312  ?  S     09:47  0:00 rpc.portmap
daemon      160  0.0  0.8   824   324  ?  S     09:47  0:00 atd
root          1  0.0  0.8   824   340  ?  S     09:46  0:02 init
root          2  0.0  0.0     0     0  ?  SW    09:46  0:00 (kflushd)
root          3  0.0  0.0     0     0  ?  SW<   09:46  0:00 (kswapd)
root         19  0.0  0.0     0     0  ?  SW    09:46  0:00 (nfsiod)
root         20  0.0  0.0     0     0  ?  SW    09:46  0:00 (nfsiod)
root         21  0.0  0.0     0     0  ?  SW    09:46  0:00 (nfsiod)
root         22  0.0  0.0     0     0  ?  SW    09:46  0:00 (nfsiod)
root         57  0.0  0.6   804   260  ?  S     09:47  0:00 update
➥(bdflush)
root        106  0.0  0.8   824   328  ?  S     09:47  0:00 inetd
root        188  0.0  1.5  1108   604  ?  S     11:51  0:00 httpd -f
➥/etc/httpd/a
```

Killing a Process: `kill`

You are able to terminate processes using the `kill` command. The `kill` command should be used as a last resort for terminating a program that is not working correctly. The `kill` command sends a signal (there are many kinds of signals; `kill` is just one of them) to the program, which should cause it to react appropriately. Otherwise, it will get killed:

```
kill pid
```

Assuming that I wanted to kill my Web server (the `httpd` process listed previously), I would issue this command:

```
[root@digital /]# kill 188
```

If you are not the owner of the process (see the owner on the first column on the ps output), you would need to be root to kill it.

Sometimes, a rogue program will not respond properly to the default kill signal. At times like this, it is sometimes necessary to use a stronger kill, the KILL (unconditional kill) signal, also known as "signal 9" in Linux. Signal 9 is very strong medicine and should only be used when a rogue program refuses to die in any other way. To kill a program with the KILL signal in Linux, use either of the following:

```
kill -KILL pid
kill -9 pid
```

Replace *pid* with the number of the process you wish to terminate. No process can ignore or escape the KILL signal.

Some processes that run as daemon, such as httpd, can be restarted by sending them a `-HUP` (hangup) signal. The restart will make the process reread its configuration files and restart, as in the following:

```
[root@digital /]# kill -HUP 188
```

"Nicing" a process: nice *and renice*

Sometimes you'll have a big job to run—say you need to process a few hundred megs of log files for some statistical information about your Web server, perhaps. Although you might want the information fast, having the computer go all out to get it for you will adversely affect the performance of everything else in your system. It could also be that you need that job run as quickly as possible, giving everything else second priority.

To start such a process with a lower priority, just type nice before the name of the command. This will launch the command in a nice state:

```
nice dobigjob
```

With nice, it is possible to set the priority a process executes. Priorities range from 19 (the nicest program) to -20 (the highest priority). Only root can assign a high (negative) priority to a process.

Nice is set up to add 10 to the current priority of any process that by default is zero.

You can also specify a priority by providing the -n flag and a priority setting followed by the PID:

```
nice -n 12 dobigjob
```

Nice only works on jobs that have not started. To make an existing process nice, you use renice. If you want to give the Web server priority before all other processes, root can adjust it like this:

```
[root@digital httpd]# renice -10 188
188: old priority 0, new priority -10
```

Monitoring Your Disk

One thing that Linux doesn't like is running out of disk space. Monitoring your disk space is easy. There are two programs that you can use: du and df.

Finding out How Much Disk Files Consume: du

The disk usage program, du, allows you to get a listing of how much space a directory eats up, given in 1K increments. By default, it will print an entry for each directory it finds, like this:

```
[alberto@digital alberto]$ du
14        ./.seyon
3         ./lg/lg_layouts
1         ./lg/.lgDESKTOP
1         ./lg/lg3_hosts
15        ./lg
```

```
40          ./.kde/share/config
1           ./.kde/share/apps/kfm/tmp
1           ./.kde/share/apps/kfm/bookmarks
6           ./.kde/share/apps/kfm
4           ./.kde/share/apps/kdehelp
2           ./.kde/share/apps/knotes/notes
1           ./.kde/share/apps/knotes/xyalarms
5           ./.kde/share/apps/knotes
1           ./.kde/share/apps/kppp/Rules
```

To summarize output, specify the -s option, as in the following:

```
[alberto@digital alberto]$ du -s
23670    .
```

To specify specific directories or files to list, provide their names as arguments, like this:

```
[root@digital /home]# du -s *
23670    alberto
32       cool
32       digital
35       flower
583      ftp
1582     httpd
1        public
1        samba
1        test_project
```

In this example, all home directories are summarized.

Finding the Amount of Free Disk Space: df

To find the amount of disk space to devices available in your system, use the df (disk free) command, as shown in the following:

```
[root@digital /home]# df
Filesystem        1024-blocks  Used Available Capacity Mounted on
/dev/hda1             686892  606189    45223     93%    /
```

The command produces a nice table specifying how much space is available. Numbers are expressed in kilobytes.

In UNIX/Linux, just because there's free space doesn't mean that you can create files. If the file system's inode table fills up (unlikely, but possible if a disk holds a great deal of tiny files), your system would be unable to create additional files. To see how you are doing on inodes, provide the -i option to df:

```
[root@digital /home]# df -i
Filesystem          Inodes   IUsed   IFree  %IUsed Mounted on
/dev/hda1           177480   34971  142509    20%   /
```

259

If you compare the regular df output, you'll see that under normal circumstances, there are plenty of inodes left. On my disk, I have used 93% of my disk, yet only 20% of the inodes.

Log Files

Many of the programs that run in the background, Web server, email, FTP, and so on generate logs for errors or just as a record of someone accessing it. This type of information is recorded, for example, every time a user logs in or out of the system.

Monitoring Logins: last

Linux keeps very good track of users and their logins. This information is particularly useful when you are in a networked environment, and as a security precaution, you check to make sure that no "weird" traffic is going on in your machine.

By default, Linux is set up to keep track of logins and logouts. You can browse the login record using the last command.

To filter output to a specific user, provide the username as an argument to last:

```
[alberto@digital log]$ last alberto
alberto   ttyp0        192.168.0.3      Fri Oct  2 18:32     still logged
➥in
alberto   ttyp0        192.168.0.3      Fri Oct  2 18:29 - 18:32
➥(00:02)
alberto   tty2                          Fri Oct  2 15:20 - 17:01
➥(01:40)
alberto   ttyp1        192.168.0.3      Fri Oct  2 14:55 - down
➥(03:32)
alberto   ftp          192.168.0.3      Fri Oct  2 13:41 - 13:42
➥(00:00)
alberto   ftp          192.168.0.3      Fri Oct  2 13:12 - 13:28
➥(00:16)
alberto   tty1                          Fri Oct  2 13:02 - down
➥(05:25)
alberto   tty1                          Wed Sep 30 17:41 - down
➥(00:18)
alberto   tty1                          Tue Sep 29 11:10 - down
➥(00:10)
alberto   tty1                          Mon Sep 28 17:36 - down
➥(00:47)
```

The last command prints the username, the terminal used to access the system, where the user came from (IP address) if the login was remote, and the date and duration of the session.

If the log file /var/log/wtmp doesn't exist in your system, the system will not keep track of login information. To enable (or disable) this feature, just create or delete this file.

Monitoring Bad Logins: lastb

The lastb command keeps track of bad (unsuccessful) logins. To enable bad login accounting, as root create the file /var/log/btmp. You can do this using the touch command (touch /var/log/btmp).

To review bad logins, use the lastb command. Unfortunately, Caldera OpenLinux doesn't currently support lastb use.

If an account has an unusual number of bad logins, it is possible that the account is under attack by someone. Such accounts should be disabled and the user owning the account should be notified.

Disabling an Account

The easiest way to disable an account is to put an asterisk (*) before the encrypted password in the /etc/passwd file. (The password is the second field in /etc/passwd.) Fields are separated by colons (:), like this:

```
me:*Ms.7kvaAYyHbU:500:100:Me:/home/me:/bin/sh
```

If you are using shadow passwords, the easiest way to disable an account is to use usermod and expire it with a date in the past:

```
usermod -e MM/DD/YY login
[root@digital alberto]# usermod -e 09/01/98 me
```

(Usermod is introduced in Chapter 18, "Users, Groups, and Passwords.")

261

Sharing Files over the Network

<div style="border:1px solid">

In This Chapter

➤ The Network File System

➤ Using the mount and umount Commands

➤ Navigating the File System with FTP

➤ Uploading and Downloading Files

➤ Controlling File Access

</div>

Sharing files over the network allows you to collaborate more easily with others. Linux has the capability to provide file-sharing services in many ways. You can also be a client to almost all popular network file-sharing schemes.

The most popular ways for sharing files under UNIX are FTP (File Transfer Protocol), NFS (Network File System), and HTTP (the Web). Other protocols, such as Gopher, have given way to Web counterparts. Windows-based PCs share files using the SMB (Server Message Block) protocol. Linux can easily be a client to an SMB server and provides you with an FTP-like interface to a server.

If the information here should awaken your interest, feel free to read the online documentation (see Chapter 15, "Help Please"). Accessing a service (being a client) is easy. Setting up a server is slightly (a few orders of magnitude) more complicated, and entire books have been written on the various subjects. Given the limited space, I have covered what I consider the least you should need to know to publish data and to access data from other servers.

NFS

The NFS is how you share files between UNIX-based machines. Originally developed by Sun, NFS is very flexible and could be used to share information between networks. However, exporting directories to networks outside your control requires careful security considerations. By design, NFS was not intended for sharing across the Internet, but given today's high-speed communication networks, it is feasible to share files over the Net.

NFS allows a directory tree to be grafted into the file system by other computers on the network in much the same way you mount a floppy disk or CD-ROM.

One issue with NFS is that file system security is based on the same mechanism your local file system uses: User IDs (UIDs) and Group IDs (GIDs) of files. If the UID of a user accessing a remote NFS volume doesn't match the user's own, the user will lack the necessary privileges. This means that in order to use NFS effectively, there needs to be a mechanism that shares login and password information. Luckily, such a system does exist; it is called NIS (Network Information Services). A long time ago, NIS was called Yellow-Pages. Configuring NIS and NFS requires more depth of information than a few paragraphs can offer. This section will only show you how to export and import an NFS volume. For in-depth configuring information, you should consult the online documentation and how-to guides and perhaps even acquire a book on NIS and NFS. Linux implementation is fairly standard, and you should have no problem adapting that information to your system.

Exporting an NFS Volume

Before you can export NFS volumes, you'll need to enable the NFS Server services in your computer. This is done through LISA under Configure daemon/server autostart under the System Configuration area; then you'll need to reboot your computer. LISA, as you learned in Chapter 21, "LISA: Linux Installation and System Administration Utility," is a command line program that manages your hardware and software configuration for the more important portions of your system.

With NFS, you don't need to export an entire disk volume; a directory of your choosing will suffice. To export a directory, you merely need to edit the file /etc/exports. When you export a directory, you choose how you make it available and the permissions that others may have on the volume. Typically, unless you know what you are doing, you should just export the volume read-only. This way, users can see and access files, but they won't be able to modify or delete files.

```
/share        (ro,insecure,all_squash)
```

In the entry shown, /share is exported with several options; here's what they mean. The ro option requests that the file system be exported as read-only: Users will be able to see and access the files, but they won't be able to modify them. Insecure allows NFS clients that don't use a reserved port to access this volume. Typically, NFS

will want to allow only clients of the service that connect on a specific port. The all_squash options maps all the UIDs and GIDs found in the files in /share to those of the anonymous user. This setting would export the /share directory to the world!

For more information on other options, read the man page on exports.

Mounting an NFS Volume

Mounting an NFS volume is very similar to mounting a CD-ROM or floppy drive. Typically, the mount command is privileged, and only the superuser, or root, can specify it. The only way a user can mount a file system is if the mount description contains the user option on the /etc/fstab file.

The mount Command

The mount command grafts a file system in a device or in the network to a directory on your local system. If the directory has files, those files are hidden from view until the mount is removed. The file /etc/fstab contains a list of all the mounts in your computer. If a line of the fstab file contains the user option, then a nonroot user can use the mount command to mount it. It is enough to specify the name of the device or mount or its mount point to access the file system. Consider the following:

```
[root@digital nfs]# more /etc/fstab
/dev/hda1 / ext2 defaults 0 1
/proc /proc proc defaults 0 0
/dev/hda5 none swap defaults 0 0
/dev/fd0 /mnt/floppy auto user,defaults,noauto 0 0
digital:/share /net/digital nfs ro
/
```

My /etc/fstab file contains mount entries for my root partition (/dev/hda1) and for other things such as my floppy (/dev/fd0). Floppies are mountable by any user (see the user option), and they are mounted in the /mnt/floppy directory. The network mounts begin with the name of the machine, followed by a colon (:) and the path they are exporting, followed by the mount point, its type (nfs), and the ro option (read-only).

To mount my floppy, I just need to type this:

```
mount /mnt/floppy or mount /dev/fd0
```

To mount an NFS volume, it's not much different:

```
mount host:/path dir
mount -ro digital:/share /net/digital
```

If you only plan to mount an NFS volume temporarily, it isn't necessary to add it to your /etc/fstab file. However, volumes that are routinely mounted should be added both for convenience and correctness.

The umount *Command*

To remove a mount from a file system, you use the umount command. As an argument provide the mount location:

```
umount mountpath
umount /net/digital
```

FTP

In Chapter 9, "Communication: Web, FTP, Email, and News," you learned how to use KDE and Netscape to download files from FTP sites. As you can imagine, there's a command line equivalent that you can use to download files, called ftp.

FTP is both a service and an end-user tool. First, we'll take a look at how to use the ftp command, and then, we'll discuss how to enable users to use ftp to get into your machine.

Connecting to an FTP Site

The ftp command is easy to use. Just specify the name of the host to which you want to connect, like this:

```
ftp hostname
[root@digital /etc]# ftp localhost
Connected to localhost.
220 digital.bordersoft.com FTP server (Version wu-2.4.2-academ[BETA-
➥15](1) Wed J
an 7 01:03:55 MST 1998) ready.
Name (localhost:alberto): alberto
331 Password required for alberto.
Password:********
230 User alberto logged in.
Remote system type is UNIX.
Using binary mode to transfer files.
ftp> ls
200 PORT command successful.
150 Opening ASCII mode data connection for /bin/ls.
total 7931
-rw-r--r--   1 alberto   alberto      7165 Sep 16 20:48 #registrar.cgi#
-rw-------   1 alberto   alberto        14 Sep  1 13:22 #rm.sh#
drwxr-xr-x  24 alberto   alberto      2048 Sep 26 15:01 .
drwxr-xr-x  10 root      root         1024 Sep 25 21:39 ..
-rw-rw-r--   1 alberto   alberto       998 Sep 26 15:42 .bash_history
```

After you connect, you are required to log in. If you have an account on the system that you are connecting to, you can use your login and password, and you'll be taken to your home directory. If you don't have an account, you can try to log in as the user "ftp" (or sometimes "anonymous") and with a password matching your email address. This is called anonymous FTP. Anonymous FTP is restricted to a specific area of the system.

Navigating the Remote File System Using the FTP Program

After you log in, you can use a number of commands. These should be familiar to you: ls, cd, and exit. You can use these commands to move about the system as you would normally do when using a shell. To exit the FTP session, just use the exit command.

Downloading a File

To download a file, first make sure that you are using the binary mode to transfer the file by typing the bin command. If the text-based file you are transferring is coming from a foreign operating system (OS), such as Windows, you might want to set your download mode to ascii by typing the ascii command. The ascii command will translate line ending sequences into the proper settings for your OS. (Typically, it converts carriage returns and newline pairs into a single newline character.) Consider the following code:

```
ftp> bin
200 Type set to I.
ftp> get ziptool.rpm
local: ziptool.rpm remote: ziptool.rpm
200 PORT command successful.
150 Opening BINARY mode data connection for ziptool.rpm (6806 bytes).
226 Transfer complete.
6806 bytes received in 0.0355 secs (1.9e+02 Kbytes/sec)
```

To download a file, just type the get command followed by a filename. If the file is large, you might want to see a progress indicator. You can enable the indicator by typing the hash command before you start the download. As the file download progresses, you'll see hash marks (#) printed on your screen. When you set a command like bin, ascii, and hash, they stay active until you reset them. To turn hash off, enter the hash command a second time. The bin and ascii commands can be toggled by setting one and then the other. Note that if you transfer binary data in ascii mode, your file will be garbage.

```
ftp> hash
Hash mark printing on (1024 bytes/hash mark).
ftp> get ziptool.rpm
local: ziptool.rpm remote: ziptool.rpm
200 PORT command successful.
```

```
150 Opening BINARY mode data connection for ziptool.rpm (6806 bytes).
######
226 Transfer complete.
6806 bytes received in 0.00224 secs (3e+03 Kbytes/sec)
```

Downloading Multiple Files

You can download multiple files with one command. When you issue the mget command followed by some regular expression, FTP will ask you if you want to download each of the matches. For a description on how to use regular expressions, see Chapter 14, "Putting the Shell to Work." The syntax looks like this:

```
mget *.rpm
```

If you want to download the files without being prompted for each one, type the command prompt. This will toggle interactive mode on or off.

Changing the Directory Where You Want to Put Your Files

To change the directory where your downloads are landing, type lcd (local cd) followed by the path to the directory you want to go into, like this:

```
lcd /tmp
```

This will put any subsequent downloads into the /tmp directory on my local machine.

Resuming a Download

Sometimes as you download files, the connection will drop. Don't despair. Most sites support the capability to restart a download right where you left off. To do this, type reget and the name of the file you were downloading. For reget to work, the local file must be shorter than the remote file, and it must be in your current directory on the local system. The syntax looks like this:

```
ftp> reget ziptool.rpm
local: ziptool.rpm remote: ziptool.rpm
200 PORT command successful.
350 Restarting at 6806. Send STORE or RETRIEVE to initiate transfer.
150 Opening BINARY mode data connection for ziptool.rpm (6806 bytes).
226 Transfer complete.
```

Uploading Files

To upload a file, you use the put command and must have permissions to write to the remote directory. The syntax looks like this:

```
ftp> put file.zip
local: file.zip remote: file.zip
200 PORT command successful.
150 Opening BINARY mode data connection for file.zip.
226 Transfer complete.
8269 bytes sent in 0.0315 secs (2.6e+02 Kbytes/sec)
```

Uploading Multiple Files

To upload multiple files, use the mput command using a regular expression. Any matching file will be uploaded to the server.

Hosting an FTP Service

Although most of the time you'll be a client to FTP sites, you might want to make some files available through FTP. To enable FTP access from other machines, you must enable the FTP service in /etc/inetd.conf. For information on how to enable these services, see the "Network Services" note.) After you enable the service in /etc/inetd.conf, you can use FTP to get to your machine and use your login and password.

To enable an FTP service, you need to ensure that the wu-ftpd package is installed. If you did a standard installation, it was installed.

The FTP service installed by default in Linux is called wu-ftpd. Wu-ftpd was originally developed at the Washington University in St. Louis. This robust FTP server software is used by sites that support thousands of users.

Providing anonymous FTP is enabled by default as your /etc/passwd contains an entry for the FTP user. Users who log in to the system as FTP login are put into the /home/ftp directory. This directory is treated differently by the FTP daemon (the software running the FTP service). As far as anonymous users are concerned, /home/ftp looks like a root file system. Users cannot change directories outside it and only have access to directories within it. The FTP daemon accomplishes this by changing the server's root for the FTP process to the /home/ftp directory. This directory contains minimum/etc and /bin directories with just enough information and software to allow anonymous users access to the system. You should not modify the contents of the /home/ftp/etc and /home/ftp/bin directories unless you know what you are doing.

To publish files, as root, create a directory inside /home/ftp/pub and make sure that permissions for the directory are 755. Anonymous users will be able to download files from there but not write to the (put) file.

269

Network Services: /etc/inetd and tcpd

Network services are handled by a program called inetd. Inetd listens for network connections, and when it gets one, it makes sure that the right server is connected with the client.

Because of security concerns, you might want to offer certain services to only certain clients. For example, you might not want everyone to be able to try to connect to your system via FTP. To accommodate such needs, there's a program called tcpd that handles requests for programs like FTP and Telnet. When a connection request is received, the system tries to determine if it should allow the connection based on where the user is coming from. Tcpd consults the files /etc/hosts.allow and /etc/hosts.deny to see if the client (the system trying to connect) falls into any of these categories. By default, any client not explicitly allowed is explicitly denied access.

To enable access for other hosts, you'll need to edit the /etc/hosts.allow file. Information on the configuration for these files is found in the online manual. (Do a man 5 hosts_access to read about the configuration format.)

For example, to enable access to hosts from all domains for all services, you would enter the following in the /etc/hosts.allow file:

ALL: ALL

Read the man page for tcpd, inetd, and hosts_access for more information.

Creating an incoming directory (one in which anonymous users can drop files) is a little trickier. If your computer is on the Internet and you put such a directory without taking adequate precautions, it will be no time before your computer becomes a distribution node for pirated software and questionable documents and images. To create an incoming directory less susceptible to this type of problem, enter the following:

```
[root@digital /root]# cd /home/ftp/pub
[root@digital pub]# mkdir incoming
[root@digital pub]# chmod 1733 incoming
```

This will create a directory that allows anonymous users to place files, but they won't be able to list the files that they uploaded. Users who know the name of a file in the incoming directory will still be able to download it, but they won't be able to list the contents of the directory.

There are many options and restrictions that you can put on anonymous users to control access to the site, including controlling the number of concurrent users and where they are coming from. Ftpd also has a number of options to log everything that comes in and goes out. To take advantage of these features, read the man documentation on ftpd. (Do an rpm -qd wu-ftpd to see a list of all the documentation and where it is installed.)

HTTP

HTTP stands for Hypertext Transfer Protocol. This is the protocol that drives the Web. When you load a file into your Web browser, you are using HTTP. HTTP provides a very secure way of publishing information for others to see. If you want to share information, your Linux system is more than capable of serving to thousands of users.

There are many popular Web servers that run on a variety of systems. By far, the most popular is Apache. Apache is a freely available Web server software distributed under the GNU Public License. Apache powers about 50% of all Web servers on the Internet. If that figure doesn't seem high to you, consider that the second most popular server is Microsoft's Internet Information Server, which only absorbs 22% of the market. Netscape servers follow at 8%, and the rest of the server software is under 2% and powers less than 1% of the sites. These statistics are based on more than 3 million Web sites (see www.netcraft.com). Apache is very good indeed. Your system already has it running, even if you didn't know it.

Configuring an Apache Server

Apache's default configuration, as installed, is fairly adequate and secure. If you need to tinker and you are maintaining a public Web server, you should really take a look at a book on Apache. A good one is my book *The Apache Server Survival Guide*, ISBN: 1-57521-175-0. It covers all the topics that you need to know about setting up and maintaining an Internet server. It doesn't assume much but provides in-depth information and many examples. It also orients you on HTML and CGI programming.

Apache's configuration files can be found at /etc/httpd/apache/conf. Configuration of an Apache server is done in three text files: httpd.conf, access.conf, and srm.conf. Configuration for Apache is straightforward. Directives appear one per line. The first word on the line is the directive; the rest are the parameters or configuration settings. Fire up your editor and open /etc/httpd/apache/conf/httpd.conf to see what I am talking about. You'll see the following:

> ➤ The httpd.conf file is the primary Web server configuration file. This file sets the default behavior of the server, such as its name, the port it runs under, the location of configuration, logs, and error files. Without getting into the depths of it, here is the only directive that you need to change in this file:
>
> ServerName—This should reflect a valid DNS name for your system. If you don't know the fully qualified DNS name for your system, leave this as localhost.

➤ The `srm.conf` configuration file keeps track of where information published by the Web server resides. It also provides a mapping between icons and files that the Web server uses when generating automatic file indexes. There are two directives that are important for you to know about:

`DocumentRoot`—This directive specifies where your HTML documents are found. By default on Linux, this points to `/home/httpd/html`. This directory contains HTML help Linux documentation pages (if you are running Caldera's distribution) or the Apache Server documentation.

`UserDir`—This directive specifies the name of a directory users can create in their accounts. Files in this directory are accessible using a browser and a URL such as `http://servername/~username/` (note the tilde (~) before the username).

`DirectoryIndex`—This directive specifies the name of files that will be loaded when a user requests a directory instead of an HTML file. If you take a look at the URL in the preceding item (`http://servername/~username/`), this URL doesn't request a file, it requests a directory. (This is similar to when you request `http://www.caldera.com`; this is just the name of a machine!). This directive specifies a filename to search when incomplete URLs are specified; if the file is found, it is sent to the browser. Otherwise, the server will generate an automatic server index, listing all files contained in the directory. You can define multiple `DirectoryIndex` files like this:

```
          DirectoryIndex index.html index.htm dir.html
➥dir.txt
```

➤ Other files such as `mime.types` provide information to the server as to the MIME (Multipurpose Internet Mail Extensions) format of files per their file extension. When a Web server sends a file to the browser, the Web server tells the browser the type of data it is sending through a MIME type.

Maintaining a Web server or any other sort of public Internet service is serious business. In the coziness of an intranet, you only have to worry about security from your peers. On the Internet, you need to worry about the entire world. There are some evil people out there that could do serious damage to your system.

Controlling Access

Another skill that you'll need when publishing Web pages is to protect materials from general users, unless they are able to provide an acceptable login and password. This is very simple to do, and it requires that you do a couple of things.

To protect a number of documents, create a directory. You can call it anything you want. Inside this directory, create a file called `.htaccess` (note that the name of the file begins with a period [.]).

Inside this file, put the following text:

```
AuthUserFile /home/yourusername/.htpasswd
AuthName Alberto's Secured Area
AuthType Basic
require  valid-user
```

`AuthUserFile` specifies the location for a password file that will be used to validate users. Note that this file lives outside the `public_html` directory or the `DocumentRoot` tree. Replace *yourusername* with your login name.

`AuthName` is a name that identifies this set of documents. It's typically displayed by the browser on the password request dialog.

`AuthType` defines the type of authentication used. We'll use `Basic`.

`Require` specifies that the only authenticated users should be let in (valid-user option).

After you put this file in the secured directory, all files and directories under this are protected.

Creating an htpassword *File*

Web server passwords are managed by a tool called `htpasswd`. This tool exists in `/home/httpd/bin/htpasswd`. The arguments are simple:

```
htpasswd [-c] filename username
```

The –c option creates the password file using the *filename* specified (in my case, I defined mine in /home/*yourusername*/.htpasswd), followed by the name of the user to add to the file:

```
[alberto@digital stuff]$ /home/httpd/bin/htpasswd -c
➥/home/alberto/.htpasswd alberto
Adding password for alberto.
New password:**********
Re-type new password: **********
```

That's all. Anyone trying to access the directory will be asked to authenticate. If the authentication succeeds, they have access to the page(s).

SMB: Sharing Disks and Printers to PCs

If your computer is on a heterogeneous network, more than likely there are Windows-based PCs sharing the network with you. Linux, again, can provide file sharing to other OSs, such as those running Windows. Windows PCs see the file shares as another PC sharing a network drive. As a client, Linux can connect to a Windows PC, allowing you to transfer files to your Linux box.

SAMBA is the common name for the service that allows you to do this. SAMBA is an acronym for the SMB protocol (Server Message Block), which allows Windows-based PC access to disks and printers from Linux and from Linux to Windows-based PC printers and disks.

This service is complex and well-developed; however, it has many gotchas—especially if you are trying to connect to Windows NT 4.0 SP3 or Windows 98 computers.

To use SAMBA, you first need to download the latest version from `http://samba.gorski.net/samba/samba.html`. The versions shipped by most manufacturers are out of date. There are RPM packages you can install available right at the site.

Accessing a PC Network Drive from Linux: `smbclient`

You use `smbclient` to access a PC network drive. The command has many options, and some systems—such as Windows NT and Windows 95—are picky about wanting to talk with Linux. For this reason I will refer you to the SAMBA documentation in the `/usr/doc/samba-1.9.18p8-Caldera.1` directory for more information on installation and configuration.

Listing Services

To see a list of the services provided by a PC host, provide the `-L` option to the `smbclient` command. By default, Linux will attach your UNIX login name. If your login is different on the PC, specify it with the `-U` option, like this:

```
smbclient -L smbhostname -U pcloginname
```

It is possible that some hosts will give you grief if you supply a login name that is not in all caps. Here's a transcript of such a session with an NT4.0 Workstation. Note that the NT host required me to provide a password:

```
[alberto@digital alberto]$ smbclient -L pri -U ARICART
Added interface ip=192.168.0.2 bcast=192.168.0.255 nmask=255.255.255.0
Got a positive name query response from 192.168.0.1 ( 192.168.0.1 )
Server time is Sat Sep 26 18:39:17 1998
Timezone is UTC-5.0
Password: ********
Domain=[WORKGROUP] OS=[Windows NT 4.0] Server=[NT LAN Manager 4.0]
security=user

Server=[PRI] User=[] Workgroup=[WORKGROUP] Domain=[]

        Sharename      Type      Comment
        ---------      ----      -------
        ADMIN$         Disk      Remote Admin
        C$             Disk      Default share
```

```
            CD              Disk
            HD              Disk
            HPLaserJ        Printer    HP LaserJet 4/4M Plus PS 600
            IPC$            IPC        Remote IPC
            print$          Disk       Printer Drivers
            shared          Disk
This machine has a browse list:

            Server                 Comment
            ---------              -------
            DIGITAL                Samba 1.9.18p8
            PRI

This machine has a workgroup list:

            Workgroup              Master
            ---------              -------
            WORKGROUP              PRI
```

From the listing, I know that this machine has several resources I can use, including a printer and access to a disk.

Accessing a Disk

To access the shared resource (called shared), use the smbclient program again—this time without the –L option and providing a full network path, like this:

```
[alberto@digital alberto]$ smbclient \\\\pri\\shared -U ARICART
Added interface ip=192.168.0.2 bcast=192.168.0.255 nmask=255.255.255.0
Got a positive name query response from 192.168.0.1 ( 192.168.0.1 )
Server time is Sat Sep 26 18:48:33 1998
Timezone is UTC-5.0
Password: ******
Domain=[WORKGROUP] OS=[Windows NT 4.0] Server=[NT LAN Manager 4.0]
security=user
smb: \> ls
  .                                 D        0  Sat Sep 26 18:25:35
➥1998
  ..                                D        0  Sat Sep 26 18:25:35
➥1998
  adir                              D        0  Sat Sep 26 18:25:06
➥1998
  Afile.rtf                         A     1972  Sat Sep 26 18:25:35
➥1998

            49580 blocks of size 65536. 33307 blocks available
```

```
smb: \> get Afile.rtp
ERRDOS - ERRbadfile (File not found.) opening remote file \Afile.rtp
smb: \> get Afile.rtf
getting file \Afile.rtf of size 1972 bytes as Afile.rtf (50.6783 kb/s)
↪(average
50.6785 kb/s)
```

Note that four slashes are used, instead of the typical two. That is because the slash is an escape character for the shell; doubling it up actually results in the correct network path: \\pri\shared.

After login, you are left in an environment very similar to the FTP program described in the section "FTP." You can use the ls, cd, get, mget, more, put, rm, and many others. To see a complete list, enter a question mark (?) or type help.

Customizing Your Linux Kernel

In This Chapter

➤ Customizing your kernel with LISA

➤ Customizing your kernel by recompiling

➤ Building a new kernel

➤ Configuring, compiling, and installing new kernels and modules

Customizing Your Linux Kernel with LISA

The easiest way to customize your kernel is to add and remove driver modules using LISA. The standard installation of Caldera OpenLinux contains a large number of drivers for various types of hardware. These drivers can be inserted and removed from your system automatically by LISA without the need for further work on your part. Although some users—such as those requiring advanced power management—will need to recompile their kernel to make use of their hardware, others will be served just as well by the kernel-management facilities offered by LISA.

For more information on using LISA to configure your system, see Chapter 21, "LISA: Linux Installation and System Administration Utility."

Customizing Your Linux Kernel by Recompiling

Kernel configuration sounds like a scary topic, but it really isn't. The one caveat is that if you are not careful, you can make your system unbootable. But then again, understanding Linux and avoiding problems are the reasons why you bought this book.

As you already know, the Linux kernel installed on your system by default seems to provide support for most of the hardware installed by most machines. This is very cool because it enabled you to do a great number of things before you even knew that kernel building was something you wanted to do. If you are happy with what you've got, read no further, you don't need to customize your kernel. Even Caldera will tell you this.

Customizing your kernel can improve the performance of your system, but given today's speedy boxes it is not likely that you'll be able to tell a great difference between a custom kernel and a generic one. There are several reasons why you'd want to build your own kernel:

➤ You have a laptop and need power management support.

➤ You want to enable file system quotas.

➤ You need Symmetric Multi-Processing support.

➤ Amateur Radio Network drivers.

➤ You want a kernel that is customized for your processor.

➤ You have some other special hardware or needs.

Kernel building is especially important if you have special hardware, such as a laptop. Building a new kernel for a laptop enables you to include support for the power management features provided by Linux.

If you want to see how fast Linux can go, customizing the kernel gives you a glimpse of this. A custom kernel requires less memory, speeds up the bootup process, and increases performance. The kernel will be built to take advantage of your processor (instead of an i386 processor); that alone will help zip a few things along.

In order for you to be able to build your kernel, you need to have a compiler installed. Warning: this process takes a while, and the actual compilation itself can take an hour, depending on the hardware you have and how much you need to support.

Getting Started

There are several steps that you need to accomplish in order to build and install a new kernel:

1. Selecting drivers and feature support
2. Compiling the kernel and any necessary modules
3. Copying the kernel to its proper place
4. Installing the new modules
5. Configuring and reinstalling LILO to see the new kernel
6. Configuring the new modules and rebooting

```
In addition to the gcc compiler, you need the following packages.
(Note that the version of your package might be better than the one I
list.) The linux-source-doc package is not necessary to build the
kernel but is good to have around. If you do a standard install, this
package is already on your disk; otherwise it is included on your
CD.linux-kernel-include-2.0.35-1.i386.rpm
linux-source-common-2.0.35-1.i386.rpm
linux-source-i386-2.0.35-1.i386.rpm
linux-source-doc-2.0.35-1.i386.rpm
```

If you do a standard install, your kernel sources will be located in the /usr/src/linux directory. This directory is just a link to the current kernel sources Linux-2.0.35 or whatever you have.

As usual, it is a good idea to read the documentation included with the kernel. A nice README file contains information on how to build the kernel. Some steps might be missing or not as well elaborated, but between this book and that document you will have enough support to build your own kernel.

Kernel Building Approaches

As you configure your kernel, you'll be offered the option to include support of a feature in two different ways:

➤ Building the support into the kernel itself
➤ Building the support as an external module

Use built-in support instead of module support when the supported device is required in order to boot your computer. If you have a specific networking or SCSI card, and you make use of that card as the computer is starting, compile support into the kernel. This makes the kernel bigger, so limit it to things you know will be loaded no matter what.

Features that you might use on and off (such as PPP support) might be better as a module. When not in use for extended periods of time the module can be removed from memory using LISA, thus releasing your valuable resources.

Caldera uses the module approach for its generic kernel. If your hardware requires the service, the module is loaded. If not, it just occupies a little of your disk.

Configuring the New Kernel

Kernel compiling is done with special tools included in the Linux kernel source. You have three tools to choose from:

➤ config

➤ menuconfig

➤ xconfig

Config is an interactive script that asks you questions for each of the options about which it needs information to configure properly. I find an interactive program is better for this sort of exercise. Use menuconfig if you are using a shell or xconfig if you are working under X (or KDE as it is also called).

To start the configuration tool, first change to the /usr/src/linux directory and enter:

```
make toolname
```

Xconfig provides buttons to configure the various options.

Linux Kernel Configuration

- Code maturity level options
- Loadable module support
- General setup
- Floppy, IDE, and other block devices
- Networking options
- SCSI support
- SCSI low-level drivers
- Network device support
- ISDN subsystem
- CD-ROM drivers (not for SCSI or IDE/ATAPI drives)
- Filesystems
- Character devices
- Sound
- Kernel hacking
- STREAMS subsystem

Save and Exit Load Configuration from File

Quit Without Saving Store Configuration to File

Where *toolname* is the name of the tool you want to use. Here's the screen you'll see if you use xconfig.

In this window, take a look at the options included. Xconfig gives you buttons for the following configuration settings:

➤ Code maturity level options

➤ Loadable module support

➤ General setup

➤ Floppy, IDE, and other block devices

➤ Networking options

➤ SCSI support

➤ SCSI low-level drivers

➤ Network device support

➤ ISDN subsystem

➤ CD-ROM drivers (not for SCSI or IDE/ATAPI drives)

➤ Filesystems

➤ Character devices

➤ Sound

➤ Kernel hacking

➤ STREAMS subsystem

If you know for a fact that your system doesn't contain specific hardware, disable it in the configuration. If you aren't positive, it's best to leave the default setting. Limit your initial experimentation with kernel building to the general setup, networking options, sound, SCSI support and SCSI low-level drivers. Provided that you know the hardware you have, you will be able to eliminate a lot from these options and leave only those items that apply to your specific hardware. If you are unsure about an item, leave it be. (It's not a bad idea to check out the online help system if you come across something you need to know more about...it's what it's there for!)

After you have configured all your drivers, click the Save, then the Exit button. This saves a new configuration file.

Say what? You want sound?

With Linux, you either have sound or you don't. I know, it seems like a joke, but it's the truth. Sound cards for all Linux users are either easy or hard to configure (not much gray area to that).

If you happen to be among those who have an easy sound card, then the process of recompiling the kernel discussed in this chapter will get you on the road to cranking out sound. During the recompilation configuration process, you'll see a series of sound questions such as the following:

```
Sound card support (CONFIG_SOUND) [Y/n/m/?]
/dev/dsp and /dev/audio support (CONFIG_AUDIO) [Y/n/?]
MIDI interface support (CONFIG_MIDI) [Y/n/?]
FM synthesizer (YM3812/OPL-3) support (CONFIG_YM3812) [Y/n/?]
ProAudioSpectrum 16 support (CONFIG_PAS) [N/y/?]
Sound Blaster (SB, SBPro, SB16, clones) support (CONFIG_SB)
➥[Y/n/?]
Generic OPL2/OPL3 FM synthesizer support (CONFIG_ADLIB) [Y/n/?]
Gravis Ultrasound support (CONFIG_GUS) [N/y/?]
```

For basic sound support, always answer yes to the CONFIG_SOUND, CONFIG_AUDIO, and CONFIG_ADLIB options. You'll also need to choose at least one sound card to support. If you know the model and make of your sound card, then you're in good shape and can answer Y to the right one. After you choose your card, you'll need to answer a couple of questions about it (IRQ, base address, and so on). With an easy sound card, the setup isn't much different than setting up SCSI controllers, multiport serial boards, or parallel devices.

If you're one of the unfortunate souls who has a hard sound card, like the Creative AWE Plug'N'Play cards, you're better off without sound for a while. The concepts you'll need to know to get this type of sound card going are something for the more seasoned Linux user rather than the beginner, so hang in there!

Compiling the Kernel and Necessary Modules

Compiling builds binary files that your computer is able to execute. To build your new kernel, enter the following commands in a root shell. Note that these commands generate a lot of output that I have omitted:

```
[root@digital linux]# make dep
[root@digital linux]# make clean
[root@digital linux]# make zImage
[root@digital linux]# make modules
```

The preceding commands (especially make zImage) will take a while. It can be anywhere from a few minutes (on a Pentium computer) to several days (on a 386 computer), depending on your choices and the speed of your hardware. If they all finish without any errors, you are ready to install your new kernel.

Installing the New Kernel

The newly built kernel exists in /usr/src/linux/arch/i386/boot/zImage. Before you install it, you need to make sure that you don't overwrite the existing kernels. These are stored as /vmlinuz and in /boot/vmlinuz-2.0.35-modular (the version will depend on your installation). You don't need to move them, simply make sure that you don't overwrite them. If you do and your new kernel fails to work properly, your system might become unbootable.

Copy your new kernel, with a new name, into the /boot directory:

```
# cp /usr/src/linux/arch/i386/boot/zImage /boot/vmlinuz-2.0.35-apm
```

I named my new kernel for its version and added the apm (Advanced Power Management) portion so that I can distinguish it from the existing kernels. Any additional name is fine, provided you don't overwrite an existing kernel.

Installing the New Modules

Installation of the modules is a little trickier because, by default, the module installation will want to overwrite existing modules. Modules are installed in the /lib/modules directory in a directory called after the kernel version. (Kernel version can be had with the uname -r command.) For my setup, this means a path of /lib/modules/2.0.35.

To save the current modules, move them out of the way:

```
[root@digital linux]# mv /lib/modules/2.0.35 /lib/modules/2.0.35-old
```

Install the new ones with

```
[root@digital linux]# make modules_install
```

After the new modules install, set things back to the way they were so that the old kernel can still find them. You can do this by

```
[root@digital linux]# mv /lib/modules/2.0.35 /lib/modules/2.0.35-apm
[root@digital linux]# mv /lib/modules/2.0.35-old /lib/modules/2.0.35
```

If the new kernel you are installing is a different version, then this step is unnecessary because the new modules will have a different version and directory.

Configuring LILO

The final step in installing your kernel is setting up *LILO*. LILO (the Linux Loader) is the program that boots Linux from your disk. The LILO configuration file will look something like this:

```
[root@digital /]# more /etc/lilo.conf
#
# general section
#

boot = /dev/sdb1
install = /boot/boot.b
# default entry
#

image = /vmlinuz
        initrd = "/boot/initrd.gz"
        label = OpenLinux
        root = /dev/sdb1
        read-only
        append = "load_ramdisk=1 ramdisk_size=2880"

#
# additional entries
#
```

Depending on the configuration of your system, you might not see the exact lines as in the example. But in looking at the example, you can see that there is already at least one Linux entry defined. The default entry is the one that boots after the time-out period has elapsed. You can install your new kernel as the default, as long as you save the previous entry just in case your new kernel doesn't behave the way you thought.

Insert the entry for the new kernel above the entry for the old kernel. Use the old entry as a partial guide. You'll need to specify values for the image (kernel file), label (name to display at boot), and root (same as in the old kernel entry). Add the "read-only" line at the end to specify that your filesystems are to be checked each time you boot this kernel. The resulting /etc/lilo.conf will be similar to

```
[root@digital /]# more /etc/lilo.conf
#
# general section
#
boot = /dev/sdb1
install = /boot/boot.b
# default entry
#

image = /boot/vmlinuz-2.0.35-apm
     label = newkernel
     root = /dev/sdb1
     read-only

image = /vmlinuz
        initrd = "/boot/initrd.gz"
        label = OpenLinux
        root = /dev/sdb1
        read-only
        append = "load_ramdisk=1 ramdisk_size=2880"

#
# additional entries
#
```

After editing the /etc/lilo.conf file, test to see that it works with

```
[root@digital /boot]# lilo -v -t
LILO version 20, Copyright 1992-1997 Werner Almesberger

Reading boot sector from /dev/hda
Merging with /boot/boot.b
Mapping message file /boot/message
Boot image: /boot/vmlinuz-2.0.35-apm
Added vmlinuz-apm *
Boot image: /boot/vmlinuz-2.0.35-modular
Added modular
Boot image: /vmlinuz
Added linux
The boot sector and the map file have *NOT* been altered.
```

If everything is all right, then you can create the boot sector by issuing

```
[root@digital /boot]# lilo -v
LILO version 20, Copyright 1992-1997 Werner Almesberger
Reading boot sector from /dev/hda
Merging with /boot/boot.b
Mapping message file /boot/message
Boot image: /boot/vmlinuz-2.0.35-apm
```

285

```
Added vmlinuz-apm *
Boot image: /boot/vmlinuz-2.0.35-modular
Added modular
Boot image: /vmlinuz
Added linux
/boot/boot.0300 exists - no backup copy made.
Writing boot sector.
```

You are now ready to test your new kernel. Shut down and reboot the system to begin module configuration. If you have any problems, hit Tab when rebooting and type the label of your previous kernel.

Configuring the New Modules and Rebooting

Once you have successfully booted into your new kernel, you might think you are finished, but this isn't the case. The drivers you compiled as modules haven't yet been made active. To make them active, you need to do a little bit of configuration.

The Caldera boot system looks for a directory in the /etc/modules directory named after the version of the kernel you built. (In my example the full path of this directory is /etc/modules/2.0.35.) In this directory it expects to find a file named after the time and date when the kernel was built followed by a .default:

```
#1 Tue Jan 6 16:44:51 MET 1998.default
```

This is a weird name for a file. The name the system expects is stored in the kernel itself. To access it, you can use the following command:

```
[alberto@digital 2.0.35]$ uname -v
#2 Sat Oct 3 13:17:24 CDT 1998
```

Using this text, you'll create the new module list so that the system will load your modules each time it boots. The command you'll use to do this is a little bit complicated, but with a look at the BASH man page you might be able to figure out that you're using a technique called command substitution:

```
# find /lib/modules/2.0.35-apm -name "*.o" -print >
"/etc/modules/2.0.35/
➥$(uname -v).default"
```

This command finds all the modules in the new modules directory, makes a list of them, and sends it to the correct file in the /etc/modules/2.0.35 directory. Without such a complex command, this is tedious work and no tool currently automates this process. If you don't do this, your new modules won't load automatically when the computer starts.

Once this has been done, shut down again and reboot using your new kernel. If everything goes as planned, your new modules will now be active. Welcome to your new system!

Part 4
Appendixes

Are you ready for an adventure? Anxious to check out Linux and see what it can do? Then let's get you on the right path by installing Linux. The information in Appendix A helps you get the Linux operating system up and running. Appendix B is a hardware compatibility guide to help you figure out if any part of your box isn't Linux–compatible. Now, let's get started and breathe some life into your computer!

 # Linux Installation

In This Appendix

➤ Getting to Know Your Hardware

➤ Basic Requirements for Installing Caldera OpenLinux

➤ The Multiboot System

➤ Installing Linux

➤ Starting the Install

➤ Configuring X-Windows

The process of installing Linux on your computer is not any more difficult than installing Windows or any other operating system (OS). If you have ever installed an OS on a PC, you already know how frustrating it can be. For some reason, "plug and play" devices sometimes are not recognized, or a driver shipped with your hardware is not really compatible with the version of the OS you are installing; or worse, the driver included with the OS is not compatible with your hardware. As I'm sure you're aware, installing an OS is tricky business.

You can save yourself a lot of grief and frustration by following a few basic guidelines and preparing for the task at hand. First, you really ought to have a clue about the hardware you are installing the OS on. If you don't, you can try to install Linux, but I bet you are going to spend lots of time working out what hardware you have. To

reduce your general stress levels, you really need to know your hardware a little more than you'd probably care to.

The basic steps for installing follow:

➤ Gather information about your hardware

➤ Check compatibility lists to ensure your hardware is supported

➤ Decide if your Linux installation will share the computer with another OS

➤ Install the software

➤ Provide some configuration

Getting to Know Your Hardware

Before you even attempt to do anything, making a list of what's inside will save you eons. People who install OSs typically know what's in their boxes, and they have the documentation for every little bit of hardware they have. Live by example—do as they do!

Sources of Information

There are several sources of information you can use to identify your hardware:

➤ **Original equipment manuals:** (You saved them, right?)

➤ **Hardware specifications from the manufacturer:** The Web can be a very good starting place for this information. More and more manufacturers are putting their complete specifications on the Web. It's a good idea to look them up before you start your install. And don't forget to check back periodically for updated drivers and information after your system is up and running.

➤ **The manufacturer itself:** You can ask the system manufacturer for what's under the hood. If you lost your manuals, you can also ask the manufacturer to sell you a replacement manual. (A greater number of manufacturers are also putting their manuals, or portions thereof, on the Web.)

➤ **The store where you bought the computer:** If it's not a chain store or a fly-by-night merchant, its salespeople are likely to know what they sold you.

➤ **Software tools such as msd** (Microsoft System Diagnostics): These tools can examine your hardware to great depths and provide quite a bit of information. In the past, msd was included with DOS, Windows, and retail versions of Windows 95. You can also get it from `ftp://ftp.microsoft.com/Softlib/MSLFILES/MSDZIP.EXE`. It is best to run msd from DOS, so copy it to a bootable DOS floppy and start your computer with it. When the computer boots, type **a:\msd,** and you should see a screen like the one in the following figure. (The Device Manager, a Win95/98 control panel tool, might be able to

provide as much information as msd. With WinNT, you can also try Windows
NT Diagnostics. Or, if you have Norton Utilities, you can also try that.)

If you would like to save msd's output to a file, enter the command **a:\msd /F
a:\report**.

➤ **The computer's innards:** Finally, as a last resort, you can always take the
computer apart and take a peek inside. However, this is only recommended for
those who have already done so before and know how to handle static-sensitive
components.

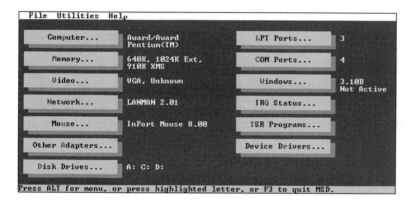

Msd can give you a lot of information about your computer's hardware.

In particular, you'll want to know the details about your cards and setup—you know,
things like chipsets (the type of computer chips), which are important for your video
setup. For example, the following figure gives you an idea of the information you'll
want to know. These details should include the brand and model of the card, and it
doesn't hurt to know the IRQ and memory addresses for it, if available. Msd can be of
great help if you have fairly standard PC hardware; however, things like SCSI, sound,
and network cards are not always properly recognized. Oh well, the saga of owning a
computer continues.

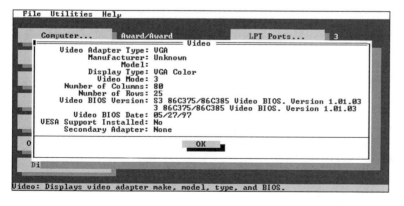

Notice how msd was able to provide information about the video card chipsets. The chipsets information is found the line with the S3 86C375/86C385 on it. Look for this sort of information about your own hardware.

291

Hardware and Network Inventory

Before you proceed, make a list—and check it twice! To help you out, you can use Tables A.1 and A.2 for guidance.

Table A.1 Hardware Inventory

Device	Make	Model	Comments
CD-ROM			
Ethernet Card			
Mouse			COM (serial) port number or PS2
Video card			Memory size in MB
Monitor			Maximum scan rate and resolution
Modem			COM (serial) port number
RAM			How much RAM do you have?

Table A.2 Network Information

Item	Address
Machine's host name	
Domain name for your network	
IP address assigned to your computer	
Netmask	
Broadcast address	
Gateway/Router address	
DNS name servers (2)	

The information about your hardware is essential before you install. But in the event that your computer doesn't support booting from a CD-ROM disk, you might need two 3 1/2" floppy disks (1.44MB) that are PC formatted.

Basic Requirements for Installing Caldera OpenLinux

So, what kind of hardware do you need to have to install Linux? Linux runs on a slew of platforms. The CD included with this book is only intended for Intel-based PCs. Other distributions have software for Digital Alpha hardware, Sun SPARC, PowerPC, and PA-RISC workstations from Hewlett-Packard. But keep in mind, the basic PC requirement is any 386, 486, Pentium, Pentium Pro, or compatible PC or clone.

In terms of memory, the basic requirements for an install are actually quite modest, especially when compared with other OSs. You should be able to install Linux on an Intel-based computer that has 8MB of RAM. If you intend to use a graphical environment, I strongly recommend that you consider 16MB as the reasonable minimum. Although this is on the questionable side of being enough, it might be all you need for minimum installations. Don't expect a minimal system to be speedy, because the resources are going to be taxed to the max. Given today's beyond reasonable memory prices, a 32MB system should be the minimum you consider if you will be working with Linux using a graphical environment. Having 32–40MB will keep Linux zooming right along and should prove to be more responsive than your current OS.

In terms of disk space, a minimal installation can probably fit on 54MB (100MB if you're installing X Windows), but at this size, many important functions will have been omitted. A small installation takes about 136MB. But keep in mind that 418MB is the recommended space for a standard install; this book assumes that you have at least that. More or less space will be required, depending on the options you choose to install. A full install will take around 1000MB, but the majority of users will never need these extra functions.

In addition to these basic requirements, you'll also need a mouse and a supported video card if you intend to take advantage of a graphical interface.

If your computer meets or exceeds these standards (any modern $350 PC seems to do), you are ready to check if your hardware is supported.

As a rule of thumb, Win devices (Winmodems, Winprinters, and so on) are not supported. Bleeding-edge hardware, as opposed to leading-edge, is also likely not to be supported. Standard clone stuff will work due to the high-quality standard components and wide availability.

See Appendix B, "OpenLinux Compatibility Guide," for the most current list of compatible hardware at the time of this writing. Make a list of the required modules, if any. If your hardware is not listed, it is probably not supported. Some components, such as Ethernet cards, will work if you try the NE2000/NE1000 and provide the IRQ and memory address for the card.

The Multiboot System

If your hardware is supported, you only need to make one more decision before you install. If you are not sure that Linux is for you, it is possible to install Linux alongside your current OS. This involves a little more preparation but gives you the opportunity to boot your computer with Linux or your other OS.

If you are considering having a dual-boot computer and have not yet installed the other OS, go ahead and do so now. Your installation will be easier if the other OS is already there. It is likely that Linux will be aware of other OSs, but your other OS probably doesn't know how to handle Linux.

Sharing the Disk with Another OS

Whether or not you are considering sharing the disk with another OS, you'll need to create at least two new partitions solely for Linux. *Partitions* are portions of a disk that are owned and used by a single OS. One partition will accommodate Linux itself, and the other will be used for virtual memory storage (swap space). The minimum size of the swap partition is 16MB, but typically, you'll want to allocate a swap space of the same size as you have RAM memory. Therefore, if you have 32MB of RAM, you'll want a 32MB swap area.

If your current OS's partition is using all available disk space, you still might be able to install Linux, provided there is free space available within the partition. Included with the Linux distribution is software to allow you to repartition the hard disk without destroying the current contents of your disk. This software is called fips.

Before you run fips, you'll need to defragment the disk to ensure that there's enough space for the repartitioning process. Your OS should have a tool such as `defrag.exe` or `optimize.exe` for this purpose. If not, there are several available from commercial vendors (Norton Utilities is one) that will do the job. Fips is only able to handle DOS and Windows 95-style partitions. If you are running Windows NT or OS2, you might need to take a look at a commercial product like PartitionMagic (see `http://www.powerquest.com`) that also supports NTFS and HPFS—even Linux drives.

The fips program, along with some readme files you should definitely read before installing, is located on the CD-ROM under `col\tools\fips15`. Let's take a quick look at how to repartition your disk space using fips:

1. Back up any important data before repartitioning. If something goes wrong, *you will lose all your existing data.*

2. Defragment your system.

3. Boot your computer into DOS. (You might need to create a DOS boot diskette; follow your computer's manuals on how to do this.)

4. Insert the Linux CD-ROM into your computer. If your boot diskette does not enable use of the CD-ROM, you might have to copy the fips program to another diskette.

5. If your CD-ROM is located on drive D, at the prompt type **d:col\tools\fips15\ fips.exe**. If your CD-ROM is accessible by another letter, substitute it for the correct drive.

Follow the onscreen instructions to reserve the amount of space you expect to need for Linux. A good estimate should include allowances for the size of your Linux install (usually 418MB), the size of your swap space (same size as your memory), and extra space for data you create while using Linux (usually a few hundred megabytes). To resize your DOS partition, use the arrow keys on your keyboard. Press Enter to set the appropriate size. Confirm your changes and reboot your computer.

Installing Linux

How you install Linux will depend on whether your BIOS supports booting from a CD-ROM. If your computer's BIOS doesn't support booting from a CD-ROM, you'll have to create two floppy disks: One disk will be a boot disk, and the other will be a modules (drivers) disk.

If your computer supports booting from a CD, you can skip building the floppies; go directly to the section "Starting the Install."

Building the Boot and Modules Floppies

If your computer doesn't support booting from a CD-ROM device, you'll need to create two floppies that start the Linux installation. One disk is required to boot the computer (the boot disk). The other disk (the modules or drivers disk) will contain additional software that is necessary if you

➤ Need access to a PC card (PCMCIA device support) while installing. (Maybe you are using a PCMCIA network or SCSI card or some other peripheral.)

➤ Are installing from the Network.

➤ Are installing from a SCSI CD-ROM.

If your system is fairly standard, it is unlikely that you'll need the second disk, but build it anyway just in case you do. To build the floppies, follow these steps:

1. Boot your computer into DOS or Windows.
2. Insert the Linux CD-ROM into your computer. (I am assuming that your CD-ROM is located in drive D. If it is located elsewhere, substitute the correct drive letter).
3. Insert a 3 1/2" 1.44MB diskette into the floppy drive.
4. At a DOS prompt, enter **d:\col\launch\floppy\rawwrite3**.
5. Enter the full pathname to the disk image file:
 d:\col\launch\floppy\install.144.
6. Provide the drive letter for the floppy diskette (typically A) and press Enter.

To build the modules diskette, repeat steps 3–6 but provide the name of the modules image instead: **d:\col\launch\floppy\modules.144**.

Note that rawwrite3 sometimes has trouble with Windows NT 4.0 systems and with some computer system BIOS chips. If rawwrite3 fails to produce working disks on your computer, you might need to borrow a friend's computer for a few moments to make working install and modules disks.

Starting the Install

If your computer doesn't support booting from a CD-ROM, insert the install diskette and start your computer. After a few seconds you'll see the Linux boot prompt. Hit return to start the installation process.

If your computer supports booting from a CD, put your CD into the CD-ROM, verify that your BIOS is set to boot from the CD (see your computer's manual), and start your computer. Booting from the CD is the fastest way to install Linux on your computer.

Either way, after a few seconds you'll see the installation screen and a boot: prompt. Hit Enter to expedite the process; otherwise, you'll have to wait about 20 seconds before the installation boot begins. After the boot process begins, you'll see text scrolling up your display for up to a minute; it is safe to ignore these progress reports.

Language Selection

After the boot process is complete, you'll be prompted for the language you want to use during the installation. Select whatever language is appropriate for you. Use the arrow keys to change the selection. When the option you want is highlighted, press Enter. Note that while installing, the button with the white text is the selected option. This is not always obvious.

Keyboard Layout Selection

Next you'll be asked to select a keyboard layout matching your locale (country). Do so and press Enter.

Using a Previously Saved Configuration

Next, you'll be asked if you want to resume installation from a known configuration. The No option should be selected (white letters); press Enter. If you are a system administrator–type person, it might be useful to know that at the end of an install, you can save your configuration to disk. If you are installing Linux on multiple machines, you can use the configuration information on the disk so you don't have to repeat the same configuration selection data.

Changing LISA Setup

The next screen will provide various options that LISA (Linux Installation and System Administration utility) will use to obtain configuration information. The options displayed on this screen are as follows:

➤ **Disable "Plug and Play" cards:** Operating systems handle Plug and Play cards in different ways, so for the moment, you should avoid altering any Plug and Play settings. The default setting should prove the safest.

➤ **Automatic network configuration with BOOTP:** This searches for information from a boot parameter server. Leave it off.

➤ **Automatic network configuration with netprobe:** Leave this one off also. This setting and the preceding one are good for system administrators that have a configured network.

➤ **Use this setup and continue:** This is the option that sets the previous settings and continues with the install.

Select the Use this setup and continue option and press Enter. LISA will now probe your computer and try to locate some basic hardware.

Hardware Found (IDE/ATAPI)

After its initial probe, LISA will report the IDE and ATAPI (CD-ROM) disks that it found. Verify that your IDE and ATAPI devices are found.

Press Enter and confirm that all devices have been recognized. If they haven't, LISA will perform a more detailed probe of your system.

Cautious Autoprobing

If you answered No when asked if all your IDE and ATAPI devices were found, LISA will probe for additional devices. Go ahead with the cautious autoprobe. After a few moments, LISA will display additional devices it found during the probe, if any. Make note of the devices found. (You might have to use your up/down arrows to see them all.) Press Enter to continue.

If your system freezes during the cautious probe, you can press your reset button and try the install again. If your system freezes on the second try, you've probably discovered a hardware conflict that needs to be resolved—a topic beyond the scope of this book. For now, you'll either have to live without the devices Linux didn't find, or you'll have to look into technical support options from Caldera. (Linux user groups also might provide some great information resources.)

Hardware Found (Hard Disks/CD-ROM/Ethernet)

If all of your devices were found, answer Yes to the recognized hardware question. Otherwise, answer No to manually load additional kernel modules with the Kernel Module Manager.

The Kernel Module Manager

If not all of your hardware was found, you'll need to manually specify the missing devices and pick the appropriate module (driver) for it. If you made your list and verified that your components are compatible with Linux, this is not really all that difficult.

Select the Load kernel modules option and press Enter to manually select any missing devices. On the Load Kernel Module panel that is displayed, select the type of driver you want to load. For example, if your Ethernet card was not recognized, select Load driver for network card and press Enter.

You will then be presented with a list of all available drivers. If your card is listed, select it and press Enter to continue. You might be required to provide some parameters before the card is successfully recognized. If so, read the next section, "Module Options."

Module Options

On your keyboard, press Alt+F2 and type **help** at the login prompt. This will display the Installation Help System. Select the List of possible parameters for module loading option. A list of the modules and required parameters will be displayed. Press **j** to scroll down and **k** to scroll up a line at a time. To move an entire screen at a time, press **f** or **b** to go forward or backward, respectively. Find the documentation on the driver you need.

For example, my network card is a LynkSys Ether16, a card that is not automatically recognized by Linux. However, many PC Ethernet cards are compatible with the NE2000/NE1000. If you scroll down the document, you'll see an entry for it, telling you that NE2000/NE1000 takes two parameters—the IO and IRQ settings. Make a note of this, and press **q** to exit the help document. This will return you to the Installation Help System. Select the Exit this help system (quit) option and press Enter. Press Alt+F1 to return to your installation window, pick the correct module (in my case, NE2000/NE1000), and provide the parameters as per your installation list.

If you absolutely can't figure out the proper parameters to provide to the module, try using the module without specifying any parameters. Although this is not recommended, some modules will work this way.

When you attempt to load the module, you will be informed whether this worked. Keep in mind that you might be prompted to insert the modules floppy at some point. Press Alt+F6 to see any diagnostic errors that might have been raised when the module was loading. Press Alt+F1 to return to the installation screen. You should see a message indicating whether your card was recognized. Repeat the process for any other devices that weren't recognized.

The Hardware found screen should now list any added devices. Press Enter to continue the installation. If you are done loading modules, select Return to previous menu and press Enter. Then select Finish kernel module management and press Enter.

Changing the Partition Table

At this point you might need to define partitions for Linux and its swap area. If you do, answer Yes to the Change Partition Table panel.

This will prompt you to select a disk. Pick the disk you want to change, and answer Yes to the Change Partition Table panel.

Using Fdisk

You will be dumped into an fdisk session. Fdisk is used to define partitions. It is a dangerous program because it gives you the ability to delete a partition that contains data.

Creating the Primary Linux Partition

Follow these steps to create the primary partition:

1. Enter **p** to list all current partitions. Make a note of where the partition ends.
2. To create the main Linux partition, enter **n**.
3. Enter **p** to create a primary partition. You'll then be asked to provide a primary partition number. Disks are only allowed to have four primary partitions. Enter a number one higher than the existing number of partitions on your disk. For example, if your disk currently contains a single partition, enter the number **2**. If there are no partitions on your disk, enter the number **1**.
4. When it asks you for the first cylinder, enter the first number you see in the parentheses. This should be a number larger than the ending cylinder of the existing partition. If there is no partition already on your disk, enter the number **1**.
5. Specify the size of the new partition in megabytes by entering, for example, **+1024MB**—making sure that you create a partition large enough for the type of installation that you intend to do plus some extra space for your files.
6. Enter **p** to list all partitions. Your new partition should be listed there.

Creating the Swap Partition

Follow these steps to create the swap partition:

1. To create a new partition, enter **n**.
2. Enter **p** to create a primary partition. When prompted for a partition number, enter a number one higher than the number of partitions that exist so far, including the primary partition you just created.
3. Enter the number suggested for the first cylinder. This number should be one higher than the end cylinder in the previous partition.

4. Your swap partition should be at least 16MB. I suggest that you allocate a partition the same size as the amount of real RAM you have installed. If you have 64MB of RAM, enter **+64M**.

5. Enter **t** to change the partition type. When prompted, enter the number of your swap partition. Then, enter the type code for a swap partition: **82**.

Saving Your Changes

To save your changes, enter **w**. This will write your new partitions to disk and exit the program. When returned to the Hard Disk Selection panel, select No further hard disk changes and press Enter.

You will now be warned that you might need to reboot your system to ensure that your partitions were properly allocated on disk. This is not normally necessary with recent computers; most users can continue with the install process safely. If you do have an older system and decide to reboot, you'll have to redo many of the Linux install steps up to this point.

The Configure Swap Space Panel

The partition that you designated for the swap area should be highlighted. Click Continue to initialize it. This will enable Linux to access it.

Installation Source Selection

Next, you are prompted for the Installation Source Selection; don't freak out—this is just a fancy way of asking you where your Linux installation disk is. Select CD and press Enter. A window with a list for all possible CD devices is displayed. If you have a standard ATAPI CD-ROM, you should see your CD-ROM selected. Otherwise, select the appropriate drive as per your configuration list.

LISA will confirm the version of the CD you are using for installation. Press Enter to acknowledge that this is what you want.

Creating the Root Partition

Next, you are asked to select the root partition. LISA should highlight the partition you created earlier for this purpose; press Enter.

LISA will confirm that the selected partition will be erased and all data it currently contains will be lost. Press Enter to confirm your choice or press your arrow key to select No to cancel the operation.

LISA will ask you if you want to check the new partition for errors. This is generally necessary only for older 386 or 486 computers or for cautious individuals. If your computer is a newer system, you can safely skip the error check. (This type of error check can take many hours if you happen to be running it on the newer, larger hard drives.) After a few moments, you'll be asked if you want to mount additional partitions. Select No. You will see information as LISA formats and prepares the partition. The format process can take anywhere from a few moments to a few hours, depending on the size of the disk and whether you chose to verify the format.

Selecting the Installation Type

You are then prompted to select the type of install. Select standard system. This book assumes that you will use this type of installation. (Note that 418MB of disk space is required for this installation, and that this number does not include space for your own data files.)

Selecting the X-Server

Next, you need to pick the X11 server appropriate for your video card. The X11 server is the software that displays a graphical user interface on your screen. This software is matched to the type of video card you have. Moving up and down through the list with your arrow keys, use the Spacebar to select both of the following servers:

➤ The server that matches the chipset on your video card
➤ The server called XFree86-SVGA

By default, the XFree86-VGA16 server will also be installed. This 16-color server will allow you to configure the server that more closely matches your card. If the server that matches your card doesn't work, you can then try the SVGA server. If you are unable to find another server that works with your card, the generic VGA16 server will always be available. Keep in mind, however, that choosing this type of server will limit you to a small screen with only 16-color support.

From here on, Linux will begin to copy and install files. When it finishes doing so, it will ask you for some additional information. In the meantime, go and take a coffee break. This process will take anywhere from 10 minutes to several hours, depending on the speed of your CD-ROM drive, speed of your CPU (386, 486, or faster), and type of install you selected (although you shouldn't have chosen any other type of install when we've coached you to choose standard system).

Configuring the Network

When file copying is completed, you will be prompted for various Network settings.

Hostname Entry

In the Hostname Entry panel you are asked for the fully qualified domain name of your computer. If your computer is in a networked environment, enter that name here. Otherwise, name your computer anything you want, but use a domain like the default `.nodomain.nowhere` (a domain that doesn't exist).

Network Card Configuration

Next, you are asked if you have a network card. Enter Yes if you do, No otherwise. If you have a network card, its name is probably `eth0` (multiple network cards are named by exchanging the `0` for some other number). Enter **eth0** as the device name for the network interface.

The next step is to provide an IP address for the card. If your computer is on a small, local network without a registered IP number(s), use an IP like **192.168.0.1** or **10.0.0.1**. (You can replace the 1 with any number up to 254, depending on this machine's location in the network.) These IP sets are reserved for private networks that are not registered with Internet IP numbers. If this computer will have a registered IP number on the Internet, provide a real IP number.

Enter a network mask if yours differs from the one that Linux calculated for you; same for the broadcast address. If you have a router or gateway, press Enter to set its IP; otherwise, select No and press Enter.

If you have a DNS name server, press Enter to enter this IP; otherwise, answer No. Or, if you have NIS information from your system administrator, enter it now. Otherwise, you should select Do not use NIS and press Enter.

Configuring the Clock

If your clock is set to Greenwich Mean Time, select this option. If not, select Local Time. If you don't know, your computer is almost certainly set to local time. When asked to do so, pick your time zone.

Configuring the Mouse Type

In the Configure Mouse Type panel, you get to pick the type of mouse you have. Select the appropriate setting and press Enter. If you're asked to select a serial port for your mouse, select the port to which your mouse is connected.

Selecting your Printer

Select your printer from the list of available printer types. If a driver or module for your exact printer is not available, select another model by the same manufacturer. I have an Epson Photo Stylus 700 printer and use the Epson Stylus Color setting. You'll then be asked for the port to use in communicating with the printer, the default resolution, and the default paper size. Provide the appropriate values.

Setting the Root Password

At the Password for root prompt, guess what you'll be asked? Here's where you'll set the root password. Now, you might be asking, what in the world is root? *Root* is a special administrative account that should only be used for system configuration. This password is essential. Whatever you set it to, make sure that you don't forget it. Otherwise, you might have to reinstall the system. Note that your characters will not show as you type the password in. This is so that someone can't look over your shoulder and steal your password. After entering it once, you'll be asked to enter it again so that the computer is sure you typed it correctly.

Accounts are covered in more detail in the first few chapters in the book. For now, just remember this password.

Creating the First Account

If you should only use the root account for system configuration, what account do you use on a day-to-day basis? The step following the root password setup is where you create your own home account. This is the account that you normally use when working with Linux. Select a username (eight characters, no spaces). Typically, your account will be your first name or a combination of your first and last names, although it could be your nickname. Enter the first letter of your name followed by your last name, or anything else you like.

Leave the UID displayed as it is (100).

Select **users** standard group.

Press Enter to set the user's home directory. It should read /home/*username* where *username* is the username you selected for your account.

On the shell selection, leave GNU bash as the default option.

Enter your full name and provide a password for your account. Again, your characters will not display as you type them, and you'll be asked to enter the password twice.

Don't forget your username and password; you'll need them to log in. Note that passwords and logins are case sensitive.

Configuring LILO

The next few steps configure the LILO boot manager. LILO is the software responsible for starting your computer when you use Linux. If Linux is sharing your computer with another OS, LILO can provide you with a choice of OSs when you start your computer. To do this, LILO must be installed on the first hard disk's MBR (master boot record).

Some OSs, like Windows NT, don't like LILO very much. For a multiboot system with NT, you'll need to install LILO on the Linux root partition instead of on the MBR and

configure the NT loader to give you a choice when you start your box (computer). Other OSs like MS-DOS, Windows 95, and Windows 98 work fine with LILO on the MBR.

When installing LILO, you will be asked to choose a Linux kernel for your system. Select the default (/boot/vmlinuz) and press Enter. If you are asked to provide an initial ramdisk file image, select the default file by pressing Enter. If you are asked to name the boot image, the default name linux should be used. At the boot parameter box, press Enter to accept whichever values appear by default, unless you do need to add some special parameters for your hardware. When the LILO installation menu displays again, select No further entries to add to LILO and press Enter to display the configuration file LISA has built for you. Press Enter to continue, and when the Install LILO as configured dialog box is displayed, press Enter once more to install LILO.

Configuring Daemon Services

Say OK to the options listed for the daemon/server autostart. These options should be left alone unless you know what you are doing. If you need to alter these settings at some point in the future, you can do them using LISA without having to reinstall Linux.

Configuring X Windows

To configure X Windows, select the X11 server appropriate for your card and press Enter.

Select Yes to call XF86Setup right now. For LISA, "right now" really means "postpone this until the installation is finished," so you won't see XF86Setup until later.

If you have another floppy disk handy, save your configuration to a diskette in case you need to restore it later. This will save you from having to manually reconfigure the install.

Congratulations! You have installed most of Linux on your system. Your computer will now boot into Linux, and afterward, you'll be able to setup the X server. During the boot process, you'll notice some scrolling status information while Linux starts. This process will take anywhere from several seconds to several minutes, depending on the speed of your computer.

XF86Setup

After your computer finishes booting into Linux, you should see a graphics screen with an X-shaped mouse pointer. After a few seconds, the XF86Setup program will be displayed.

If your mouse is working, you can use the mouse to click on boxes and select various options. Otherwise, you might have to use your arrow and Tab keys to move among the various options. Use the Enter key to activate the option.

Mouse Settings for X Windows

The mouse configuration screen allows you to set the details about your mouse (see the next figure). Linux likes mouse devices that have three buttons. If your mouse only has two, you might want to consider purchasing an inexpensive three-button mouse. Your other alternative is to select the Emulate3Buttons option. This will require that you press both mouse buttons at the same time to simulate the middle one.

Note that configuring a nonworking mouse can be tricky. For example, some newer Logitech mouse devices use the Microsoft protocol, whereas some older Microsoft mouse devices use the Logitech protocol. If yours is an older mouse, try to match the name of the mouse to the name of the protocol. If yours is a newer serial mouse, it is most likely a Microsoft mouse, regardless of its manufacturer. If your mouse is connected to a PS/2 mouse port, select the PS/2 protocol. If your mouse is already working, just let it be!

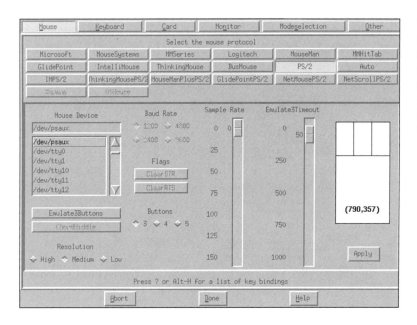

The mouse configuration option allows you to fine-tune and configure your mouse settings. If your mouse is working, you should leave most of the settings as they are by default.

Keyboard Configuration

To begin keyboard configuration, select the Keyboard button at the top of the display (see the following figure). More than likely your keyboard is already working properly. One setting that many people like is assigning the Caps Lock key (to the right of the A key) as the Ctrl key. This is only one of the possible options. The keyboard selection also has settings for specific keyboards from Dell and other vendors, including laptop models. Check this option to see if you have one of those listed. Click the Apply button when you have completed your configuration.

The keyboard option allows you to select a keyboard and to control various options such as the location of the Ctrl key.

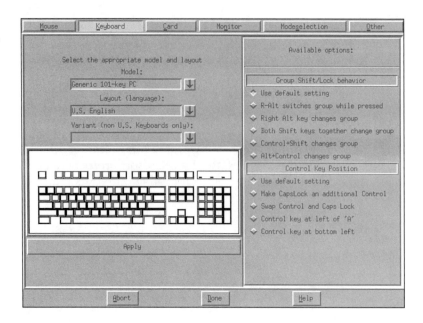

Video Card Configuration

To begin video card configuration, select the Card button at the top of the display. The following figure shows you your video card configuration. Provided you selected the appropriate X11 server to match your card, you should be able to specify a minimum number of settings to have your card recognized. You will want to specify the amount of Video RAM you have and the chipset. If you know the exact card and chip settings (an S3 86C375/86C385 type of thing), you can click on the Card List button, pick the correct card, and then press Detailed Setup.

If you don't know a specific value, use the Probed options. XF86Setup will try to query the card for the unknown information. If your card is unknown, you might want to try the SVGA settings. The system won't be able to make use of advanced features available for your card, but you'll be able to work while you find more information about your system.

Configuring Your Monitor

To begin monitor configuration, select the Monitor button at the top of the display, as shown in the next figure. You'll need to know the specs for your monitor and supply the appropriate range for horizontal and vertical refresh rates. If you don't know them, you'll need to pick one of the options listed. Note that it's very important that you supply the correct options for your monitor. Using incorrect refresh rates will overdrive your monitor, possibly wrecking it. This is more of an issue with non-multisync–type monitors. If you have your monitor manual, you should enter the settings yourself by hand.

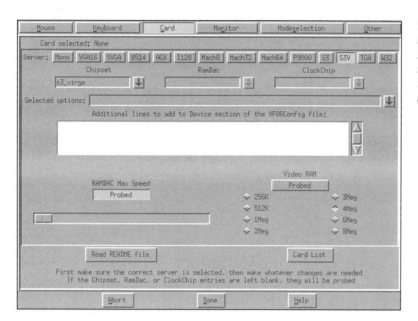

This is the configuration screen for your video card. Note that you can assign multiple settings by clicking the Card List button and picking your card.

Laptop monitors can be especially tricky. Newer laptops might work without problems using standard 640×480, 800×600, or 1024×768 modes. (Select the resolution that matches your laptop's display.) Some laptops, on the other hand, might exhibit display problems. On my laptop I have been unable to find the proper setting, so when I boot into X-Windows, my screen dances. My fix for a number of years has been to switch between monitor output options (internal and external), and that somehow fixes the problem for the session.

Monitor resolution selects the refresh rates your monitor is capable of supporting. Overclocking a refresh rate will kill a monitor.

Selecting Resolutions

To begin resolution configuration, select the Modeselection button at the top of the display. You'll see the screen shown in the next figure. Depending on the amount of video RAM your video card has, it might be possible to specify various resolutions and color settings. By default, X-Windows will use the biggest resolution the card can handle. In some environments, this means enabling a virtual screen in which the screen drops off the right and bottom edges. Moving the cursor to the right or bottom edges scrolls what you see. To me, this sort of setting is disturbing, so I specify settings that match what my monitor can do.

The color depth selection is activated by the four buttons at the bottom of the panel: 8 bpp (bits per pixel) will yield 256 colors, 16bpp will yield 32768 colors, and 24 and 32bpp will yield 65535 and millions of colors, respectively. Note that not all video cards will support all display depths.

The Modeselection panel allows you to set the resolutions you want to use on your monitor along with the default color depth.

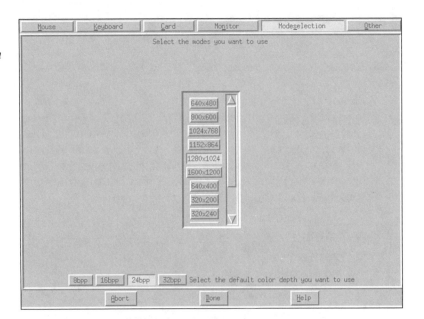

Other Configurations

The Other configuration has to do with options for switching resolutions and exiting the X server (see the following figure). The Ctrl+Alt+Numeric Pad plus (+) and minus (-) keys allow you to switch between different display resolutions on the fly. The Ctrl+Alt+Backspace sequence is used to exit immediately from the X server. If you boot into X Windows and cannot read the screen, Ctrl+Alt+Backspace will take you back to the command prompt. You might need to do this once or twice before you get your configuration right.

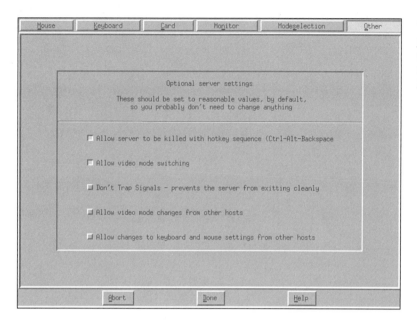

The Other configuration panel allows you to set options regarding switching resolutions and exiting X-Windows.

Finishing the Configuration

When you click Done to exit the XF86Setup program, XF86Setup will prompt you to make sure you're done setting up your system. If you select OK, XF86Setup will try to start your card-specific X server using the settings you specified for your monitor and video card. If your settings appear normal, you are done. If your screen is scrunched up and your monitor geometry buttons don't correct the problem, you might need to use xvidtune, a program that will fine-tune the video rates. Xvidtune is a potentially dangerous program and should be used only if you cannot adjust the picture using your monitor's controls.

If your settings are correct, you should see a black-and-white mesh as the background for your screen and a window without any title bars that aligns with the top-left corners of the screen. If this is correct, click Save the configuration and exit button. Your system will now boot into multiuser mode and is ready for use.

Congratulations! Now that you've installed and configured Caldera OpenLinux, turn to Chapter 1, "The First Login on the KDE Desktop" to get started using your new OS.

OpenLinux Compatibility Guide

This appendix is reproduced with permission from the Caldera Web site. For up-to-date information, see http://www.calderasystems.com/products/openlinux/hardware.html. If your hardware is not listed, more than likely it is not supported. Contact your manufacturer for more information or purchase a compatible replacement. It is important to make sure that your model matches the supported designation exactly.

CD-ROM Drives

Following is the list of CD-ROM drives and interface cards that are supported by the Caldera OpenLinux release 1.3.

CD-ROM Drives

Supported CD-ROM Drives

Company	Model
Aztech	CDA268-01A
Conrad	TXC
Creative Labs	CD-200F (CD-200 not fully supported)
CyCDROM	CR520
	CR520ie
	CR540
	CR940ie

continues

Supported CD-ROM Drives, Continued

Company	Model
ECS-AT	Vertos 100
Funai	E2550UA
	MK4015
	2800F
Goldstar/Reveal	R420
IBM	External ISA drive
Kotubuki	See Panasonic
Lasermate	CR328A
Longshine	LCS-7260
Matsushita	See Panasonic
Mitsumi	CRMC LU005S
	FX001S (single speed)
	FX001S (multisession)
	FX001D (double speed)
	FX001D (multisession)
Okano/Wearnes	CDD110
Optics Storage	DOLPHIN 8000 AT
Orchid	CDS-3110
Panasonic	CR-521
	CR-522
	CR-523
	CR-562
	CR-563
Philips/LMS	cm206 (w/ cm206 card)
Sanyo	CDR-H94A
Sony	CDU-31A (not auto-probed)
	CDU-33A (not auto-probed)
	CDU-510
	CDU-515
	CDU-531
	CDU-535
Teac	CD-55A

Supported CD-ROM Interface Cards

Supported CD-ROM Interface Cards

Company
ISP16
MAD16
Mozart

Most SCSI drives with a block size of 512 or 2048 bytes should work. You will need to have a supported SCSI controller card to use one of these drives. Note: Some CD-ROM drives are shipped with nonstandard SCSI adapters that might not be supported.

Most drives connected via IDE/ATAPI interfaces should work. A few of the vendors currently shipping compatible drives include Aztech, Mitsumi, NEC, Sony, Creative Labs, and Vertos. Some multi-CD changers like the NEC CDR-251 and Sanyo's "non-standard" 3-CD changer are supported as ATAPI drives and, hence, do not have a special driver on the preceding list. A sample CD change program is included at the end of the following document:

```
/usr/src/linux/Documentation/cdrom/ide-cd
```

The CyCDROM 940i and 520ie drives, although connected to IDE interfaces, are not IDE devices; they use the Aztech driver.

Parallel Port CD-ROM Drives

Compatible Parallel Port CD-ROM Drives

Company	Model	Module
Arista	ParaCD 525 (4/8 bit only)	arcd
DataStor	EP2000	dscd
Freecom	Power CD*	pwcd
KingByte Information Sys.	KBIC-951A	kicd
Microsolutions	Backpack (modern)	bpcd
	Backpack (old)	bpmcd
OnSpec Electronics	90c26	oicd
Shuttle Technologies	EPIA	eicd
	EPAT	epcd
	EPEZ	epcd

** Must be initialized with POWER-CD.SYS in DOS first; then boot to Linux with LOADLIN.*

313

Network Cards

Following are the lists of ethernet, frame relay, token ring, and radio modem cards that are supported by the Caldera OpenLinux release 1.3 (includes Standard, Base, and Lite).

Ethernet Cards

Ethernet Cards

Company	Model	Module
3Com	Etherlink	3c501
	Etherlink II	3c503
	Etherlink II/16	3c503
	Etherlink Plus	3c505
	Etherlink16	3c507
	Etherlink III (3c509)	3c509
	Etherlink III (3c579)	3c509
	Fast Etherlink (3c590, 3c592, 3c595, 3c597)	3c59x
	Fast Etherlink XL (3c900, 3c905 3c905B)	3c59x
	Corkscrew Etherlink XL (ISA)	3c515
Accton	EtherDuo PCI	tulip
	EN1207 (all three types)	tulip
Adaptec	ANA6901/C	tulip
	ANA6911/TX	tulip
Allied Telesis	AT1500	lance
	AT1700 (ALPHA)	at1700
	LA100PCI-T	tulip
AMD Lance	PCnet-ISA	lance
	PCnet-ISA+	lance
	PCnet-PCI	lance32
	PCnet-PCI II	lance
	PCnet-32	lance32
Ansel Com.	AC3200 EISA	ac3200
Apricot	Xen-II	apricot

Company	Model	Module
ARCnet	All (ALPHA)	arcnet
AT-Lan-Tec/Realtek	RTL8002 (chipset)	atp
	RTL8012(chip)	atp
Bay Networks	Netgear FX310 TX 10/100	tulip
BOCA	AMD 79C960 based cards	lance
Cabletron	E2100	e2100
C-NET	CNE-935	tulip
Cogent	EM100	tulip
	EM110	tulip
	EM400	tulip
	EM960	tulip
	EM964 Quartet	tulip
Compaq	Netelligent 10(PCI)	tlan
	Netelligent 10/100(PCI)	tlan
	Integrated NetFlex-3/P(PCI)	tlan
	NetFlex-3/P(PCI)	tlan
	ProLiant Netelligent 10/100(PCI)	tlan
	Dual Port Netelligent 10/100(PCI)	tlan
	Deskpro 4000 5233MMX (PCI)	tlanCompex
	Readylink ENET100-VG4(EISA/PCI)	hp100
Danpex	EN-9400P3	tulip
D-Link	DE-530CT	tulip
	DE-600	de600
	DE-620	de620
	DFE500-Tx	tulip
DEC	DEPCA	depca
	DE-100	depca
	DE-101	depca
	DE-200 Turbo	depca
	DE-201 Turbo	depca
	DE-202 Turbo (TP BNC)	depca
	DE-203 Turbo (BNC)	ewrk3
	DE-204 Turbo (TP)	ewrk3
	DE-205 Turbo (TP BNC)	ewrk3
	DE-210	depca
	DE-422 (EISA)	depca

continues

315

Ethernet Cards, CONTINUED

Company	Model	Module
	DE-425 (TP BNC EISA)	de4x5
	DE-434 (TP PCI)	de4x5
	DE-435 (TP BNC AUI PCI)	de4x5
	DE-450 (TP BNC AUI PCI)	de4x5
	DE-500 10/100	de4x5
	EtherWORKS	depca
	EtherWORKS III	ewrk3
	EtherWORKS 10 (PCI)	tulip
	EtherWORKS 10/100 (PCI)	tulip
	QSILVER	tulip
	DEC chips 21040/21041/21140	tulip
	DEC chips 21142/21443	tulip
	DEC chips 21040(no SROM)/21041A	de4x5
	DEC chips 21140A	de4x5
Digi	RightSwitch SE/x	dgrs
Fujitsu	FMV-181	fmv18x
	FMV-182	fmv18x
	FMV-183	fmv18x
	FMV-184	fmv18x
Hewlett-Packard	100VG-AnyLan	hp100
	27248B (Cascade)	hp100
	AMD 79C960 based cards	lance
	J2405A	lance
	J2577 (Cascade)	hp100
	J2577 (REVA Cascade)	hp100
	J2573 (Cascade)	hp100
	J2573 (REVA Cascade)	hp100
	J2585	hp100
	J2585[AB]	hp100
	J2970	hp100
	J2973	hp100
	PC-Lan	hp
	PC-Lan Plus	hp-plus
ICL	EtherTeam 16i	eth16i
	EtherTeam32 (EISA)	eth16i

Company	Model	Module
Intel	EtherExpress Pro/10	eepro
	EtherExpress Pro/10(PCI)	eep10pci
	EtherExpress Pro/100B	eepro100
	EtherExpress 16	eexpress
	Other i82557 based cards	eepro100
Kingston	DEC 21x4x based cards	de4x5
	AMD 79C960 based cards	lance
	EtherX KNE100TX	tulip
	EtherX KNT40T	tulip
Linksys	AMD 79C960 based cards	lance
	DEC 21x4x based cards	de4x5
	EtherPCI	tulip
NE1000		ne
NE1500		lance
NE2000		ne
NE2100		lance
NI5210		ni52
NI6510		ni65
Pure Data	PDI8023-8	wd
	PDUC8023	wd
	PDI8023-16	wd
RealTek	See AT-Lan-Tec	
Schneider & Koch	G16	sk_g16
SMC	83c790 chips	smc-ultra32
	8432	de4x5
	8432BT	tulip
	9000 Series	smc9194
	Ultra	smc-ultra
	EtherEZ	smc-ultra
	EtherPower 10 (PCI)	tulip
	EtherPower 10/100 (PCI)	tulip
	Ultra32 EISA	smc-ultra32
	EtherPower II	epic100

continues

Ethernet Cards, Continued

Company	Model	Module
Surecom	EP-320X	tulip
Thomas Conrad	TC5048	tulip
Western Digital	WD80x3 based cards	wd
Zenith	Z-Note	znet
Zynx	ZX312 EtherAction	tulip
	ZX314	tulip
	ZX315 EtherArray	tulip
	ZX316 10/100 4 port	de4x5
	ZX34x/351	tulip

Frame Relay Cards

Frame Relay Cards

Company	Model	Module
Sangoma	S502A	sdla
	S502E	sdla
	S507	sdla
	S508	sdla

FDDI Cards

FDDI Cards

Company	Model	Module
DEC	FDDI controller (EISA/PCI)	defxx

Radio Modem/Network Cards

Radio Modem/Network Cards

Company	Model	Module
AT&T	GIS Wavelan	wavelan
Baycom	par96	baycom
	par97	baycom
	picpar	baycom
	ser12	baycom
Creative Labs	SoundBlaster	sm
Gracilis	PackeTwin	pt
Ottawa Amateur Radio Club	PI	pi2
	PI2	pi2
WSS	WSS(half duplex)	sm
z8530 SCC		scc

Token Ring Cards

Token Ring Cards

Company	Model	Module
IBM	Any non-DMA cards	ibmtr

Floppy Drives

The number of floppy drives that are not supported by OpenLinux is so small that it is hardly even worth mentioning. Regardless, in the kernel sources, a few laptop drives are mentioned because of special boot/module parameters that are required to get them working correctly. Also, there are additional boot parameters that can be used to adjust floppy support. OpenLinux Base and OpenLinux Standard customers may contact Caldera for details on these parameters or check the BootPrompt-HOWTO.

Compatible Laptop Floppy Drives

Company	Model	Module
HP	Omnibook	floppy
IBM	L40SX ThinkPad	floppy

IDE Drives

Following is the list of IDE Drives that are supported by the Caldera OpenLinux release 1.3.

IDE Hard Drives, CD-ROM Drives, and Tape Drives

A disk geometry translation with "255 heads" is detected and supported by the genhd module.

These drivers support up to four IDE interfaces on one or more IRQs with up to eight disk/CD=ROM/tape/floppy drives. OpenLinux, by default, ships with support for IDE hard drives on the first two controllers (2 drives per controller = 4 drives total) and includes device files for up to four more devices without partitions. The only devices that can use partitions without creating new device files are the first four hard drives that are connected to the first two IDE controllers only.

Users who have hard drives connected to a sound card IDE interface will need to have new device files made. OpenLinux Base and OpenLinux Standard customers can contact tech support for details on how to make these device files.

Compatible Drives

Model	Module
Hard Drives	ide
CD-ROM Drives	ide-cd
Tape Drives	ide-tape

IDE Floppy (Removable) Drives

A word of warning: This arena of hardware support is considered to be fairly unstable with current "full release" kernels, including 2.0.35 (which OpenLinux 1.3 systems run by default). Use caution when operating with removable IDE drive support, and consider using other types of hardware if this is going to run on a production or mission critical system.

Floppy Drives

Company	Model	Module
EASYSTOR	LS-120	ide-floppy
Iomega	ZIP Drive	ide-floppy

Mouse Pointing Devices

The generic serial port drivers in the Linux kernel support serial mouse devices. If the port is recognized, the mouse connected to it should be recognized as well. Note that busmouse devices are assumed to be running at IRQ 5, and PS/2 mouse devices are assumed to be running at IRQ 12. Any variations could require some adjustment in the kernel sources to get the mouse devices recognized and working correctly.

Mouse Pointing Devices

Company	Model	Module
ATI	XL	atixlmouse
Logitech	Busmouse	busmouse
Microsoft	Busmouse	msbusmouse
PS/2	Compatibles	psaux

PC Card Support (PCMCIA)

Most PC Cards are supported. For more information, see
http://www.caldera.com/LDP/HOWTO/PCMCIA-HOWTO.html.

SCSI Adapters

Following is the list of SCSI adapters that are supported by the Caldera OpenLinux release 1.3.

SCSI Adapters

Company	Model	Module
AMD	AM53C974	AM53C974
	AM79C974	AM53C974
Adaptec	1520	aha152x
	1522	aha152x

continues

SCSI Adapters, CONTINUED

Company	Model	Module
	1542(A,CP,CF,?)	aha1542
	1740	aha1740
	274x/274xT	aic7xxx
	284x	aic7xxx
	2910B	aic7xxx
	2920 (PCI)	fdomain
	294x	aic7xxx
	3940	aic7xxx
	3985	aic7xxx
	aic7770 (motherboard)	aic7xxx
	aic7850 (motherboard)	aic7xxx
	aic7855 (motherboard)	aic7xxx
	aic7860 (7850 ultra)	aic7xxx
	aic7870 (motherboard)	aic7xxx
	aic7880 (motherboard)	aic7xxx
	aic7895 (motherboard)	aic7xxx
Advansys	ABP-510	advansys
	ABP-542	advansys
	ABP-742	advansys
	ABP-752	advansys
	ABP-842	advansys
	ABP-852	advansys
	ABP-920	advansys
	ABP-930	advansys
	ABP-930U	advansys
	ABP-930UA	advansys
	ABP-940	advansys
	ABP-940U	advansys
	ABP-940UW	advansys
	ABP-950	advansys
	ABP-960	advansys
	ABP-960U	advansys
	ABP-970	advansys
	ABP-970U	advansys
	ABP-980U	advansys

Company	Model	Module
	ABP-5140	advansys
	ABP-5142	advansys
	ABP-5150	advansys
Always	IN2000 (ISA)	in2000
BusLogic	BT-445C	BusLogic
	BT-445S	BusLogic
	BT-540CF	BusLogic
	BT-542B	BusLogic
	BT-542D	BusLogic
	BT-545C	BusLogic
	BT-545S	BusLogic
	BT-742A	BusLogic
	BT-747C	BusLogic
	BT-747D	BusLogic
	BT-747S	BusLogic
	BT-757C	BusLogic
	BT-757CD	BusLogic
	BT-757D	BusLogic
	BT-757S	BusLogic
	BT-946C	BusLogic
	BT-948	BusLogic
	BT-956C	BusLogic
	BT-956CD	BusLogic
	BT-958	BusLogic
	BT-958D	BusLogic
	Flashpoint	BusLogic
Control Concepts	SCSI/IDE/SIO/PIO/FDC cards	qlogicfas
DPT	EATA_PIO/DASD devices	eata_pio
	PM2011	eata_dma
	PM2011B/9X	eata
	PM2012A	eata
	PM2012B	eata
	PM2021	eata_dma
	PM2021A/9X	eata
	PM2022	eata_dma

continues

SCSI Adapters, CONTINUED

Company	Model	Module
	PM2022A/9X	eata
	PM2024	eata_dma
	PM2041	eata_dma
	PM2042	eata_dma
	PM2044	eata_dma
	PM2122	eata_dma
	PM2122A/9X	eata
	PM2124	eata_dma
	PM2144	eata_dma
	PM2322	eata_dma
	PM2322A/9X	eata
	PM3021	eata
		eata_dma
	PM3122	eata_dma
	PM3222	eata
		eata_dma
	PM3224	eata
		eata_dma
	PM3222W	eata
	PM3224W	eata
	PM3332	eata_dma
	PM3334	eata_dma
DTC	3180	dtc
	3280	dtc
Future Domain	TMC-885	seagate
	TMC-950	seagate
	TMC-1610M	fdomain
	TMC-1610MER	fdomain
	TMC-1610MEX	fdomain
	TMC-1650	fdomain
	TMC-1660	fdomain
	TMC-1670	fdomain
	TMC-1680	fdomain
	TMC-3260 (PCI)	fdomain

Company	Model	Module
GVP	Series II SCSI	gvp11
HP	4020i CD-R card	advansys
IBM	TMC-1680 based	fdomain
ICP vortex	GDT3000/3020	gdth
Computersysteme		
GmbH	GDT3000/3020	gdth
	GDT3000A/3020A/3050A	gdth
	GDT3000B/3010A	gdth
	GDT2000/2020	gdth
	GDT6000/6020/6050	gdth
	GDT6000B/6010	gdth
	GDT6110/6510	gdth
	GDT6120/6520	gdth
	GDT6530	gdth
	GDT6550	gdth
	GDT6117/6517	gdth
	GDT6127/6527	gdth
	GDT6537	gdth
	GDT6557/6557-ECC	gdth
	GDT6115/6515	gdth
	GDT6125/6525	gdth
	GDT6535	gdth
	GDT6555/6555-ECC	gdth
	GDT6117RP/GDT6517RP	gdth
	GDT6127RP/GDT6527RP	gdth
	GDT6537RP	gdth
	GDT6557RP	gdth
	GDT6111RP/GDT6511RP	gdth
	GDT6121RP/GDT6521RP	gdth
	GDT6117RP1/GDT6517RP1	gdth
	GDT6127RP1/GDT6527RP1	gdth
	GDT6537RP1	gdth
	GDT6557RP1	gdth
	GDT6111RP1/GDT6511RP1	gdth
	GDT6121RP1/GDT6521RP1	gdth
	GDT6117RP2/GDT6517RP2	gdth

continues

SCSI Adapters, CONTINUED

Company	Model	Module
	GDT6127RP2/GDT6527RP2	gdth
	GDT6537RP2	gdth
	GDT6557RP2	gdth
	GDT6111RP2/GDT6511RP2	gdth
	GDT6121RP2/GDT6521RP2	gdth
Iomega	Jazz Jet PCI	advansys
	PPA3 (parallel port Zip drive)	ppa
NCR	5380	g_NCR5380
	53c400 (no DMA)	g_NCR5380
	53c406a	NCR53c406a
	53c700 (chipset)	53c7,8xx
	53c720 (chipset)	53c7,8xx
	53c810 (chipset)	ncr53c8xx
		53c7,8xx
	53c810A (chipset)	ncr53c8xx
	53c815 (chipset)	ncr53c8xx
	53c820 (chipset)	ncr53c8xx
		53c7,8xx
	53c825 (chipset)	ncr53c8xx
	53c825A (chipset)	ncr53c8xx
	53c860 (chipset)	ncr53c8xx
	53c875 (chipset)	ncr53c8xx
	53c876 (chipset)	ncr53c8xx
	53c895 (chipset)	ncr53c8xx
Pro Audio	Spectrum 16	pas16
	Studio 16	pas16
Qlogic	FastSCSI! (ISA VLB)	qlogicfas
	FastSCSI! (PCMCIA- must be initialized by QL41DOS.SYS and QL40ENBL.SYS in DOS first; then reboot to Linux w/LOADLIN)	qlogicfas
	IQ-PCI (no disconnect)	qlogicisp
	IQ-PCI-10	qlogicisp

Company	Model	Module
	IQ-PCI-D	qlogicisp
	PCI-Basic	AM53C974
Quantum	ISA-200S	fdomain
	ISA-250MG	fdomain
Seagate	ST01	seagate
	ST02	seagate
SIIG	i540 SpeedMaster	advansys
	i542 SpeedMaster	advansys
	Fast SCSI Pro PCI	advansys
TekRam	DC390	tmscim
	DC390	scsiiom
Trantor	T128	t128
	T128F	t128
	T130B	g_NCR5380
	T228	t128
UltraStor	14F	u14-34f
		ultrastor
	24F	ultrastor
	34F	u14-34f
		ultrastor
Western Digital	WD7000-FASST2	wd7000
	WD7000-ASC	wd7000
	WD7000-AX (ALPHA)	wd7000
	WD7000-MX (ALPHA)	wd7000
	WD7000-EX (ALPHA)	wd7000

IDE-SCSI Devices

With the IDE-SCSI driver, you can use the Linux SCSI drivers instead of the native IDE ATAPI drivers. These drivers support ATAPI devices for which no native driver has been written (for example, an ATAPI PD-CD drive).

Serial Boards

Following is the list of serial boards that are supported by the Caldera OpenLinux release 1.3.

327

Serial Boards

Company	Model	Module
Cyclades	Cyclom-Y Boards	cyclades
DigiBoard	PC/Xe	pcxx
	PC/Xeve	pcxx
	PC/Xi	pcxx
SDL Comm	RISCom/8	riscom8
Stallion	Brumby	istallion
	EasyIO	stallion
	EasyConnection 8/32	stallion
	EasyConnection 8/64	istallion
	ONboard	istallion
	Stallion	istallion
Specialix	IO8+ multiport	specialix

Tape Drives

Most QIC-40, QIC-80, and QIC-117 floppy tape drives should be supported by the ftape driver. The following is a listing of drives mentioned by name in the ftape sources. There are no individual, per-drive drivers as with SCSI or Ethernet cards; all are covered under the same driver.

Tape Drives

Company	Model	Module
AIWA	CT-803	ftape
Archive	31250Q (Escom)	ftape
	5580i	ftape
	S.Hornet (Ident./Escom)	ftape
	XL9250i (Conner/Escom)	ftape
CMS	11c3	ftape
	11c5	ftape
Colorado	700	ftape
	1400	ftape
	DJ-10	ftape
	DJ-20	ftape
	T1000(HP)	ftape

Company	Model	Module
Conner	C250MQ	ftape
	C250MQT	ftape
	TSM420R	ftape
	TSM850R	ftape
	TSM1700R	ftape
	TST800R	ftape
	TST3200R	ftape
COREtape	QIC80	ftape
Exabyte	EXB-1500	ftape
Iomega	250	ftape
	700	ftape
	3200	ftape
	Ditto 800	ftape
Insight	80mb	ftape
Irwin	80SX	ftape
Jumbo	700	ftape
Mountain	FS8000	ftape
Reveal	TB1400	ftape
Summit	SE 150	ftape
	SE 250	ftape
Teac	700	ftape
Wangtek	3040F	ftape
	3080F	ftape
	3200	ftape

SCSI and IDE Tape Drives

There are no specific drivers for SCSI and IDE tape drives; support for them is loaded along with the driver for the interface they are connected to, so no special modules or drivers are required to use them. If the interface is up and running (SCSI or IDE), the drive connected to it should be usable.

Video Cards Supported by XFree86 v3.3.2

Following is the list of video cards that are supported by the XFree86 3.3.2 servers. Most video cards currently on the market are supported by at least one of the server packages provided in the XFree86 distribution.

Video Cards Supported by XFree86 v3.3.2

Company	Card	Server
2 the Max	MAXColor S3 Trio64V+	S3
928Movie		S3
AGX (Generic)		AGX
ALG-5434(E)		SVGA
ASUS	3Dexplorer	SVGA
	PCI-AV264CT	Mach64
	PCI-V264CT	Mach64
	VideoMagic PCI V864	S3
	VideoMagic PCI VT64	S3
AT25		SVGA
AT3D		SVGA
ATI	3D Pro Turbo	Mach64
	3D Xpression	Mach64
	3D Xpression+ PC2TV	Mach64
	8514 Ultra (no VGA)	Mach8
	All-in-Wonder	Mach64
	Graphics Pro Turbo	Mach64
	Graphics Pro Turbo 1600	Mach64
	Graphics Ultra	Mach8
	Graphics Ultra Pro	Mach32
	Graphics Xpression w/ 68875 RAMDAC	Mach64
	Graphics Xpression w/ AT&T 20C408 RAMDAC	Mach64
	Graphics Xpression w/ CH8398 RAMDAC	Mach64
	Graphics Xpression w/ Mach64 CT (264 CT)	Mach64
	Graphics Xpression w/ STG1702 RAMDAC	Mach64
	Mach32	Mach32
	Mach64	Mach64
	Mach64 3D RAGE II, Internal RAMDAC	Mach64
	Mach64 3D RAGE II+, Internal RAMDAC	Mach64
	Mach64 CT (264 CT), Internal RAMDAC	Mach64
	Mach64 GT (264 GT), aka RAGE, Internal RAMDAC	Mach64
	Mach64 VT (264 VT), Internal RAMDAC	Mach64
	Mach64 w/ AT&T 20C408 RAMDAC	Mach64

330

Company	Card	Server
	Mach64 w/ CH8398 RAMDAC	Mach64
	Mach64 w/ IBM RGB514 RAMDAC	Mach64
	Ultra Plus	Mach32
	Video Xpression	Mach64
	Win Boost w/ AT&T 20C408 RAMDAC	Mach64
	Win Boost w/ CH8398 RAMDAC	Mach64
	Win Boost w/ Mach64 CT (264CT)	Mach64
	Win Boost w/ STG1702 RAMDAC	Mach64
	Win Turbo	Mach64
	Wonder SVGA	SVGA
	Xpert@Play PCI and AGP, 3D RAGE Pro	Mach64
	Xpert@Work 3D RAGE Pro	Mach64
ATrend	ATC-2165A	SVGA
Actix	GE32+ 2MB	S3
	GE32i	S3
	GE64	S3
	ProStar	SVGA
	ProStar 64	SVGA
	Ultra	S3
Acumos	AVGA3	SVGA
Alliance	ProMotion 6422	SVGA
Ark Logic	ARK1000PV (Generic)	SVGA
	ARK1000VL (Generic)	SVGA
	ARK2000MT (Generic)	SVGA
	ARK2000PV (Generic)	SVGA
Avance Logic	2101	SVGA
	2228	SVGA
	2301	SVGA
	2302	SVGA
	2308	SVGA
	2401	SVGA
Binar Graphics	AnyView	SVGA
Boca	Vortex (Sierra RAMDAC)	AGX
California Graphics	SunTracer 6000	SVGA
Canopus Co.	PowerWindow 3DV	SVGA
	Total-3D (not fully supported)	VGA16

continues

Video Cards Supported by XFree86 v3.3.2, CONTINUED

Company	Card	Server
Cardex	Challenger (Pro)	SVGA
	Cobra	SVGA
	Trio64	S3
	Trio64Pro	S3
Chips & Technologies	CT64200	SVGA
	CT64300	SVGA
	CT65520	SVGA
	CT65525	SVGA
	CT65530	SVGA
	CT65535	SVGA
	CT65540	SVGA
	CT65545	SVGA
	CT65546	SVGA
	CT65548	SVGA
	CT65550	SVGA
	CT65554	SVGA
	CT65555	SVGA
	CT68554	SVGA
Cirrus Logic	GD542x	SVGA
	GD543x	SVGA
	GD544x	SVGA
	GD5462	SVGA
	GD5464	SVGA
	GD62xx (Laptop)	SVGA
	GD64xx (Laptop)	SVGA
	GD754x (Laptop)	SVGA
Colorgraphic	Dual Lightning	SVGA
Compaq	Armada 7380DMT	S3
	Armada 7730MT	S3
Creative Labs	3D Blaster PCI (Verite 1000)(not fully supported)	VGA16
	Graphics Blaster 3D	SVGA
	Graphics Blaster MA201	SVGA
	Graphics Blaster MA202	SVGA
	Graphics Blaster MA302	SVGA

Company	Card	Server
	Graphics Blaster MA334	SVGA
DFI-WG1000		SVGA
DFI-WG5000		SVGA
DFI-WG6000		SVGA
DSV3325		SVGA
DSV3326		S3
DataExpert	DSV3325	SVGA
	DSV3365	S3
Dell	S3 805	S3
	onboard ET4000	SVGA
Diamond	Edge 3D	SVGA
	Stealth 3D 2000	SVGA
	Stealth 3D 2000 Pro	SVGA
	Stealth 3D 3000	SVGA
	Speedstar (Plus)	SVGA
	Speedstar 24	SVGA
	Speedstar 24X (not fully supported)	SVGA
	Speedstar 64	SVGA
	Speedstar HiColor	SVGA
	Speedstar Pro (not SE)	SVGA
	Speedstar Pro 1100	SVGA
	Speedstar Pro SE (CL-GD5430/5434)	SVGA
	Speedstar 64 Graphics 2000/2200	SVGA
	Stealth 24	S3
	Stealth 32	SVGA
	Stealth 64 DRAM SE	S3
	Stealth 64 DRAM w/ S3 SDAC	S3
	Stealth 64 DRAM w/ S3 Trio64	S3
	Stealth 64 VRAM	S3
	Stealth 64 Video VRAM (TI RAMDAC)	S3
	Stealth Pro	S3
	Stealth VRAM	S3
	Stealth Video 2500	SVGA
	Stealth Video DRAM	S3
	Stealth 64 Graphics 2001 series	SVGA
	Stealth 64 Graphics 2xx0 series (864 + SDAC)	S3

continues

333

Video Cards Supported by XFree86 v3.3.2, CONTINUED

Company	Card	Server
	Stealth 64 Graphics 2xx0 series (Trio64)	S3
	Stealth 64 Video 2001 series (2121/2201)	S3
	Stealth 64 Video 2120/2200	S3
	Stealth 64 3200	S3
	Stealth 64 Video 3240/3400 (IBM RAMDAC)	S3
	Stealth 64 Video 3240/3400 (TI RAMDAC)	S3
	Viper 330	SVGA
	Viper PCI 2MB	P9000
	Viper VLB 2MB	P9000
EIZO (VRAM)		AGX
ELSA	Gloria-4	S3
	Gloria-8	S3
	Victory ERAZOR	SVGA
	Victory 3D	SVGA
	Victory 3DX	SVGA
	Winner 1000/T2D	S3
	Winner 1000AVI (AT&T 20C409 version)	S3
	Winner 1000AVI (SDAC version)	S3
	Winner 1000ISA	S3
	Winner 1000Pro w/ S3 SDAC	S3
	Winner 1000Pro w/ STG1700 or AT&T RAMDAC	S3
	Winner 1000Pro/X	S3
	Winner 1000TRIO	S3
	Winner 1000TRIO/V	S3
	Winner 1000TwinBus	S3
	Winner 1000VL	S3
	Winner 2000	S3
	Winner 2000AVI	S3
	Winner 2000AVI/3D	SVGA
	Winner 2000PRO-2	S3
	Winner 2000PRO-4	S3
	Winner 2000PRO/X-2	S3
	Winner 2000PRO/X-4	S3
	Winner 2000PRO/X-8	S3
	Winner 3000	SVGA

Company	Card	Server
	Winner 3000-L-42	SVGA
	Winner 3000-M-22	SVGA
	Winner 3000-S	SVGA
ET3000 (Generic)		SVGA
ET4000 (Generic)		SVGA
ET4000/W32i, W32p (Generic)		SVGA
ET4000/W32		W32
ET6000 (Generic)		SVGA
ET6100 (Generic)		SVGA
ExpertColor	DSV3325	SVGA
	DSV3365	S3
Generic VGA Compatible		VGA16
Genoa	5400	SVGA
	8500VL (-28)	SVGA
	8900 Phantom 32i	W32
	Phantom 64i w/ S3 SDAC	S3
	VideoBlitz III AV	S3
Hercules	Dynamite	W32
	Dynamite 128/Video	SVGA
	Dynamite Power	SVGA
	Dynamite Pro	SVGA
	Graphite HG210	AGX
	Graphite Power	AGX
	Graphite Pro	AGX
	Graphite Terminator 64	S3
	Graphite Terminator 64/DRAM	S3
	Graphite Terminator Pro 64	S3
	Stingray	SVGA
	Stingray 64/V w/ ICS5342	SVGA
	Stingray 64/V w/ ZoomDAC	SVGA
	Stingray Pro	SVGA
	Stingray Pro/V	SVGA
	Terminator 3D/DX	SVGA
	Terminator 64/3D	SVGA

continues

335

Video Cards Supported by XFree86 v3.3.2, CONTINUED

Company	Card	Server
	Terminator 64/Video	S3
Integral	Flashpoint	SVGA
Intel	5430	SVGA
Interay	PMC Viper	SVGA
JAX	8241	S3
Jaton	Video 58P	SVGA
	Video 70P	SVGA
Jazz Multimedia	G-Force 128	SVGA
LeadTek	WinFast 3D S600	SVGA
	WinFast 3D S680	SVGA
	WinFast S200	SVGA
	WinFast S430	S3
	WinFast S510	S3
MELCO	WGP-VG4S	S3
	WGP-VX8	S3
Matrox	Comet	SVGA
	Marvel II	SVGA
	Millennium (MGA)	SVGA
	Millennium II	SVGA
	Millennium II AGP	SVGA
	Mystique	SVGA
MediaVision	Proaxcel 128	SVGA
Mirage	Z-128	SVGA
Miro	Crystal 10SD w/ GenDAC	S3
	Crystal 12SD	S3
	Crystal 16S	S3
	Crystal 20SD PCI w/ S3 SDAC	S3
	Crystal 20SD VLB w/ S3 SDAC (BIOS 3.xx)	S3
	Crystal 20SD w/ ICD2061A (BIOS 2.xx)	S3
	Crystal 20SD w/ ICS2494 (BIOS 1.xx)	S3
	Crystal 20SV	S3
	Crystal 22SD	S3
	Crystal 40SV	S3
	Crystal 80SV	S3
	Crystal 8S	S3

Company	Card	Server
	MiroVideo 20TD	SVGA
	Video 20SV	S3
	MiroMedia 3D	SVGA
NeoMagic	(not fully supported)	VGA16 (Laptop/Notebook)
Number Nine	FX Motion 331	S3
	FX Motion 332	SVGA
	FX Motion 531	S3
	FX Motion 771	S3
	FX Vision 330	S3
	GXE Level 10/11/12	S3
	GXE Level 14/16	S3
	GXE64	S3
	GXE64 Pro	S3
	GXE64 w/ S3 Trio64	S3
	Imagine I-128 (2-8MB)	I128
	Imagine I-128 Series 2 (2-4MB)	I128
	Visual 9FX Reality 332	SVGA
Oak (Generic)		SVGA
Ocean (octek)	VL-VGA-1000	SVGA
Orchid	Celsius (AT&T RAMDAC)	AGX
	Celsius (Sierra RAMDAC)	AGX
	Fahrenheit 1280	S3
	Fahrenheit VA	S3
	Fahrenheit 1280+	S3
	Fahrenheit Video 3D	SVGA
	Kelvin 64	SVGA
	Kelvin 64 VLB Rev. A	SVGA
	Kelvin 64 VLB Rev. B	SVGA
	P9000 VLB	P9000
Paradise	Accelerator Value	SVGA
Paradise/WD	90CXX	SVGA
Rendition	Verite 1000 (not fully supported)	VGA16
RIVA128		SVGA
S3	801/805 (Generic)	S3

continues

Video Cards Supported by XFree86 v3.3.2, Continued

Company	Card	Server
	801/805 w/ ATT20C490 RAMDAC	S3
	801/805 w/ ATT20C490 RAMDAC and ICD2061A	S3
	801/805 w/ Chrontel 8391	S3
	801/805 w/S3 GenDAC	S3
	801/805 w/ SC1148{2,3,4} RAMDAC	S3
	801/805 w/ SC1148{5,7,9} RAMDAC	S3
	864 (Generic)	S3
	864 w/ ATT20C498 or 21C498	S3
	864 w/ SDAC (86C716)	S3
	864 w/ STG1703	S3
	868 (Generic)	S3
	868 w/ ATT20C409	S3
	868 w/ ATT20C498 or 21C498	S3
	868 w/ SDAC (86C716)	S3
	86C260 (Generic)	SVGA
	86C325 (Generic)	SVGA
	86C357 (Generic)	SVGA
	86C375 (Generic)	SVGA
	86C385 (Generic)	SVGA
	86C764 (Generic)	S3
	86C765 (Generic)	S3
	86C775 (Generic)	S3
	86C785 (Generic)	S3
	86C801 (Generic)	S3
	86C805 (Generic)	S3
	86C864 (Generic)	S3
	86C868 (Generic)	S3
	86C911 (Generic)	S3
	86C924 (Generic)	S3
	86C928 (Generic)	S3
	86C964 (Generic)	S3
	86C968 (Generic)	S3
	86C988 (Generic)	SVGA
	86CM65	S3

Company	Card	Server
	911/924 (Generic)	S3
	924 w/ SC1148 DAC	S3
	928 (Generic)	S3
	964 (Generic)	S3
	968 (Generic)	S3
	Aurora64V+ (Generic)	S3
	Trio32 (Generic)	S3
	Trio64 (Generic)	S3
	Trio64+ (Generic)	S3
	Trio64V2 (Generic)	S3
	Trio64V2/DX (Generic)	S3
	Trio64V2/GX (Generic)	S3
	ViRGE	S3V
	ViRGE (Generic)	SVGA
	ViRGE/DX (Generic)	SVGA
	ViRGE/GX (Generic)	SVGA
	ViRGE/GX2 (Generic)	SVGA
	ViRGE/VX (Generic)	SVGA
	Vision864 (Generic)	S3
	Vision868 (Generic)	S3
	Vision964 (Generic)	S3
	Vision968 (Generic)	S3
SNI	PC5H W32	SVGA
	Scenic W32	SVGA
SPEA	Mercury 64	S3
	Mirage	S3
SPEA/V7	Mercury	S3
	Mirage P64	S3
	Mirage P64 w/ S3 Trio64	S3
	Mirage VEGA Plus	SVGA
	ShowTime Plus	SVGA
STB	Horizon	SVGA
	Horizon Video	SVGA
	LightSpeed	SVGA
	LightSpeed 128	SVGA
	MVP-2	SVGA

continues

Video Cards Supported by XFree86 v3.3.2, Continued

Company	Card	Server
	MVP-2 PCI	SVGA
	MVP-2X	SVGA
	MVP-4 PCI	SVGA
	MVP-4X	SVGA
	Nitro (64)	SVGA
	Nitro 3D	SVGA
	Nitro 64 Video	SVGA
	Pegasus	S3
	Powergraph 64	S3
	Powergraph 64 Video	S3
	Powergraph X-24	S3
	Powergraph 3D	SVGA
	Velocity 3D	SVGA
	Velocity 64 Video	S3
	Velocity 128	SVGA
SiS	SG86C201	SVGA
Sierra	Screaming 3D (not fully supported)	VGA16
Sigma	Concorde	W32
	Legend	SVGA
Spider	Black Widow	AGX
	Black Widow Plus	AGX
	Tarantula 64	S3
	VLB Plus	SVGA
TechWorks	Thunderbolt	W32
	Ultimate 3D	SVGA
Toshiba	Tecra 540CDT	SVGA
	Tecra 550CDT	SVGA
	Tecra 750CDT	SVGA
	Tecra 750DVD	SVGA
Trident	8900/9000 (Generic)	SVGA
	8900D (Generic)	SVGA
	Cyber9382 (Generic)	SVGA
	Cyber9385 (Generic)	SVGA
	Cyber9388 (Generic)	SVGA
	Cyber9397 (Generic)	SVGA

Company	Card	Server
	TGUI9400CXi (Generic)	SVGA
	TGUI9420DGi (Generic)	SVGA
	TGUI9430DGi (Generic)	SVGA
	TGUI9440 (Generic)	SVGA
	TGUI9660 (Generic)	SVGA
	TGUI9680 (Generic)	SVGA
	TGUI9682 (Generic)	SVGA
	TGUI9685 (Generic)	SVGA
	TVGA9200CXr (Generic)	SVGA
Unsupported VGA compatible		VGA16
VI720		SVGA
VL-41		S3
VidTech	FastMax P20	S3
VideoLogic	GrafixStar 300	S3
	GrafixStar 400	S3
	GrafixStar 500	S3
	GrafixStar 550	SVGA
	GrafixStar 600	SVGA
	GrafixStar 700	S3
ViewTop PCI		SVGA
WD	90C24 (Laptop)	SVGA
	90C24A or 90C24A2 (Laptop)	SVGA
XGA-1 (ISA bus)		AGX
XGA-2 (ISA bus)		AGX

Information about XFree86-supported hardware was extracted from the XF86Setup configuration utility that ships with XFree86 v 3.3.1.

For additional information, refer to the main XFree86 Web pages at http://www.xfree86.org/.

Compatible XT Hard Drives

Following is the list of XT Hard Drives that are supported by the Caldera OpenLinux release 1.3.

Compatible XT Hard Drives

Company	Model	Module
DTC	5150CX	xd
	5150X	xd
OMTI	5520	xd
Seagate	ST11M/R	xd
	ST11R	xd
Western Digital	WD1002-27X	xd
	WD1002AWX1	xd
	WD1004A27X	xd
	WDXT-GEN2	xd
XEBEC		xd

Sound Cards

For detailed is not necessarily complete, but it is some of the hardware known not to work with Caldera OpenLinux Release 1.3 out of the box. Some of it might work with the use of additional software from other vendors or kernel patches. The list follows:

➤ Microchannel-based PCs

➤ Parallel Port Tape Drives

➤ Xircom Ethernet Cards

➤ "WinModems" (modems made specifically for Windows systems)

➤ "WinPrinters" (printers made specifically for Windows systems, like the Lexmark 2070 printer)

Index

GNU GENERAL PUBLIC LICENSE

Version 2, June 1991

Copyright (C) 1989, 1991 Free Software Foundation, Inc.

675 Mass Ave, Cambridge, MA 02139, USA

Preamble

The licenses for most software are designed to take away your freedom to share and change it. By contrast, the GNU General Public License is intended to guarantee your freedom to share and change free software—to make sure the software is free for all its users. This General Public License applies to most of the Free Software Foundation's software and to any other program whose authors commit to using it. (Some other Free Software Foundation software is covered by the GNU Library General Public License instead.) You can apply it to your programs, too.

When we speak of free software, we are referring to freedom, not price. Our General Public Licenses are designed to make sure that you have the freedom to distribute copies of free software (and charge for this service if you wish), that you receive source code or can get it if you want it, that you can change the software or use pieces of it in new free programs; and that you know you can do these things.

To protect your rights, we need to make restrictions that forbid anyone to deny you these rights or to ask you to surrender the rights. These restrictions translate to certain responsibilities for you if you distribute copies of the software, or if you modify it.

For example, if you distribute copies of such a program, whether gratis or for a fee, you must give the recipients all the rights that you have. You must make sure that they, too, receive or can get the source code. And you must show them these terms so they know their rights.

We protect your rights with two steps: (1) copyright the software, and (2) offer you this license which gives you legal permission to copy, distribute and/or modify the software.

Also, for each author's protection and ours, we want to make certain that everyone understands that there is no warranty for this free software. If the software is modified by someone else and passed on, we want its recipients to know that what they have is not the original, so that any problems introduced by others will not reflect on the original authors' reputations.

Finally, any free program is threatened constantly by software patents. We wish to avoid the danger that redistributors of a free program will individually obtain patent licenses, in effect making the program proprietary. To prevent this, we have made it clear that any patent must be licensed for everyone's free use or not licensed at all.

The precise terms and conditions for copying, distribution and modification follow.

GNU GENERAL PUBLIC LICENSE

TERMS AND CONDITIONS FOR COPYING, DISTRIBUTION AND MODIFICATION

0. This License applies to any program or other work which contains a notice placed by the copyright holder saying it may be distributed under the terms of this General Public License. The "Program", below, refers to any such program or work, and a "work based on the Program" means either the Program or any derivative work under copyright law: that is to say, a work containing the Program or a portion of it, either verbatim or with modifications and/or translated into another language. (Hereinafter, translation is included without limitation in the term "modification".) Each licensee is addressed as "you".

 Activities other than copying, distribution and modification are not covered by this License; they are outside its scope. The act of running the Program is not restricted, and the output from the Program is covered only if its contents constitute a work based on the Program (independent of having been made by running the Program). Whether that is true depends on what the Program does.

1. You may copy and distribute verbatim copies of the Program's source code as you receive it, in any medium, provided that you conspicuously and appropriately publish on each copy an appropriate copyright notice and disclaimer of warranty; keep intact all the notices that refer to this License and to the absence of any warranty; and give any other recipients of the Program a copy of this License along with the Program.

 You may charge a fee for the physical act of transferring a copy, and you may at your option offer warranty protection in exchange for a fee.

2. You may modify your copy or copies of the Program or any portion of it, thus forming a work based on the Program, and copy and distribute such modifications or work under the terms of Section 1 above, provided that you also meet all of these conditions:

 a)You must cause the modified files to carry prominent notices stating that you changed the files and the date of any change.

 b)You must cause any work that you distribute or publish, that in whole or in part contains or is derived from the Program or any part thereof, to be licensed as a whole at no charge to all third parties under the terms of this License.

 c)If the modified program normally reads commands interactively when run, you must cause it, when started running for such interactive use in the most ordinary way, to print or display an announcement including an appropriate copyright notice and a notice that there is no warranty (or else, saying that you provide a warranty) and that users may redistribute the program under these conditions, and telling the user how to view a copy of this License. (Exception: if the Program itself is interactive but does not normally print such an announcement, your work based on the Program is not required to print an announcement.)

 These requirements apply to the modified work as a whole. If identifiable sections of that work are not derived from the Program, and can be reasonably considered independent and separate works in themselves, then this License, and its terms, do not apply to those sections when you distribute them as separate works. But when you distribute the same sections as part of a whole which is a work based on the Program, the distribution of the whole must be on the terms of this License, whose permissions for other licensees extend to the entire whole, and thus to each and every part regardless of who wrote it.

 Thus, it is not the intent of this section to claim rights or contest your rights to work written entirely by you; rather, the intent is to exercise the right to control the distribution of derivative or collective works based on the Program.

In addition, mere aggregation of another work not based on the Program with the Program (or with a work based on the Program) on a volume of a storage or distribution medium does not bring the other work under the scope of this License.

3. You may copy and distribute the Program (or a work based on it, under Section 2) in object code or executable form under the terms of Sections 1 and 2 above provided that you also do one of the following:

a)Accompany it with the complete corresponding machine-readable source code, which must be distributed under the terms of Sections 1 and 2 above on a medium customarily used for software interchange; or,

b)Accompany it with a written offer, valid for at least three years, to give any third party, for a charge no more than your cost of physically performing source distribution, a complete machine-readable copy of the corresponding source code, to be distributed under the terms of Sections 1 and 2 above on a medium customarily used for software interchange; or,

c)Accompany it with the information you received as to the offer to distribute corresponding source code. (This alternative is allowed only for noncommercial distribution and only if you received the program in object code or executable form with such an offer, in accord with Subsection b above.)

The source code for a work means the preferred form of the work for making modifications to it. For an executable work, complete source code means all the source code for all modules it contains, plus any associated interface definition files, plus the scripts used to control compilation and installation of the executable. However, as a special exception, the source code distributed need not include anything that is normally distributed (in either source or binary form) with the major components (compiler, kernel, and so on) of the operating system on which the executable runs, unless that component itself accompanies the executable.

If distribution of executable or object code is made by offering access to copy from a designated place, then offering equivalent access to copy the source code from the same place counts as distribution of the source code, even though third parties are not compelled to copy the source along with the object code.

4. You may not copy, modify, sublicense, or distribute the Program except as expressly provided under this License. Any attempt otherwise to copy, modify, sublicense or distribute the Program is void, and will automatically terminate your rights under this License. However, parties who have received copies, or rights, from you under this License will not have their licenses terminated so long as such parties remain in full compliance.

5. You are not required to accept this License, since you have not signed it. However, nothing else grants you permission to modify or distribute the Program or its derivative works. These actions are prohibited by law if you do not accept this License. Therefore, by modifying or distributing the Program (or any work based on the Program), you indicate your acceptance of this License to do so, and all its terms and conditions for copying, distributing or modifying the Program or works based on it.

6. Each time you redistribute the Program (or any work based on the Program), the recipient automatically receives a license from the original licensor to copy, distribute or modify the Program subject to these terms and conditions. You may not impose any further restrictions on the recipients' exercise of the rights granted herein. You are not responsible for enforcing compliance by third parties to this License.

7. If, as a consequence of a court judgment or allegation of patent infringement or for any other reason (not limited to patent issues), conditions are imposed on you (whether by court order, agreement or otherwise) that contradict the conditions of this License, they do not excuse you from the conditions of this License. If you cannot distribute so as to satisfy simultaneously your obligations under this License and any other pertinent obligations, then as a consequence you may not distribute the Program at all. For example, if a patent license would not permit

royalty-free redistribution of the Program by all those who receive copies directly or indirectly through you, then the only way you could satisfy both it and this License would be to refrain entirely from distribution of the Program.

If any portion of this section is held invalid or unenforceable under any particular circumstance, the balance of the section is intended to apply and the section as a whole is intended to apply in other circumstances.

It is not the purpose of this section to induce you to infringe any patents or other property right claims or to contest validity of any such claims; this section has the sole purpose of protecting the integrity of the free software distribution system, which is implemented by public license practices. Many people have made generous contributions to the wide range of software distributed through that system in reliance on consistent application of that system; it is up to the author/donor to decide if he or she is willing to distribute software through any other system and a licensee cannot impose that choice.

This section is intended to make thoroughly clear what is believed to be a consequence of the rest of this License.

8. If the distribution and/or use of the Program is restricted in certain countries either by patents or by copyrighted interfaces, the original copyright holder who places the Program under this License may add an explicit geographical distribution limitation excluding those countries, so that distribution is permitted only in or among countries not thus excluded. In such case, this License incorporates the limitation as if written in the body of this License.

9. The Free Software Foundation may publish revised and/or new versions of the General Public License from time to time. Such new versions will be similar in spirit to the present version, but may differ in detail to address new problems or concerns.

Each version is given a distinguishing version number. If the Program specifies a version number of this License which applies to it and "any later version", you have the option of following the terms and conditions either of that version or of any later version published by the Free Software Foundation. If the Program does not specify a version number of this License, you may choose any version ever published by the Free Software Foundation.

10. If you wish to incorporate parts of the Program into other free programs whose distribution conditions are different, write to the author to ask for permission. For software which is copyrighted by the Free Software Foundation, write to the Free Software Foundation; we sometimes make exceptions for this. Our decision will be guided by the two goals of preserving the free status of all derivatives of our free software and of promoting the sharing and reuse of software generally.

NO WARRANTY

11. BECAUSE THE PROGRAM IS LICENSED FREE OF CHARGE, THERE IS NO WARRANTY FOR THE PROGRAM, TO THE EXTENT PERMITTED BY APPLICABLE LAW. EXCEPT WHEN OTHERWISE STATED IN WRITING THE COPYRIGHT HOLDERS AND/OR OTHER PARTIES PROVIDE THE PROGRAM "AS IS" WITHOUT WARRANTY OF ANY KIND, EITHER EXPRESSED OR IMPLIED, INCLUDING, BUT NOT LIMITED TO, THE IMPLIED WARRANTIES OF MERCHANTABILITY AND FITNESS FOR A PARTICULAR PURPOSE. THE ENTIRE RISK AS TO THE QUALITY AND PERFORMANCE OF THE PROGRAM IS WITH YOU. SHOULD THE PROGRAM PROVE DEFECTIVE, YOU ASSUME THE COST OF ALL NECESSARY SERVICING, REPAIR OR CORRECTION.

12. IN NO EVENT UNLESS REQUIRED BY APPLICABLE LAW OR AGREED TO IN WRITING WILL ANY COPYRIGHT HOLDER, OR ANY OTHER PARTY WHO MAY MODIFY AND/OR REDISTRIBUTE THE PROGRAM AS PERMITTED ABOVE, BE LIABLE TO YOU FOR DAMAGES, INCLUDING ANY GENERAL, SPECIAL, INCIDENTAL OR CONSEQUENTIAL DAMAGES ARISING OUT OF THE USE OR INABILITY TO USE THE PROGRAM (INCLUDING BUT NOT LIMITED TO LOSS OF DATA OR DATA BEING RENDERED INACCURATE OR LOSSES SUSTAINED BY YOU OR THIRD PARTIES OR A FAILURE OF THE PROGRAM TO OPERATE WITH ANY OTHER PROGRAMS), EVEN IF SUCH HOLDER OR OTHER PARTY HAS BEEN ADVISED OF THE POSSIBILITY OF SUCH DAMAGES.

END OF TERMS AND CONDITIONS

Linux and the GNU system

The GNU project started 12 years ago with the goal of developing a complete free Unix-like operating system. "Free" refers to freedom, not price; it means you are free to run, copy, distribute, study, change, and improve the software.

A Unix-like system consists of many different programs. We found somecomponents already available as free software—for example, X Windows and TeX. We obtained other components by helping to convince their developers to make them free—for example, the Berkeley network utilities. Other components we wrote specifically for GNU—for example, GNU Emacs, the GNU C compiler, the GNU C library, Bash, and Ghostscript. The components in this last category are "GNU software". The GNU system consists of all three categories together.

The GNU project is not just about developing and distributing free software. The heart of the GNU project is an idea: that software should be free, and that the users' freedom is worth defending. For if people have freedom but do not value it, they will not keep it for long. In order to make freedom last, we have to teach people to value it.

The GNU project's method is that free software and the idea of users' freedom support each other. We develop GNU software, and as people encounter GNU programs or the GNU system and start to use them, they also think about the GNU idea. The software shows that the idea can work in practice. People who come to agree with the idea are likely to write additional free software. Thus, the software embodies the idea, spreads the idea, and grows from the idea.

This method was working well—until someone combined the Linux kernel with the GNU system (which still lacked a kernel), and called the combination a "Linux system."

The Linux kernel is a free Unix-compatible kernel written by Linus Torvalds. It was not written specifically for the GNU project, but the Linux kernel and the GNU system work together well. In fact, adding Linux to the GNU system brought the system to completion: it made a free Unix-compatible operating system available for use.

But ironically, the practice of calling it a "Linux system" undermines our method of communicating the GNU idea. At first impression, a "Linux system" sounds like something completely distinct from the "GNU system." And that is what most users think it is.

Most introductions to the "Linux system" acknowledge the role played by the GNU software components. But they don't say that the system as a whole is more or less the same GNU system that the GNU project has been compiling for a decade. They don't say that the idea of a free Unix-like system originates from the GNU project. So most users don't know these things.

This leads many of those users to identify themselves as a separate community of "Linux users", distinct from the GNU user community. They use all of the GNU software; in fact, they use almost all of the GNU system; but they don't think of themselves as GNU users, and they may not think about the GNU idea.

It leads to other problems as well—even hampering cooperation on software maintenance. Normally when users change a GNU program to make it work better on a particular system, they send the change to the maintainer of that program; then they work with the maintainer, explaining the change, arguing for it and sometimes rewriting it, to get it installed.

But people who think of themselves as "Linux users" are more likely to release a forked "Linux-only" version of the GNU program, and consider the job done. We want each and every GNU program to work "out of the box" on Linux-based systems; but if the users do not help, that goal becomes much harder to achieve.

So how should the GNU project respond? What should we do now to spread the idea that freedom for computer users is important? We should continue to talk about the freedom to share and change

software—and to teach other users to value these freedoms. If we enjoy having a free operating system, it makes sense for us to think about preserving those freedoms for the long term. If we enjoy having a variety of free software, it makes sense for to think about encouraging others to write additional free software, instead of additional proprietary software.

We should not accept the splitting of the community in two. Instead we should spread the word that "Linux systems" are variant GNU systems—that users of these systems are GNU users, and that they ought to consider the GNU philosophy which brought these systems into existence.

This article is one way of doing that. Another way is to use the terms "Linux-based GNU system" (or "GNU/Linux system" or "Lignux" for short) to refer to the combination of the Linux kernel and the GNU system.

Copyright 1996 Richard Stallman

(Verbatim copying and redistribution is permitted without royalty as long as this notice is preserved.)

The Linux kernel is Copyright © 1991, 1992, 1993, 1994 Linus Torvaldis (others hold copyrights on some of the drivers, file systems, and other parts of the kernel) and and is licensed under the terms of the GNU General Public License.

The views and conclusions contained in the software and documentation are those of the authors and should not be interpreted as representing official policies, either expressed or implied, of the Regents of the University of California.

www@FreeBSD.ORG

CALDERA SYSTEMS OPENLINUX 1.3 *31 AUG 1998*

OpenLinux is a Caldera Systems-maintained distribution of the Linux operating system. Caldera Systems OpenLinux 1.3 uses a standard 2.0.35 Linux kernel. It also includes other unique features, making OpenLinux the most reliable and easy-to-use Linux available.

This document contains the following:

➤ How-to procedures
➤ OpenLinux features
➤ Getting help

How-To Procedures

Depending on what you want to do, do one of the following.

To do this...	...do this
To automatically update to OpenLinux 1.3	1. Insert the Installation CD and mount the CD-ROM drive.
	2. Change to the "/" directory.
	3. To extract the contents of the update file type tar zxvf /mnt/cdrom/update.col-1.3.0.2.tgz and press Enter, where "/mnt/cdrom" indicates the CD-ROM drive mount point.
	4.Read the "README" file in the /usr/doc/update.col-1.3.0.2" directory. This file contains important information about updating to OpenLinux 1.3.
To install OpenLinux with a bootable CD-ROM drive	1. Insert the Installation CD.
	2. Turn on your computer.
	NOTE: For details on installing OpenLinux, see the "Getting Started Guide."
Install OpenLinux with a floppy diskette	See the "README" file in the "col/launch/floppy" directory on this Installation CD.
Install OpenLinux from a DOS system	See the "README" file in the "col/launch/dos" directory on this Installation CD.
Install OpenLinux from an existing	See the "README" file in the Linux system "col/launch/"linux" directory on this Installation CD.
Install individual software packages ROM drive.	1. Insert the Installation CD and mount the CD-
	2. Type "lisa —pkg" and press Enter, then follow the prompts.
Install StarOffice	See the documentation in the StarOffice_40 directory on this Installation CD.
View Caldera Systems' online resources	From a Web browser, access the technical index.html file in the "col/doc" directory on this Installation CD.

OpenLinux Features

Caldera Systems OpenLinux is a powerful system suited for many uses. The following list highlights some of the key features of OpenLinux:

➤ Full 32-bit architecture, supporting both ELF and a.out binaries
➤ Multi-tasking, multi-user

- ➤ X Window System (graphical interface)
- ➤ Powerful Desktop interface
- ➤ Graphical and character-based text editing
- ➤ Client access to UNIX, DOS, and Windows systems (NT and 95/98)
- ➤ Server to UNIX and Windows systems (NT and 95/98)
- ➤ Remote management (telnet, rlogin, and SNMP protocol)
- ➤ Complete Internet client and server suite, including the Apache Web server and Netscape Communicator
- ➤ NetWare Client for accessing Bindery and NDS servers

Getting Help

Caldera Systems OpenLinux includes electronic support. For electronic support, send email to "support@caldera.com" or visit Caldera Systems' Web site (`http://www.caldera.com/support/`).

If you encounter any problems using OpenLinux, review the Known Bugs List. To view this list, use a Web browser to access the col/doc/index.html file on this Installation CD.

You can also send email to any of the following addresses:

info@caldera.com (general comments or questions)

support@caldera.com (technical questions)

majordomo@caldera.com (mailing list information)

faq@caldera.com (auto-responds with list of questions and answers)

Thank you for using Caldera Systems products.

Caldera Systems, Inc.
PO Box 1920
Orem, UT 84059-1920
USA

Information: info@caldera.com
WWW: http://www.caldera.com
voice: +1 (801) 765-4999
fax: +1 (801) 765-1313

Orders: orders@caldera.com
voice: +1 (888) GOLINUX
voice: +1 (800) 850-7779
+1 (801) 765-4888
fax: +1 (801) 765-1313

Disclaimer

By opening this package, you are agreeing to be bound by the following agreement:

Some of the programs included with this product are governed by the GNU General Public License, which allows redistribution; see the license information for each product for more information. Other programs are included on the CD-ROM by special permission from their authors.

You may not copy or redistribute the entire CD-ROM as a whole. Copying and redistribution of individual software programs on the CD-ROM is governed by terms set by individual copyright holders. The installer and code from the author(s) is copyrighted by the publisher and the author. Individual programs and other items on the CD-ROM are copyrighted by their various authors or other copyright holders. This software is sold as-is without warranty of any kind, either expressed or implied, including but not limited to the implied warranties of merchantability and fitness for a particular purpose. Neither the publisher nor its dealers or distributors assumes any liability for any alleged or actual damages arising from the use of this program. (Some states do not allow for the exclusion of implied warranties, so the exclusion may not apply to you.)

NOTE: This CD-ROM uses long and mixed-case filenames requiring the use of a protected-mode CD-ROM Driver.